Medieval Castles
of Ireland

David Sweetman

THE BOYDELL PRESS

First published 1999
The Collins Press, West Link Park, Doughcloyne, Wilton, Cork
in association with Dúchas – The Heritage Service
Irish ISBN 1 898256 75 6

New edition 2000
The Boydell Press, Woodbridge
ISBN 0 85115 788 2

The Boydell Press is an imprint of Boydell & Brewer Ltd
PO Box 9, Woodbridge, Suffolk IP12 3DF, UK
and of Boydell & Brewer Inc.
PO Box 41026, Rochester, NY 14604–4126, USA
web site: http://www.boydell.co.uk

A catalogue record for this book is available
from the British Library

Library of Congress Cataloging-in-Publication Data
Sweetman, P. David.
    Medieval castles of Ireland / David Sweetman. – New ed.
        p. cm.
    Originally published: Cork, Ireland : Collins Press, 1999.
    Includes bibliographical references and index.
    ISBN 0-85115–788–2 (acid-free paper)
        1. Castles – Ireland – History – To 1500. 2. Architecture, Medieval – Ireland.
    3. Ireland – History – 1172–1603.   4. Ireland – Antiquities. I. Title
    DA985.S89 2000
    941.5 – dc21   99–089487

This publication is printed on acid-free paper

Printed in Slovenia

Contents

Preface

Acknowledgements

Introduction   1

1   Earth and timber castles   3

2   The Anglo-Norman stone fortress   33

3   Hall-houses   89

4   Later medieval stone fortresses   105

5   The tower house   137

6   Fortified houses and stronghouses   175

Notes   199

Bibliography   203

Glossary   207

Placename index   209

PREFACE

Since the early 1970s when I first excavated the castles of Trim and Ferns I had an ambition to update and upgrade Harold Leask's book on Irish castles.[1] However, the more I learned about Irish castles the more daunting this task became. I came to realise that it was neither practical nor desirable to update this classic work and the idea of writing a book about castles was removed from my agenda for many years. Because of the practical problems of recording a sufficient number of castles on my own it seemed wise to wait until the Archaeological Survey of Ireland was advanced enough to take advantage of the information provided in the County Inventories. The basic data in this book is derived from the records of the Archaeological Survey and without their information I could not have undertaken this task. Many of my friends and colleagues over the years have urged me to write a book on Irish castles and when Colin Rynne suggested a publisher to undertake this project, I finally agreed with much trepidation.

There is no doubt that medieval archaeology and, in particular, castle studies have made great progress in the last ten years in Ireland. Most of this is due to many of the people mentioned in the book who are enthusiastic about the recording and research of our field monuments. Recent work for instance on the ringwork has shown this type of castle to be relatively common, whereas ten years ago they were considered a rarity. These sites have been found through excavation of a number of Anglo-Norman fortresses but also through the dedicated fieldwork of the archaeologists in Dúchas. There is no doubt that before the Archaeological Survey of the whole country is complete further earthwork castles, and in particular ringworks, will be identified. Certain problems remain, like the lack of earthwork castles in parts of the west, despite the advanced stage of the survey there. This is a problem that could be looked at by the Discovery Programme or by some individual who was sufficiently funded in order to undertake detailed survey followed by excavation.

When the Archaeological Survey commenced in the mid 1960s many of the type sites that we now recognise as earthwork castles were classified merely as earthworks or enclosures. Similarly many hall-houses have been classified as tower houses. Some stronghouses and fortified houses also almost certainly have not been correctly classified and lurking in the general category of castles are many tower houses. The entire archaeological record needs to be examined and many sites revisited so that they can be re-classified if necessary. Until this task is completed it will be extremely difficult to give a more accurate picture of the distribution and development of the castle in Ireland.

I hope that this book is a start to a new era in castle studies in Ireland and that it will form a basic framework and reference from which the student and academic can progress the subject. At the same time I hope that its contents will provide the general reader with some pleasure and that it will help further an understanding of the development of the castle in Ireland.

ACKNOWLEDGEMENTS

There are several of my friends and colleagues who were more than anxious to provide me with the information necessary to write this book. In particular, I would like to thank Terry Barry, Tom Condit, Jean Farrelly, Con Manning, Caimin O'Brien, Kieran O'Conor, Paddy O'Donovan, Denis Power and Matthew Stout. It is difficult to single out individuals but Caimin and Tom were particularly inspirational, especially when doing fieldwork with them. Also I have had many discussions with Con, Terry and Kieran which have helped me formulate and consolidate my ideas.

This book would not have been written without the help and encouragement of my friends and colleagues, most of whom are working in Dúchas. The book, to a large extent, is based on information gathered from the records of the Archaeological Survey, my own personal observations and the ideas of various colleagues. I would like to thank Dúchas for allowing me to use their records and, in particular, the photographs and line drawings. All photographs and line drawings are courtesy of Dúchas unless otherwise stated. Con Brogan is largely responsible for the photographic work with the help of Tony Roche, while Kevin O'Brien, Dick Stapleton and Gerry Woods assisted with the line drawings. Terry Barry, Willie Cumming, Bob Higham, John Kenyon, Con Manning and Matthew Stout read the manuscript and suggested many useful changes. Antoinette Robinson typed and amended the typescript. The book was designed and illustrated by Matthew Stout. I discussed my ideas for the book with many of my friends and colleagues. In addition to those already mentioned, I would like to thank Olive Alcock, Declan Hurl, Chris Lynn, Michael Moore and Mary Tunney. I doubt if this book would have been written but for gentle arm-twisting by Colin Rynne.

INTRODUCTION

Spread over the Irish countryside there is a quite surprising number of ancient buildings, both large and small, whose strong walls, narrow loopholes and meagre windows proclaim a military or at least defensive purpose. No traveller can fail to see them whilst all must feel some degree of curiosity about buildings which the maps declare to be castles (Harold Leask).[1]

The piecemeal conquest of Ireland by the Anglo-Normans, which commenced in the year 1169, had a fundamental impact on the Irish landscape. The introduction by them of large earthwork and stone castles was almost totally new to Ireland. According to Giraldus Cambrensis (Gerald of Wales), whose writings are a contemporary source for the early Anglo-Norman settlement, the Irish used bogs and woods for protection.[2] The period from 1169 to 1185 was one of great political change in Ireland and by the time Prince John arrived in 1185 the cities of Dublin, Cork and Waterford, with their immediate hinterlands, were already under the control of the king. Their military successes must be attributed to their fighting skill, especially on horseback, their organisation and their ability to build strongholds rapidly in strategic positions.

Robert FitzStephen, with a force of 30 knights, 60 men at arms and 300 archers and foot soldiers landed in Bannow Bay in May 1169. These forces were followed by others under Maurice de Prendergast. They were professional soldiers and they revolutionised the method of fighting in Ireland. The archers were probably equally or more important than the cavalry since the Irish were armed only with slings and spears. Giraldus Cambrensis stresses the importance of the archers in the conquest but their ability to build earthwork and timber castles rapidly consolidated their conquests.

Henry II was very aware of the strength of Earl Strongbow in Ireland and, probably because of an appeal from the Irish themselves, he set sail for Waterford in 1171. On 16 October he landed near Waterford and then entered the city which Strongbow surrendered to him as well as doing homage for the rest of Leinster. But Henry did not trust Strongbow and he made certain that he could assert no claim to Meath by granting it to Hugh

Diarmait MacMurchada, from Giraldus Cambrensis, *Expugnatio Hibernica.*

1

de Lacy, a marcher lord. De Lacy was also appointed justiciar and constable of Dublin. Although de Lacy had made grants in Meath in 1172-3 it appears that it was not occupied other than to build earthwork castles at Trim and Duleek. Trim and Duleek were destroyed in 1174 but repaired shortly afterwards and, by 1175, the Normans under the control of de Lacy had started a systematic occupation of Meath.

Strongbow died in 1176 but by this time Leinster appears to have been largely sub-infeudated. De Courcy, who is said to have been granted Ulster by the King, if he could conquer it, marched northwards with 22 knights and about 300 others. Despite considerable resistance de Courcy was successful in two battles and, by 1178, had exerted his control in Ulster. According to Giraldus Cambrensis, he 'erected castles throughout the province (in reality areas east of the river Bann) in suitable places and established it in firm peace'.

De Lacy was active in Dublin, Meath and North Leinster where 'he was building strong castles throughout' – presumably mainly earthwork and timber fortifications. By 1180 de Lacy was the predominant force, so-much-so that Henry feared he would throw off his allegiance to the English crown to declare himself King of Ireland. By 1185 the lands so far occupied by the Anglo-Normans were thoroughly sub-infeudated and, certainly by the time Hugh de Lacy had been killed in 1186, the annals tell us that the country was full of foreigners and castles. Only North Munster, Connacht and the western portion of Ulster and Oriel remained unconquered. The rest of the country was under tight Anglo-Norman control and expansively covered by their earthwork and timber castles. Large stone fortresses began to make their appearance at this time. The period of large stone castle building broadly covers the years from 1175 to 1310. The earliest of these fortresses are to be found in the areas controlled by de Lacy and de Courcy. Later in the medieval period the hall-houses and then the tower houses were built, and these were followed by the erection of stronghouses and fortified houses at the end of the late medieval period. This book deals with the development of the Irish castle from 1169 to 1600 and to this end the fortifications have been divided into six groups with a chapter dedicated to each:

(1)   Timber and earthwork castles
(2)   Large stone fortresses (*c*.1175 to 1310)
(3)   Hall-houses
(4)   Later medieval fortresses
(5)   Tower houses
(6)   Fortified houses and stronghouses

Hugh de Lacy from Giraldus Cambrensis, *Expugnatio Hibnernica.*

CHAPTER ONE

EARTH AND TIMBER CASTLES

The most difficult area in the study of Irish castles is the recognition in the field of the earthworks of the timber castles. The country is full of earthworks of all shapes and sizes and recent work in the Archaeological Survey of Ireland has shown that it is extremely difficult to date and classify them. When we look at medieval earthworks we have to remember that we are seeing only part of the defences of the castle and that we are missing all the woodwork connected with the defences. We have two types of earth and timber castles in Ireland, namely the motte and the ringwork. However, there are a number of sites that could fit into either category while others, which are obviously of medieval origin, will not fit neatly into one or the other. For instance, Sheeaunbeg Motte, Barrinagh, Co. Roscommon was recorded as a motte,[1] as a motte and bailey using a natural esker for part of its defences,[2] as a ringfort converted into a platform ringfort or motte,[3] and by the Archaeological Survey as a possible inauguration site. None of the recent work on medieval earthwork castles has come to grips with the morphology of the ringwork.[4] The ringwork has been described as, at its simplest, being shaped like an empty flan case.[5] It can therefore be easily confused in Ireland and possibly Wales with the ringfort. Indeed, in Wales, many sites which have been identified as ringworks look remarkably like large ringforts. If it is difficult to recognise a ringwork in the field based on its morphology alone, then other factors can come into play which might help us identify these sites, namely their siting and distribution. Higham and Barker in their book on the timber castles set out a framework for discussing these monuments by dividing them into five groups:[6]

1. Ringworks without baileys
2. Ringworks with one bailey or more
3. Mottes without baileys or with no apparent baileys
4. Mottes with one bailey or more
5. Ringworks or mottes (with or without baileys) within earlier earthworks

The only category mentioned above which has so far not been found in Ireland in any great numbers is the ringwork with a bailey. However, recent fieldwork has revealed an example of one just off the north slope of the Loughcrew Hills, Co. Meath, and two possible sites in Roscommon at

Sheeaunbeg and Dundonnell. Other Irish site types which sometimes prove to be of Anglo-Norman origin are the raised raths, cliff-edge forts and promontory forts, whether inland or coastal. I will deal with these in the first section on ringworks followed by a discussion on mottes.

RINGWORKS

The morphology of the ringwork or its exact definition presents something of a problem in that it is often difficult to distinguish its earthwork remains from the more common ringfort or other unclassified earthwork enclosures. In England and Wales it is, in its simplest form, an area enclosed by a fosse and rampart. It has also been defined as having a minimum height of 2m above the level of the outside defences with the enclosed area disproportionately small compared to the massive enclosing elements.[7] However, in Ireland we can expand on these definitions by saying the bank(s) are more pronounced and the fosse is wider than one would expect to find on a ringfort. The entrance to a ringwork is also distinguishable from a ringfort in that it will often have a pronounced ramp and each side of the gap in the rampart will be faced with stone. The example at Drumsawry, Loughcrew, Co. Meath, also has extensive stonework on top of its rampart. A number of ringworks have recently been identified in north Tipperary[8] and, in most instances, they are not circular, being either almost squared-off or irregular in shape. A ringwork, test excavated by the author at Mulphedder, Clonard, Co. Meath, was of a very irregular shape.[9] Fortunately, one of the three small cuttings on the river side of the site produced the parts of fifteen planks which were part of a wooden palisade and appear to be part of the outer defences of the ringwork. Several of the planks had dowel holes in them for securing to upright posts and cross timbers which would have been braced from the inside.

Recent excavations at Trim Castle, Co. Meath,[10] produced unequivocal evidence for a ringwork castle which was undoubtedly the fortress mentioned in the near contemporary Norman-French poem 'The Song of Dermot and the Earl'. The poem states that Hugh de Lacy fortified a house at Trim, threw a fosse around it and enclosed it with a herisson in the year 1172.[11] There was clear evidence for a palisade trench and bracing posts at the north-west section of the ringwork. In addition, excavations uncovered large post-holes of a wooden structure inside the ringwork which had been burnt down. The excavated evidence here fits nicely with the historical reference to the burning down of Hugh de Lacy's castle in 1173 by Roderick O'Connor. Also found were the remains of grain spread over a wide area as well as horseshoes and arrowheads, just what one would expect from a fortification which housed knights and their horses. Four other castles have also clear evidence of a ringwork fortification pre-dating the stone castle. At Ferns in Co. Wexford, excavation revealed the remains of an earthwork under the south-east angle of the keep.[12] A small fosse outside the castle at the east side may also have belonged to the pre-stone castle fortification. Recently at Carlow Castle, which is morphologically the same as Ferns, the fosse of a ringwork was found below the foundations of the remains of the keep.[13] At Adare Castle, Co. Limerick, a wide deep fosse encloses the keep providing protection for the inner ward. Until 1961 it had been postulated that this fosse was the remains of an earlier ringfort. However, it was convincingly demonstrated that metal and wooden objects recovered from the fosse *c.*1845 were mainly of a mid- to late-medieval date and there was no reason to assume the enclosed area was a ringfort.[14] The subcircular shape of the site with its wide deep fosse would rather suggest that it was a ringwork castle and would therefore have a direct parallel in Trim Castle. Also the siting for a ringfort on low ground beside the river would be very unusual. Another possible example of a ringwork pre-dating a stone castle is to be found at Clonmacnoise although some archaeologists claim that the earthwork is contemporary with the stone building. However, it is in a similar siting to Adare Castle beside a river on low ground and it would be unusual to build such a massive fosse and rampart contemporaneously with the erection of the stone fortress. Recent excavations at Kilkenny Castle and Limerick Castle have also revealed a substantial ringwork underneath the

Arrowheads and horseshoes from the excavated ringwork at Trim Castle. Mounted knights and archers in combination made up a formidable fighting machine.

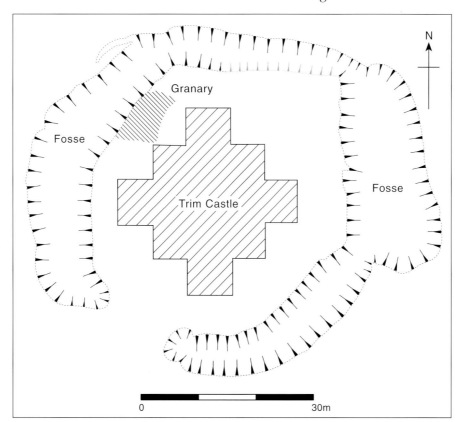

Fig. 1 Trim, Co. Meath. Remains of ringwork as discovered during recent excavations by Alan Hayden.

This 'Ham Green' wine jug, made near Bristol, was found in association with the excavated ringwork at Trim Castle. It provides evidence for the strong trading links which existed between Anglo-Norman Ireland and south-west Britain.

walls of the stone building.[15] At Limerick Castle the earthen bank was, in places, revetted by stone and there was a substantial external fosse. There is also the possibility of a ringwork surrounding Lea Castle, Co. Laois.[16]

It was stated, in 1987, that there were only five sites where excavation had uncovered possible ringworks: Pollardstown, Co. Kildare; Castletobin, Co. Kilkenny; Beal Boru, Co. Clare; Clonard, Co. Meath and Ferns, Co. Wexford.[17] Four more can be added to this list, namely Trim Castle, Kilkenny Castle, Carlow Castle and Limerick Castle. The number of excavated examples is unlikely to increase in the near future unless a research programme is undertaken. None of the partially excavated sites other than Trim, Clonard, Limerick and Carlow have given us definite evidence of defensive details such as wooden palisading and revetting so we have to rely on observation and interpretation of the remains of the earthwork. If we compare the ringwork, using recently discovered examples in Kildare, Cavan, Meath, Laois, Offaly, Roscommon and Tipperary, to a typical ringfort there are quite pronounced differences. It has been maintained that Irish ringforts could be classified as ringworks if they occurred in England,[18] and that ringworks in Ireland may have been classified as ringforts because we lacked a classification scheme which is sufficiently discerning.[19] Unfortunately, until recently, this has been the situation. Lurking in the archaeological records of the Archaeological Survey are many ringwork castles classified as large ringforts or merely as enclosures. For instance, at Danestown and Rodanstown, Co. Meath, multivallate ringworks adjacent to medieval churches have been classifed as ringforts. Fortunately, fieldworkers have come on the scene with an interest in medieval archaeology, who are no longer predominantly interested in the prehistoric and early historic periods.[20]

A number of cliff-edge forts in north Tipperary appear to be exactly the same as those identified in Glamorgan as ringworks.[21] They basically consist of single or multiple ramparts and fosses in a semi-circle enclosing a D-shaped area which is bounded on its straight side by a cliff or ravine. In Glamorgan, ringworks are often situated close to church sites as are the mottes, but in Ireland sites recently identified do not appear to have this association. There are, of course, examples of this association of ringwork and church. At Castlerahan in Co. Cavan, for instance, there appears to have been a medieval church sited inside a bailey associated with a large and impressive ringwork.[22] This ringwork is built on the summit of a drumlin and consists of a subrectangular platform 4m high, measuring 42m by 24m enclosed by two substantial banks of earth and stone. Another cliff-edge fort, Ballyprior, was identified in Co. Laois.[23] Its entranceway was via a causeway and its rampart consisted of an earth and stone bank. Seven ringwork castles, three of which are 'cliff-edge forts' were identified in Co. Wexford.[24] The one at Newtown (Ferrycarrig) was fortified by FitzStephen

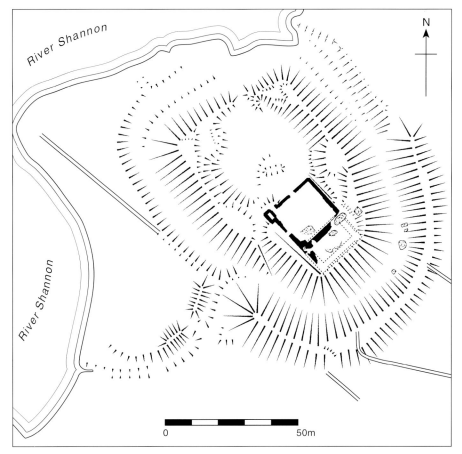

Fig. 2 Plan of Clonmacnoise Castle with its earlier ringwork. The earthwork, which encloses the stone fortress, is located on the banks of the River Shannon. The fortress was placed near the site of an early medieval monastery in a location commanding an important river crossing.

in 1169-70 and excavations here revealed a stone wall on top of an earthen bank.[25] The site is located on a spit of land which extends northwards into the estuary and is naturally defended by steep cliffs to the north and east. By 1171 the site was defended by a fosse and a bank with a palisade. The excavation showed that the fosse was 5.2m wide at the top, 1.8m at the base and 1.9m deep. Unfortunately the finds from the fosse could not be closely dated. Thirteen cliff-edge forts have been recorded in Cork and many of these are likely to be Anglo-Norman in origin.

In Co. Kildare, excavations were carried out on the remains of an earthen enclosure at Pollardstown which was situated on top of a natural gravel ridge.[26] Its siting, and the recovery of medieval finds from it, indicate that this was a ringwork. The finds included an iron arrowhead which can be dated to the twelfth century and two medieval stirrups. Another earthwork site was excavated at Beal Boru, Co. Clare, which is situated on a steep-sided triangular spur of gravel on the bank of the River Shannon.[27] Because of its position overlooking the river, its siting was believed to have been chosen to dominate or control an important crossing point. The castle and its earlier earthwork defences at Clonmacnoise, also

Fig. 3 Castlerahan, Co.
Cavan. Large ringwork
with a church and
graveyard situated
within the bailey of the
earthwork castle
(CUCAP).

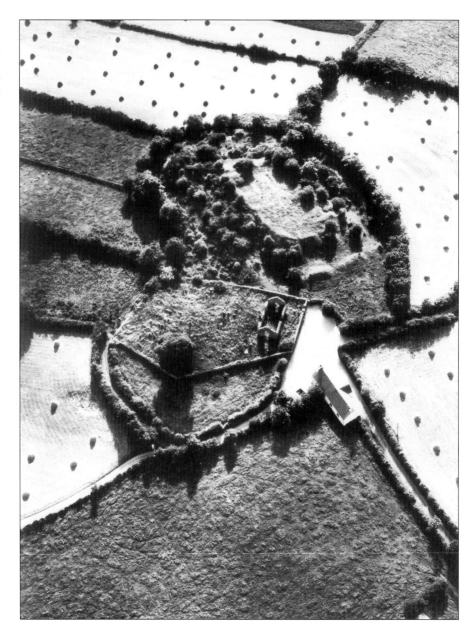

on the banks of the River Shannon, must have had a similar function. The
Beal Boru site was circular in plan, had a very large bank and was
surrounded by a broad well-marked fosse. The overall diameter of the site
was 70m to 75m but since the base of the bank was up to 17m wide, only an
area some 20m in diameter was enclosed. The entrance to this site, like so
many ringworks, was via a causeway and the bank was faced with stone.
This site was built and occupied in two distinct and separate phases, the
earliest being sometime in the eleventh century based on the coin evidence.
The second phase of construction was thought to be an unfinished motte;

however, the site could be complete and is almost certainly a ringwork castle built on a pre-existing enclosure. Its location and siting would also point to the latter interpretation.

Another ringwork is to be found on the west bank of the old course of the River Shannon, at Meelick, Co. Galway. In the *Annals of Clonmacnoise* it is mentioned that William de Burgo founded a castle here in 1203 close to the church. It was assumed that the present ecclesiastical remains had been built on the site of the early castle and had destroyed it. However, an enclosure 100m north of the friary is very similar to the ringwork castle at Clonard and has a similar siting. The site consists of an irregular-shaped enclosure defined by a bank with the enclosed area slightly higher than the surrounding land. There is quite an amount of stone on and in the bank and there is a ramped entrance at the south. Since there are no obvious signs of a fosse around the site it must have been defended by a substantial wooden palisade.

In Co. Offaly three ringworks were identified compared to eleven mottes.[28] However, mottes were a well-known feature whereas the ringworks are newly identified. One of these is a low, rectangular-shaped flat-topped mound situated just inside the earthen ramparts which enclose the monastic settlement at Churchland/Clonmore, Seirkieran. The example at Ballynacarrig is an irregular-shaped, flat-topped mound with the appearance of a truncated motte. It has the remains of a bailey-type area which is defined by a low earthen bank. The third example at Dungar is a

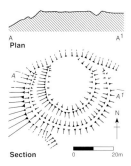

Plan and section of Summerhill, Co. Tipperary. This ringwork is located on an inland promontory (after Stout, 1984).

Fig. 4 Kilpipe, Co. Wicklow. Ringwork sited at the edge of a ridge close to a medieval church (not shown).

circular platform enclosed by a water-filled fosse. It has a causewayed entrance and the possible remains of an enclosing wall around the perimeter of the platform.

Fourteen ringwork castles have been identified in Tipperary (North Riding). Three of these are cliff-edge forts while another is sited very close to a ravine. Most of the sites are low platforms with low earth and stone banks around the perimeter, some with stone facing and others with wall footings. Where a fosse exists it is usually flat-bottomed and access is via a causeway. One site, at Greenan, is very similar to the Meelick and Clonard examples and is situated in low-lying, wet terrain. Recent fieldwork in Roscommon has revealed at least six ringworks in addition to those identified in a 1988 paper.[29] All of these sites are marked on the Ordnance Survey maps but the initial interpretation and classification was not precise enough. For instance, there is an earthen enclosure close to the bank of the River Suck at Creeharmore. It is a subcircular earthen platform, slightly raised above the level of the surrounding ground. The platform has a slight lip around its perimeter possibly indicating the remains of a palisade. The platform is enclosed by a wide flat-bottomed fosse and the site is cut off on the landward side by a bank and fosse. There is a break in the bank and its terminals turn markedly inwards to give access to a small platform which lies between the outer fosse and the inner defences. This platform is undoubtedly the remains of a timber gateway controlling the entrance and drawbridge. At the river side of the ringwork there is a passageway which is delimited by an earthen bank on each side and would appear to be some type of slipway for small boats. Another of the Roscommon sites is at Ballyglass and has been classified as a platform ringfort. It is a circular platform *c*.2m high and *c*.35m in diameter and is surrounded by a wide flat-bottomed fosse. Its location on flat low-lying ground suggests that this is a ringwork rather than a raised rath. The site at Rathnallog is very similar in its morphology and is located in the same type of terrain.

Some sites in Roscommon have initially been identified as burial mounds but their siting and morphology would indicate that they are medieval earthworks. For instance, an impressive site at Gortnasillagh was identified first as a rath and then as a barrow. It is situated on the summit of a ridge and consists of an almost circular-shaped platform with a diameter of about 24m and a maximum height of 2.7m at the west side. The platform is surrounded by a wide, flat-bottomed fosse but there is no definite evidence for a causeway entrance. Lissalway, classified as a raised rath, has a large deep fosse surrounding it and could well be a medieval earthwork castle.

Without citing further examples of ringwork castles, as well as possible sites, it has become quite obvious to field archaeologists that this type of site is there to be found. Another way of identifying the ringwork other than its morphology is its location, siting and association with other type

Plate 1 The small ringwork or low square motte was built on the boundary of the early medieval ecclesiastical enclosure at Seirkeiran, Co. Offaly.

Plate 2 Ringwork at Loughcrew, Co. Meath is situated on the side of a hill below Carnbane East megalithic tombs. The depression near the centre probably represents a collapsed wooden tower. Note also the crescentic-shaped bailey (top) possibly indicating the remains of an earlier site on which the earthwork castle was built.

Plate 3 Clonmacnoise Castle, Co. Offaly. This large earthwork, possibly an earlier ringwork, encloses the stone fortress on the banks of the River Shannon. It commands an important crossing of the Shannon at the junction of the *Eiscir Riada* – Ireland's main east/west routeway – and overlooks the adjacent early medieval 'city' of Clonmacnoise.

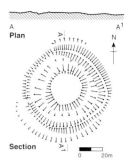

Plan and section of
Dungar, Co. Offaly
(after Cunningham, 1987).

Fig. 5 Dungar, Co.
Offaly. Ringwork
enclosed by a wide, flat-
bottomed fosse with
causewayed entrance.

sites. In England and Wales medieval earthwork castles are often associated
with ecclesiastical remains; however, in Ireland this link is not as
pronounced. A good example of this relationship is to be seen at
Castlerahan, Co. Cavan, where a church and graveyard are situated within
the bailey of a large and impressive ringwork. Another impressive site is at
Rathangan, Co. Kildare, and is situated only 100m away from the site of a
medieval church. It consists of a circular platform with a diameter of about
60m and rises 2m above the surrounding land. It has a causewayed
entrance at the east. When considering the siting and location of earthwork
castles one has to keep in mind medieval nucleated settlement in England
where one would expect to find a church, a castle and houses with their
plots. In Ireland we seldom find such a neat association of all three major
elements despite extensive fieldwork in Westmeath and elsewhere.[30]
However, keeping the political divisions of the early Anglo-Norman
settlement with its sub-infeudation in mind, we realise that we are more
likely to find discrete sites and dispersed settlement within the broad area
of the manorlands which can be roughly equated with the parish
boundaries. The historical records are therefore very important in helping
to identify medieval earthwork castles within a manor. However, there still
remains the problem of identifying sites in the sub-manor which would be
of a lower status to those in the chief manor.

Because of the poor historical records in some areas and the scattered
nature of the earthworks it will remain almost impossible to distinguish
medieval sites from earlier ones. It is undisputed, however, that where there

Fig. 6 Castlekevin, Co. Wicklow. Ringwork with bailey (bottom) similar to the earthwork castle at Seirkeiran. The remains of a stone bridge between ringwork and bailey are visible in the foliage.

is a manor there must be a medieval earthwork castle. So, for instance, at Rathangan, Co. Kildare, there is no obvious early castle to be seen until one examines the large earthwork which is classified as a ringfort by the Archaeological Survey. On close inspection it can be seen that its banks and defences have been altered to make it into a ringwork castle. There is an annalistic reference to the rath here in 801 and later references to a castle. Its position close to the site of a medieval church would be a typical model for manorial settlement in England.

When identifying ringwork castles it is very important to keep in mind their location and siting so that one can isolate them from the more numerous ringforts and other earlier enclosures. It is generally accepted that ringforts are located off the tops of high ground on the slopes of hills and are nearly always isolated. Ringworks seldom, if ever, are sited in the same type of location as ringforts and usually occupy the high ground on top of ridges and small hills. They occupy areas where there is often a degree of natural defence such as at the edge of cliffs or the end of inland promontories. Ringworks are also found in low-lying, wet ground but on a slight rise. For example, ringworks at Meelick and Clonard are beside rivers. The ringworks recently identified through the fieldwork of the Archaeological Survey indicate that most of the sites are located in strategic positions either controlling river crossings or passes through valleys. Other isolated examples appear to have been placed close to areas of historical and prehistoric interest such as at Loughcrew and Knowth in Co. Meath and

14

Rathmore, Rathcroghan, Co. Roscommon. The location of these three sites seems to be a statement to show that new rulers dominated areas of ancient importance rather than for strategic reasons alone.

West of the Shannon and in Ulster there are a considerable number of raised raths which consist of a circular raised platform enclosed by a fosse. In Co. Down, at Rathmullan, an excavated site ended as a motte but had four phases of occupation which pre-dated the Anglo-Norman fortification.[31] Another mound site in the same county at Gransha, was also excavated. Here, however, the final phase of occupation pre-dated the Anglo-Normans.[32] Raised raths are defined as flat-topped mounds, sometimes with a slight bank around the perimeter of the summit and with a ramped or causewayed entrance.[33] From the evidence of those excavated in Ulster it can be seen that their height was a result of prolonged occupation with occasional deliberate dumping of clean upcast material. However, some raised raths were formed in one operation so their height was achieved at the initial stage of building.[34] At Gransha the extra height of the mound gave it a motte-like appearance, but this was achieved in one operation prior to the Anglo-Norman invasion. In the barony of Ikerrin, Tipperary, an examination of platform ringforts concluded that they were not of medieval date because of their siting and location.[35]

A paper on the timber and earthwork fortifications in western Ireland pointed out that there was little easily recognisable physical evidence for Anglo-Norman settlement west of the Shannon and in parts of Munster.[36] Certainly, there is very little evidence for the classical motte-type castle, so we are dependent on finding other types of medieval earthwork castles for the physical remains of Anglo-Norman settlement. There are some cliff-edge forts which may be ringworks in Cork and in north Mayo recent fieldwork has turned up some hill-top enclosures which could also be of Anglo-Norman origin. In Co. Sligo almost 90 raised raths have been identified but only four mottes and one ringwork. Going on the basis of excavation results from similar sites in Ulster it is possible that between 25% and 50% of the raised raths could have Anglo-Norman remains on them. Therefore, raised raths could fill the void created by the lack of more easily recognisable, medieval earthwork fortifications in the western half of Ireland. Few raised raths, outside the Ulster counties, have been found in the eastern part of the country. In Monaghan, where there are only three mottes recorded, there are a number of raised raths similar in their morphology to those excavated in Co. Down. In Co. Cavan, eight mottes and one ringwork castle were recorded; however, a number of sites classified as ringforts in the *Archaeological Inventory* would appear to be ringwork castles. For instance at Drumcor, Drumharid, Cornaslieve and Lisnafana the enclosed area is raised considerably above the level of the surrounding land. The enclosing elements consist of a very large bank and a wide deep fosse and invariably

Fig. 7 Rathturtle Moat, Deerpark townland, Co. Wicklow. This probable ringwork was built on a high ridge overlooking the Douglas river.

they have causewayed entrances. However, as demonstrated by the excavation of a small number of raised raths in Co. Down, there is no way that we can be certain that any of these sites could be of Anglo-Norman origin. Virtually all of the sites listed as ringforts in Cavan are isolated and cannot be classified by their association with ecclesiastical remains. Since the Anglo-Normans settled areas west of the Shannon, in Munster and counties such as Monaghan and Cavan, they must have built earthwork castles. But as there are little or no obvious remains of their earthwork castles in these areas we must assume that some sites classified as ringforts, especially the raised or platform type, are in fact Anglo-Norman in origin, or Gaelic sites which have been adapted by the Anglo-Normans.

MOTTES

The most obvious physical evidence of early Anglo-Norman settlement in Ireland is the motte castle. Its classical form takes the shape of a Christmas pudding. However, fieldwork in Ireland in the last 20 years has shown that there is a wide variation in the shape and size of this type of earthwork castle. The extent to which the Norman conquest of Ireland was effective depended on how the great tenants controlled the conquered areas. The Anglo-Norman earthwork castles reflect this control in that, when the land was sub-divided, the sub-tenants built a stronghold, namely an earth and timber castle. Goddard Orpen was the first person to identify Irish mottes as the earthwork castles of the Anglo-Norman invasion.[37] He forcibly argued

16

for a Norman origin for many of our earthen mounds which up to this time had been considered pre-Norman or even pre-historic. Orpen was very well aware of the absence of mottes in the western half of Ireland. Another substantial paper on mottes and raths in Connacht observed:

> The Normans adopted the motte and bailey fortress as their ideal, using sometimes a natural rock or hillock as the citadel, or making one by piling up a mound. But they used other works freely, and abandoned it generally in Connacht in the middle of the thirteenth century for the flat motte type [i.e. the raised rath].[38]

Mottes are found almost exclusively in the eastern half of the country. Work by the Archaeological Survey of Ireland over the past 30 years has not changed this distribution to any great extent. In 1972, the total number of mottes was estimated to be *c.*340 for the whole of Ireland.[39] Since the Archaeological Survey commenced its data base for archaeological sites in the 26 counties this number has been increased to at least 456. In Leinster alone there are 275 mottes and between Antrim and Down there are at least 106, leaving only 75 in the rest of the country. Less than 16% of all mottes are found outside of Leinster, Antrim and Down. The distribution of these sites in Ulster is easily explained in terms of the Anglo-Norman settlement east of the River Bann and their lack of penetration westwards. While there are mottes in the centre of Ireland virtually none have been found in Cork, Kerry or west of the River Shannon. Since we know that the Normans conquered these regions they must have used other types of earthwork castles to hold their newly-acquired territories.

Mottes were constructed in Ireland into the second decade of the thirteenth century and they were used in Leinster in some instances at the end of that century.[40] The earthwork castle at Moydow Glebe, Co. Longford,

Fig. 8 Reconstruction of a motte and bailey (after Johnson, 1985).

17

Fig. 9 Distribution of
mottes in Ireland.

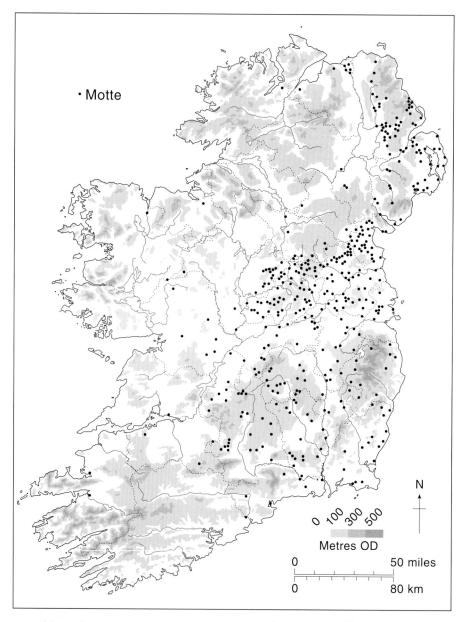

possibly a low motte, was not constructed until 1261.[41] Since it cannot therefore be argued that the motte was a redundant type of fortification by the time the Anglo-Normans conquered the west of Ireland, we are forced to accept the possibility that the raised raths and platform ringforts are the Anglo-Norman earthwork castles of the west.

The classical form of motte has the shape of a plum pudding. However, as can be seen from the detailed recording of the earthwork castles of Glamorgan, some mottes can have very low mounds rising barely above the surrounding ground level.[42] The most obvious division within the motte

Fig. 10 Clonard, Co. Meath. Motte sited on the bank of the river Deale across from a ringwork – on the opposite bank – and close to the famous early medieval monastic site (Chris Corlett).

category is whether or not they have baileys. In the six counties of Northern Ireland there are few mottes with baileys compared to English examples where it is the norm. The Ulster examples are also smaller.[43] Mottes in the eastern counties of Ulster are similar to those of Galloway, the most Gaelic part of the Scottish Lowlands.[44] Out of 336 mottes in the Republic of Ireland 149 or 44% have baileys. Mottes with baileys are concentrated on the borders of the Earldom of Ulster and only 23% of all the mottes in Ulster have baileys. Mottes and baileys are quite small in Antrim and Down, where they mainly occur, and they were often built within existing ringforts.[45]

In England the baileys were large enough to hold various buildings, including a hall, while the motte itself had a wooden tower on it for refuge. The Ulster baileys generally appear to be too small to hold a hall. Only about fourteen mottes have been archaeologically excavated in the whole of Ireland and very few of these have been excavated on a large scale. Four excavations of mottes in Co. Down gave some evidence of their defences and internal structures.[46] At Clough Castle, which is thought to be on the route followed by de Courcy when he invaded Ulster in 1177, excavations revealed post-holes of a palisade around the perimeter of the mound.[47] This excavation, which concentrated on the motte, concluded that the mound had no occupation prior to its final topping-off. The earliest defence of the site was the palisade which had been set back from the edge of the mound by up to 1m. The entrance way through the palisade was not found nor any evidence for a bridge from the bailey. A number of pits cut into the mound inside the line of the palisade were discovered and at least one of them was a weapon pit.[48]

At Lurgankeel, Co. Louth, an archaeological excavation in 1965 produced evidence for a timber palisade and a 'breastwork of timber posts

Fig. 11 Plan and section
of Glebe motte and
bailey, Co. Westmeath.

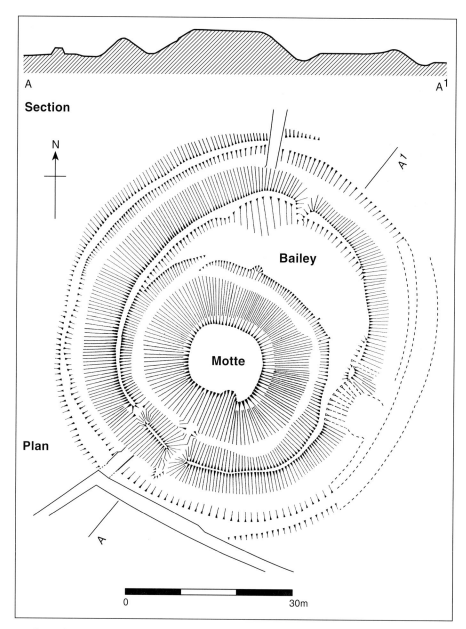

and earth'. In the centre of the mound there was evidence for a timber tower.
At Clough Castle, there was no evidence for a timber tower but a central
hollow was found and these hollows on the top of the mottes can indicate
the area where a wooden tower once stood and subsequently collapsed and
decayed. As has been noted in a study of timber castles in England, 'the very
act of demolishing a structure, a tower, a gate or a palisade will cause
disturbance of the earthworks which will tend to collapse down the sides'.[49]
The authors of this study also pointed out that there is increasing evidence
that ramparts and even the motte itself could have been revetted with

Fig. 12 Milltown, Co.
Meath. This motte, with
the ruins of a castle on
top, is sited close to a
medieval church – the
diagnostic components of
medieval nucleated
settlement
(Chris Corlett).

vertical timbers. When slippage is removed from the side of the mound a
virtual timber casing can be found and where palisade post holes are located
they may in some instances be part of an earth and timber wall.

Mottes were often constructed by using the material dug from the
enclosing fosse and piling it up on the perimeter of the intended mound so
that if it was never completed it would look like a ringfort or ringwork. Beal
Boru, Co. Clare, was originally a ringfort and the secondary fortification,
which had its banks heaped up on the primary enclosures, was intended, in
the excavator's view, to be a motte. Whether one accepts the secondary site
as a motte or a ringwork does not detract from the fact that the Anglo-
Normans were using an earlier structure on which to build their own
fortification. At Downpatrick, the Anglo-Norman mound appears to be built
at one end of an earlier fortification and seems to be an unfinished motte
rather than a ringwork. At Lismahon, also in Co. Down, a mound had three
building phases, the two earlier ones indicating pre-Norman occupation.[50]
The second phase of building consisted of heightening the mound and
enclosing it with a wooden revetment. The third phase of construction
consisted of raising the height by piling over a metre of the boulder clay on
top of the platform of phase two.

Several other mounds in eastern Ulster such as Castleskreen and
Rathmullan, Co. Down, Doonmore and Dunsilly, Co. Antrim, were occupied
and fortified prior to the Anglo-Normans taking them over. Other motte-like
mounds in Ulster which have been excavated – Gransha, Co. Down; Big
Glebe, Co. Derry; Deer Park Farms, Co. Antrim – produced only evidence
for pre-Norman occupation.[51] So the identification of low mounds as mottes

without baileys is just as much a problem as distinguishing some of the ringwork castles from large ringforts. The only sure way of identifying isolated low mottes without baileys is to excavate them. A small mound at Dunsilly, Co. Antrim, was excavated in the mid 1970s. It was sited at the edge of a low bluff near the River Burn. Its siting near the river, and the fact that it had a bailey, clearly identified this site as a motte even though the mound itself was very unimpressive.[52]

Recent fieldwork in the Republic of Ireland has shown that nearly 45% of mottes have baileys. Their siting and location beside rivers, in commanding positions, near medieval churches and directly associated with historical references can give us clear indications as to their true identity. Like the ringwork castle the smaller examples may be associated with the sub-division of the manor so that the smaller mottes should be found in the more isolated areas and would belong to sub-tenants. Twenty-five mottes were recorded in Co. Louth; fifteen of these have baileys, five are in close proximity to churches and thirteen are sited close to rivers. In Wexford, where there are only sixteen definite mottes, seven were found close to churches. In Cavan, Meath, Carlow, Laois, Wicklow, Offaly and

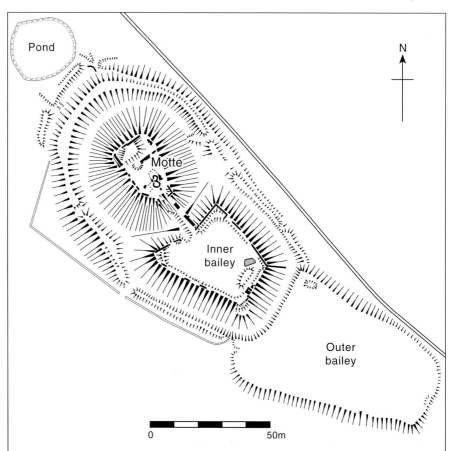

Fig. 13 Mannan Castle, Donaghmoyne, Co. Monaghan. A motte with two baileys, a causeway and the remains of a stone built castle (after O'Conor).

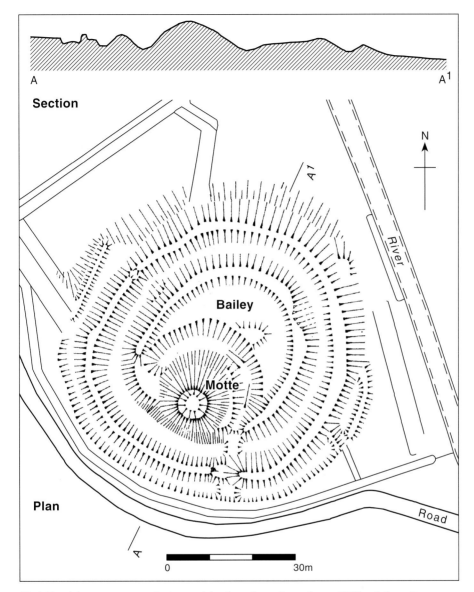

Fig. 14 Tonashammer, Co. Westmeath. Plan and section of a motte and bailey with multiple banks.

Dublin this same association with churches, in at least 25% of the sites, was noted. Their siting close to rivers and on high ground with commanding views is also typical.

As shown from the excavated mottes mentioned above, the earthworks as we see them today can be very misleading, in that their present form conceals as much as it reveals. Many of the mounds would have had much steeper sides and would have been revetted with stone or timber which has been robbed or decayed, allowing the mound to slump into a more gentle slope. Also, when we look at the earthwork remains of these early castles we tend to forget that what we see are only the foundations for wooden and, less often, stone structures which were placed on and around the mound.

Most if not all of the excavations that have taken place on mottes have concentrated on the top of the mound. This is unfortunate because if the motte had a bailey attached most of the domestic activity would have been located within the enclosure rather than on top of the mound. In other instances mottes selected for archaeological excavation can be so eroded and degraded that no evidence of their defences or occupation survived on top of the mound.

The activity on the top of the motte at Rathmullan, Co. Down, was dated to 1200 based on the finding of three coins and historical data.[53] The primary structure on the summit of this motte consisted of a rectangular wooden building which had been burnt down. No evidence was found for a palisade or any defensive element on the perimeter of the mound. The occupation of the motte phase of the mound at Lismahon, Co. Down, was tentatively dated to *c.*1200 and the date depended largely on the finding of a coin of John de Courcy. Evidence for a rectangular-shaped building, regarded as an 'English-style' hall, was found on top of the mound with evidence for a wooden tower attached to its north-east angle.

The excavation on the top of the mound of a motte and bailey at Dromore, Co. Down, produced evidence of two flimsy palisades around the perimeter.[54] This site was dated on documentary evidence to before 1211-12 because the Irish Pipe Roll from the fourteenth year of the reign of King John contains several entries which refer to a new bridge, hall and other buildings at Dromore. But like the motte at Clough, it was probably erected soon after 1177 by John de Courcy or one of his followers. A motte with a double bailey at Ballyroney, Co. Down, was partially excavated.[55] This site like many of

Fig. 15 Relagh Beg, Co. Cavan. Motte and bailey, one of the few in this county. Note the large, almost rectangular bailey.

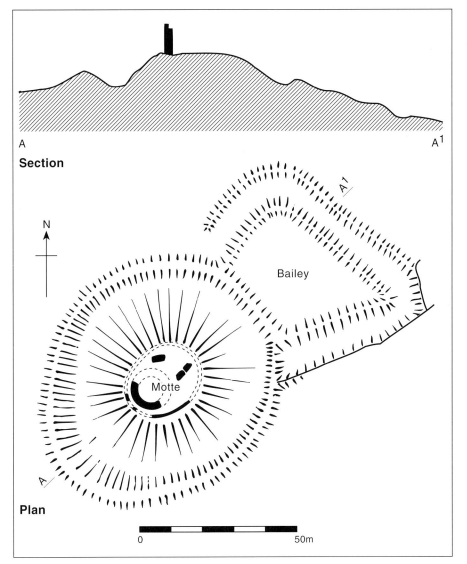

Aerial view of Shanid, Co. Limerick, from the east (Ordnance Survey).

Fig. 16 Plan and section of the motte and bailey at Shanid, Co. Limerick. The motte has a circular stone keep and curtain walls on its summit.

the mottes in Ireland is located close to a river on high ground. Both baileys were defended by a single bank and fosse. The motte was separated from the baileys by a fosse. Excavation at this site concentrated on the top of the mound but there was a reasonable quantity of small finds, including iron arrowheads and horseshoes, as well as a silver halfpenny of John (Lord of Ireland) and sherds of pottery. Another motte at Dunsilly, in Co. Antrim, was partially excavated but no remains of any structures were found on top of the mound.[56] Dunsilly had been constructed on top of a ringfort which had been occupied for some time. As can be seen from the brief description of most of the excavated mottes the amount of structural evidence is very sparse and, in some instances, there was little evidence of occupation or of any substantial defences. It is unfortunate that no one has excavated any motte and bailey thoroughly so that we could see exactly what areas of these earthwork castles were defended and occupied.

An earthwork at Castleskreen, Co. Down, was partially excavated in the early 1950s and it showed that it was constructed in three phases. The final phase, built around 1200, was intended to be a motte, but it does not appear to have had any defensive features on the top of the mound.[57] Clough Castle, Co. Down, of all the excavated sites, had the most elaborate buildings and defences, and appears to have been occupied from *c.*1200 to 1500. A number of archer pits, one with the remains of a stone loop built into the palisade, were found around the perimeter of the mound. By the middle of the thirteenth century a single-storey stone hall was constructed and, later in that century, a two-storey rectangular keep was built. A considerable quantity of small finds were found associated with the occupation on the top of the mound. Most of the pottery appears to have been local ware but some was imported from the Bordeaux region. There was also a large collection of pottery which was dated to the second half of the thirteenth century. A considerable number of iron objects and a few of bronze and bone were also discovered. So, compared to the other excavated mottes, it was relatively rich and must have been an important site, yet there are no historical references to it.

In Anglo-Norman Ulster, mottes with baileys were concentrated on the borders of the Earldom or beyond and there were none in the centre of the settlement in south Down or north Antrim.[58] In the Liberty of Meath (comprising modern Westmeath and Meath) it was claimed that mottes with baileys often had a frontier location.[59] However, work over the past twenty years by the Archaeological Survey shows a more random distribution. In

Fig. 17 Callan, Co. Kilkenny. Locations close to rivers are a common siting for earthwork castles.

Fig. 18 Cloncurry, Co. Kildare. This motte stands beside a medieval church and deserted medieval village.

Co. Louth, where a detailed survey has been carried out, most of the mottes and baileys have a riverine location rather than a political or military frontier siting. It has been suggested that the building of a seignorial castle (of earth and stone) might merely be a matter of prestige rather than defence.[60] Further, the excavated mottes at Rathmullan, Co. Down, and Dunsilly, Co. Antrim, did not appear to have defensive features on their summits, and Castleskreen, Co. Down, had its bailey occupied throughout the thirteenth century and yet had nothing built on top of the motte.[61] Some mottes were heightened with the intention of later fortifying them in the event of a likely attack. Henry III made an order in 1225 to the lesser Lords in the Vale of Montgomery to fortify their mottes with stockades. Similarly, King John made a command in 1200 that persons holding land in the marches of Ireland should fortify their castles. This probably means placing *bretasches* (wooden palisades) on top of already heightened mounds such as those at Dunsilly and Rathmullan.[62]

The vast majority of earthwork castles were built in the initial stages of the conquest. De Lacy, for instance, had built most of his fortifications in Meath for himself and his lesser Lords by 1181, according to Giraldus Cambrensis. But the vast majority of Co. Meath castles which were returned to Walter de Lacy from 1215 onwards were of earth and timber.[63] In addition, some of the important Marshal castles of Leinster in 1231 were earthworks. So we must remember that many of the earth and timber fortifications were built for long-term occupation and not merely for the initial conquest period. Despite the fact that Rohesia de Verdun had built a motte castle at

Fig. 19 The motte and
bailey of Old Connell on
the plains of Co. Kildare.

Mount Bagnall, Co. Louth, and had a manor at Castletown and a stone castle
at Castleroche, she was granted respite in 1242 regarding the colonisation of
her land in the heart of Co. Louth. In the early stages of settlement, the
baronies in Louth merely represented pre-existing boundaries. The charters
given to Pipard and de Verdun reflect these divisions in Oriel.[64] Mottes may
still have been used as fortifications until the beginning of the sixteenth
century especially in the outlying areas of a manor and, in Leinster, mottes
with baileys tend to occur at the *Capita* of the principal land grants.[65] In

Fig. 20 Aghaboe, Co.
Laois. This motte and
bailey is sited close to the
early medieval monastic
complex of the same
name. The motte is
squared off at the
summit and has
foundations of stone
walls around the
perimeter.

Plate 4   Clonmacnoise Castle, Co. Offaly, on the banks of the River Shannon with its strongly-built earthwork defences.

Plate 5   Trim Castle, Co. Meath. This magnificent castle is situated on the west bank of the River Boyne.

29

Plate 6   Adare Castle, Co. Limerick, was built on an earlier ringwork at the edge of the River Maigue.

Plate 7   Dunamase Castle, Co. Laois, was built on a large expanse of rock outcrop.

Co. Wicklow, a frontier region, few mottes with baileys occur on the periphery. Mottes without baileys in Leinster appear to have large summit areas, probably to compensate for the lack of space which would have been provided by the bailey.

Some mottes have 'squared-off' or angular summits as at Aghaboe, Co. Laois, or at Faughart Upper, Co. Louth. In some instances the 'squaring-off' of the mound may be due to refortification of the motte by building a masonry wall around its summit. Several of the mottes in Co. Louth illustrated by Wright had quite substantial stone fortifications.[66] The remains of some of these fortifications can still be seen at Faughart Upper, Ash Big, Castlering and Stormanstown. At Aghaboe there are the remains of wall footings around the edge of the summit of the mound. Some of these stone walls around the edges of the summit may not be part of the original fortification and may also contribute to the 'squared-off' look of the motte. Other motte summits such as at Racraveen, Co. Cavan, have what appear to be low earthen banks around their edges, which may be the remains of an earth and timber palisade, rather than a stone wall, and would therefore be an original feature of the motte.

Since 1986 the Archaeological Survey has been publishing county by county archaeological inventories and it is hoped by the end of the millennium the fieldwork will almost be completed. All the present information is on a data-base and readily available but, unfortunately, when the field survey first commenced, there was often a lack of knowledge which would have helped in the precise classification of the medieval earthworks. Recent fieldwork in Tipperary, Offaly and Roscommon, to name but three

Faughart Upper,
Co. Louth

Mountbagnall,
Co. Louth

Killanny,
Co. Louth

Three mottes in Co. Louth, taken from illustrations in Wright's *Louthiana* (1758).

Fig. 21 Donohill motte and bailey in Moatquarter, south Co. Tipperary. A prominent earthwork with fragmentary remains of a stone castle on top. This site is also located near a medieval church.

31

counties, has demonstrated the diversity of the medieval earthwork and probably for the first time since Orpen published his work on mottes, we are making real progress in our identification of the Anglo-Norman earthworks and their distribution. This work needs to be followed-up by a campaign of selective excavation on the baileys as well as the tops of mottes and on the various forms of possible ringworks such as cliff-edge forts. Until such investigations are carried out it is difficult to see how we can progress our knowledge of the Anglo-Norman earthwork castle in Ireland.

CHAPTER TWO

THE ANGLO-NORMAN STONE FORTRESS

The main period of stone fortress building in Ireland was from 1175 to *c*.1310. Hugh de Lacy, with the blessing of the king, and in order to offset the power of Strongbow in Ireland, whom he did not trust, set about building a network of castles in his newly acquired domain. Having established his authority in the Kingdom of Meath with earth and timber castles he began to build more permanent and more spectacular stone structures. The earliest and most important of these is the impressive stone fortress of Trim. The large stone fortresses of the late twelfth and early thirteenth centuries are the most spectacular evidence of domination by the Anglo-Normans in Ireland. Their location on high ground and in strategic positions close to river crossings and ports must have had a dramatic effect on the lives of the native Irish. Not only did they control the commerce of the country but these massive piles dominated the landscape and intimidated the people.

Harold Leask, when he wrote his pioneering book *Irish Castles*, a work which has never been surpassed, divided them into various groups or classifications.[1] These were based on various criteria including whether or not they had a keep, were built on rock or in urban areas, etc. While it helped to record Irish castles by putting them in various groups it was in some ways a restrictive approach. However, no one since Leask has attempted seriously to classify or place in groups, whether based on date or type, the stone fortresses of the Anglo-Normans.

Castles 'are at once the best known and the least understood of medieval buildings',[2] but few scholars in Ireland have taken the time or the trouble to reassess the original work of Leask. However, it is extremely doubtful if any one person will ever have the time or resources to visit every castle in Ireland and study them in detail. Fortunately, the Archaeological Survey is nearing completion of its preliminary field work in the 26 counties so that at least we will know in the next few years how many castles we have and how many of those are early fortresses. Since 1970 a number of these early stone castles have been excavated and, while it has not radically altered our knowledge of these fortresses, it has certainly added greatly to it. A large number of castles were recorded in the 1940s, despite a lack of adequate transport, by using a network of Clerks-of-Works in the Office of Public Works who worked on the conservation of monuments throughout the country – a structure which largely still exists. Some drawings from this period are very accurate while others are not so good – it all depended on the ability of the men in the field and whether or not Leask was able to find the time to transport himself and his bicycle by train to the remoter parts of Ireland. Leask's interpretation of medieval buildings is very good and has stood the test of time.

The only detailed survey work that has been carried out in recent years is that of Co. Louth where detailed drawings and descriptions were made of most of the castles in the county. Inventory-like descriptions of Irish castles have been done by other researchers,[3] but none have matched the incisive and scholarly study of the medieval fortifications of Britain.[4]

The development of the Anglo-Norman stone fortresses in Ireland is to a large extent linked to historical figures and events. The earliest castles were built by a handful of powerful knights and, in particular, Hugh de Lacy, who held sway over a large part of the southeast, and John de Courcy who controlled most of Ulster. The two earliest and greatest Anglo-Norman fortresses were erected by these Lords. De Lacy controlled his territory from the ports of Drogheda and Dublin and the greatest of the fortresses in Ireland, Trim Castle, Co. Meath. De Courcy's most impressive stone castle, Carrickfergus, Co. Antrim, stands on the shores of Belfast Lough.

SITING

A number of these early fortresses were built on pre-existing earthwork castles which had been erected in the first years of the Anglo-Norman campaign. For example, Trim's donjon or keep is built on a ringwork castle which had been constructed by Hugh de Lacy; Ferns Castle is partially built on a ringwork as is a similarly constructed castle in Carlow town.[5] Other examples are at Adare, Co. Limerick, which has the keep built on a substantial ringwork; Kilkenny, where excavations have revealed a portion of a large enclosing fosse underneath the west wing of the existing building; and Limerick where excavators found a stone-revetted earthen bank with a wide fosse positioned under part of the remains of the stone castle.[6] Most of these early fortresses are also sited close to water and this often coincides with the fact that they are built on earlier earthwork castles, usually a ringwork, which controlled a crossing or commerce on the waterway. For instance the Boyne River, which de Lacy controlled up to Trim, was navigable from the port of Drogheda albeit with flat-bottomed boats. De Lacy chose to build his major stone fortress at Trim rather than Drogheda, where he had established the town by constructing a large motte at Millmount near the River Boyne, and by setting up two parishes maintained by the Augustinians. De Lacy therefore controlled a port town which could supply with provisions his other major fortress of Trim. Recent excavations at the castle of Trim revealed a slipway and storage facilities at the east end

Fig. 22 Carrickfergus Castle, Co. Antrim, sited on the shores of Belfast Lough (John Scarry).

of the great hall at the edge of the River Boyne.[7] Trim was also a frontier town and the castle protected de Lacy's newly acquired territory to the east. It also kept the Irish under control immediately to the west as far as Athlone on the River Shannon, where another earthwork castle was erected in 1200, and a stone castle built over it *c.*1210.

King John's Castle, Carlingford, Co. Louth, was built on rock on the edge of and overlooking Carlingford Lough where it commanded a very strong position. Its exact date of building, like most Irish castles, is not known but judging by its rectangular-shaped twin gate-towers it must be at the beginning of the thirteenth century. Its position on the western shore of the Lough protected the settlement to its south where a walled town, two monasteries and a church were founded. It also controlled the harbour on which it was founded and must have had some considerable influence on commerce up and down the Lough. By the time King John arrived in Ireland the de Lacys appear to have had control of the east coast up to Carrickfergus. Hugh, who was not apparently prepared to make peace with John, fled to Carrickfergus despite the fact that Walter, his brother, placed all his castles in the king's hand. John occupied Carlingford Castle on his drive northwards along the east coast so there must have been a substantial fortress there for him to occupy. After a short siege Carrickfergus fell to the king and Hugh de Lacy escaped by sea. In just nine weeks King John had driven the de Lacys out of both the Lordships of Meath and Ulster and had taken them into his own control. William Marshal now was the only magnate of first rank left in Ireland.

Although the Anglo-Normans had taken control of Limerick in 1175 and the castle of Limerick is referred to as a royal building, presumably built at

Fig. 23 Limerick Castle on King's Island on the banks of the River Shannon (from a sketch by Robert O'Callaghan Newenham)

the command of Henry II, it is doubtful if it dates to before *c*.1200 since it was not until 1197 that the Anglo-Normans finally took full control of the city. There are several good references to the castle in the early thirteenth century and we may assume it was built by the end of the first decade. This large fortress, with its impressive twin-towered gateway, stands on the east bank of the River Shannon within the city of Limerick and forms part of the extensive defences of the medieval walled town. It also appears from recent excavations that there was an earlier earthwork castle here, apparently a ringwork dating to *c*.1175 whose enclosing elements consisted of a stone-faced bank and fosse. It is sited on King's Island where it controlled traffic into the town from the west across Thomond bridge as well as shipping coming up and down the lower reaches of the Shannon River. Adare Castle, Co. Limerick, which is sited on the north bank of the River Maigue, was built on a pre-existing Anglo-Norman earthwork and, like Trim and the other early fortresses, controlled traffic on the river. There appear to be no historical references to the earthwork castle at Adare and the stone fortress is not mentioned before 1226 but parts of the structure could date to the first decade of the thirteenth century.

Lea, Co. Laois, which is situated on low-lying ground on the south bank of the River Barrow, appears also to have been constructed on the remains of a ringwork castle.[8] Clonmacnoise on the banks of the River Shannon is built inside earthwork defences which would also appear to have been a pre-existing ringwork. Athlone, Co. Westmeath, can also be added to the list of riverside locations for early stone castles built on earlier Anglo-Norman earthwork fortifications. Dundrum, Co. Down, which was built by John de Courcy following his invasion of Ulster in 1177, appears at first also to have

Fig. 24 Limerick Castle prior to recent excavations and conservation works.

been some type of ringwork castle. A defensive bank of this period (*c*.1177) was found during the course of an archaeological excavation. However, in this case the castle is not sited on a river but on high ground overlooking Dundrum Bay. Maynooth Castle, Co. Kildare, is built on slightly elevated ground at the junction of and between two streams (Lyreen and Owenslade). The manor of Maynooth was granted by Strongbow to Maurice FitzGerald in 1176 but the stone castle was probably not built until *c*.1203. Since the grant took place in 1176 one would expect the same arrangements as most other large early Anglo-Norman fortresses, with there being clear evidence of an earthwork on the same site as the later stone castle. Excavations in 1996 in the hall-keep at ground-floor level found evidence of an earlier structure.[9] However, further investigation would be required to prove that we have an earthwork castle here.

Some of the larger early Anglo-Norman stone fortresses were not built near rivers or beside inlets and the sea. However, in most instances, these castles would have been built on pre-existing earthwork castles or within an earlier settlement. For instance Dublin Castle was built under a mandate by King John in 1204 (probably the only genuine King John's Castle in Ireland) because the Justiciar of Ireland had no safe place for the treasury, had need of a strong fortress within the City of Dublin and wanted a suitable place for administration. The location is on high ground away from the River Liffey and appears from historical records to have been built on the site of an earlier fortification. Ferns Castle, Co. Wexford, built by one of the Marshals

37

in the first quarter of the thirteenth century, is also located away from water but is situated on a pre-existing ringwork castle and is close to an early medieval monastic settlement. Carbury Castle, Co. Kildare, is a multi-period fortress sited on high ground in a very isolated area with no obvious easy access to it. It is, however, close to a graveyard and church which could originally have been contemporary with the building of the earthwork castle which is sited immediately to the west of the stone fortress. Also, like Loughcrew and Knowth, there are prehistoric burial mounds which are located on higher ground to the south of the castle. The Barony of Carbury was granted to Meiler FitzHenry but was later a manor in the ownership of William Marshal. It is first mentioned in 1234 by which time the earliest phase of the stone castle must have been built.

Dunamase Castle, Co. Laois, is dramatically sited crowning a massive rock overlooking the surrounding countryside. Unusually, this massive fortress was built on a pre-existing native Irish stone fort and recent excavations have uncovered part of this early fortification underneath one of the Anglo-Norman gateways of the inner ward. Strongbow appears to have inherited this Irish fortification and the first Anglo-Norman fortress here seems to have been built by Meiler FitzHenry near the end of the twelfth century and was further added to by William Marshal early in the thirteenth. It seems that all the standing remains of the early stone fortress were completed by 1211. Under Marshal the castle was the centre of military power and administration in this part of Leinster.[10] Theobald Walter, chief of the Butler family, built Nenagh Castle sometime between 1200 and 1220 on Ormond lands granted to him by Henry II. It stands on high ground in an

Fig. 25 Maynooth Castle, Co. Kildare. The remains of the gateway (centre) and great tower are located between two streams.

Fig. 26 Castleroche, Co. Louth, is built on a rock outcrop in a dominant position similar to Dunamase.

area which was surrounded by wood, well away from any obvious thoroughfare and some distance from the Nenagh River. Archaeological excavations in and around the gatehouse did not reveal any pre-masonry structure suggesting that it was not built on an earlier earthwork castle.[11] Despite its seemingly isolated location, Nenagh Castle became the strong point of the Anglo-Norman settlement in north Tipperary.

Carlow Castle, partially excavated in 1997,[12] is one of Leask's so-called 'towered keeps'.[13] Ferns, Co. Wexford; Lea, Co. Laois; Carlow, Co. Carlow and Terryglass, Co. Tipperary, all have large rectangular-shaped keeps with round towers at each angle and all appear to have been built by or for William Marshal the elder or the younger or a combination of both between 1207 and 1225. Carlow Castle is built on a slight rise at the confluence of the Rivers Burren and Barrow and therefore controlled traffic up and down these waterways. Excavations revealed the remains of post-holes inside the line of a curving fosse underneath the walls of the keep, clearly indicating that there was a ringwork castle here prior to the stone building. Historical sources suggest that this earth and timber castle was constructed by Hugh de Lacy in 1180. William Marshal the elder commenced work on the stone building in 1210 to control the movement of traffic on the navigable River Barrow down to New Ross, Co. Wexford.[14] In the process of constructing the stone castle the earthwork defences were flattened but remains of the fosse and the post-holes of the palisade survived because they had been originally cut so deeply into the subsoil.[15] The excavation revealed that the keep, like that at Ferns uncovered by excavation in the 1970s, had no foundations and their walls were set directly on the undisturbed boulder clay. In the case of Ferns the keep was built at two slightly different levels because the earthwork castle was not totally levelled but flattened enough to build the walls directly on top. There was also some evidence that the earlier castle may have been partially encased in stone.

Dungarvan, Co. Waterford, is one of the few Royal Castles built in Ireland, others being Rindown, Co. Roscommon, Limerick, Dublin and Athlone, Co. Westmeath. The Dungarvan area was taken into the King's hands in 1204 and work on the stone castle commenced before 1209. It is built on the shore of a sheltered bay at the mouth of the River Calligan controlling trade to the harbour and town which expanded around it. Excavations have revealed that there was a large fosse around the shell keep which may possibly pre-date it.[16] However, the excavation was too limited to discover its relationship to the shell keep. An enclosing bank of earth and stones was also partially uncovered to the east of the fosse. It appears also to be an early feature and runs up to the edge of the fosse at its north-western end. It is possible that the fosse is part of an earthwork castle (maybe a ringwork) and the stone and earthen bank is part of a bailey.

Another early stone castle is Dundrum, Co. Down, which was built by John de Courcy before his downfall in 1203. It is sited on the summit of a prominent hill on the west shore of Dundrum Inner Bay. The site was first occupied at the end of the first millennium AD and then as an Anglo-Norman earthwork castle so its position was considered by de Courcy, as well as the native Irish, to be strategically important for controlling the immediate hinterland and, in de Courcy's case, for his ambition to conquer Ulster. Rindown Castle, Co. Roscommon, is also sited on an earlier native Irish fortification and was built in 1227 by Geoffrey de Marisco on the peninsula of St John's Point on the western shore of Lough Ree. It is built at the narrowest point on the promontory and was used by de Courcy as a bridgehead for ferrying his troops across Lough Ree from Rindown after his defeat in Connacht in 1200-1201. It was therefore a strategically important fortification in the conquest of Connacht and would also have controlled traffic to some extent on the Lough. It was in Royal hands for much of the thirteenth and fourteenth centuries and was one of the most important Anglo-Norman fortifications in Connacht.

Clogh Oughter Castle, Co. Cavan, is one of only three Anglo-Norman stone fortresses in Ireland built on islands in lakes, the others being on Lough Key, Co. Roscommon, and on Lough MacNean Upper, Co. Cavan. Clogh Oughter Castle was constructed on an artificial island in shallow water not too far from the shore of Lough Oughter.[17] It was possibly first used as a crannóg but the excavation of a small area found no evidence of this. The frontier castle was constructed by Hugh de Lacy or his half-brother William Gorm de Lacy before 1224 and probably after 1220.

It can be seen from the above examples that most early thirteenth-century stone fortresses were sited on earlier Anglo-Norman earth and timber castles or less often on native Irish forts. This occurred simply because the later buildings were taking advantage of an already established area of control. Therefore, if one looks carefully at these early castles and their siting, one will invariably see evidence of an earlier earthwork fortification although, in some instances such as Ferns and Carlow, they were only revealed as a result of archaeological excavation.

OUTER DEFENCES

The expression 'An Englishman's home is his castle' may have some truth but what makes a true castle is its defences. Many so-called castles for instance in Scotland are merely 'châteaux' or grand houses of the late sixteenth or early seventeenth centuries and are not true castles because they do not have the defensive features of the medieval fortress. The castle is essentially feudal and is the fortified residence of a lord in a society dominated by the military. So the earliest Anglo-Norman castles in Ireland, although they were the homes of the conquering knights, had to be defensible because the territory in which they were being erected was hostile. Most of these early stone fortresses were built on pre-existing earthwork castles for the obvious reason that the site had already been secured. However, many of these early castles, whether of stone or earth and timber, were immediately captured or destroyed by the native Irish. For instance at Trim, Hugh de Lacy's ringwork was captured by Roderick O'Connor in 1173 and burnt to the ground; Clogh Oughter, Co. Cavan, built *c*.1221-24 to control the native Irish, was captured shortly afterwards by the O'Reillys and appears to have remained in their control for some considerable time. Also, even though grants of land in Ireland were made by Henry II, John and Henry III, to knights like de Lacy, de Courcy and de Verdon, there was no guarantee that they could get the specified land because first they had to conquer it and, secondly, they had to hold it. All the great Lords who held castles had been knights and had retinues of knights in their households. Therefore these early castles were primarily feudal fortresses and in a way can be compared to the castles built by Edward I (albeit that they were almost 100 years later than the Irish ones) in his effort to finally conquer Wales.

The outer defences of medieval castles were built to withstand a variety of medieval siege instruments. Depicted here are a siege tower and battering ram for breaking down castle walls (top), and a catapult for firing missiles over walls.

All the early Anglo-Norman stone castles in Ireland are fortresses and are built in strategic positions to control and dominate in the newly acquired territories. For instance, the large stone fortress on the Rock of Dunamase is in such a prominent position that it can be seen for miles around and, when close to it, is intimidating. On approaching the castle from the southeast one is first faced with the outer defences which now consist of a wide deep fosse which presumably had wooden palisades on its inner and outer edges since there is no evidence of a substantial bank here. There is a causeway across these

Fig. 27 Plan of
Dunamase Castle,
Co. Laois.

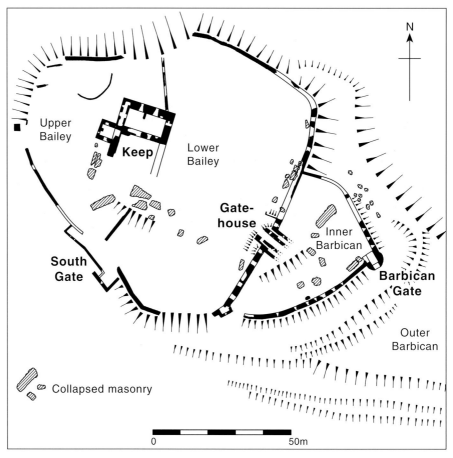

earthen and wooden defences which was probably defended by a wooden gatehouse and which gave access to the outer barbican. A further set of earthworks protecting the inner barbican would have had another causeway across them leading to the outer stone gateway. This gateway, which leads into the inner barbican area, has been partially excavated and the remains of slots for a drawbridge were found.[18] Work on the gate into the lower ward, which leads from the inner barbican, uncovered extensive remains which predated the Anglo-Norman fortress.[19] This once again illustrates the point that these sites were chosen by the Anglo-Normans to impose themselves on pre-existing places of importance to the native Irish. The early remains, which consisted of uncoursed drystone walling of large boulders and blocks, were stratified under the Anglo-Norman walls and could be of ninth-century origin. Also uncovered were the remains of a simple, rectangular-shaped, gate-building to the east of the present gatehouse. This early gate-building had at least a first-floor level since evidence was found for a stairs in one of its angles. When the present gatehouse was built the entrance in the early one was blocked-up and a base-batter added to the outer face of the building to line up with the new

THE ANGLO-NORMAN STONE FORTRESS

Fig. 28 The outer gateway of Dunamase Castle, Co. Laois (David Sweetman).

curtain wall and entranceway. The new curtain wall also had a considerable number of plunging arrow-loops at two levels with embrasures placed in it along its entire length. The new curtain placed great emphasis on archery as a means of defence.[20] This system of plunging arrow loops in two tiers is also to be seen in the curtain wall protecting the inner barbican and is attributed to the work of William Marshal between 1208 and 1210.[21] The excavation revealed four additional embrasures to those that could already be seen, giving a total of eleven protecting the southern approach. As with

Fig. 29 The inner gateway of Dunamase Castle, Co. Laois, after excavation (David Sweetman).

Fig. 30 The Dublin
gateway and barbican at
Trim Castle, Co. Meath.

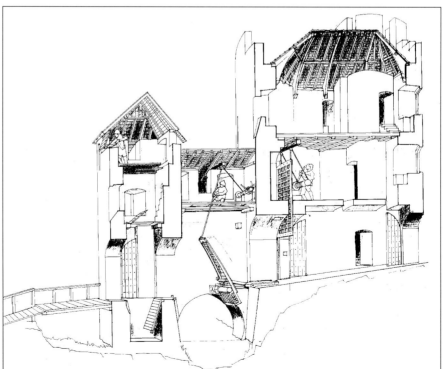

Fig. 31 Reconstruction
drawing of a section
through the Dublin
gateway (Kevin O'Brien).

Fig. 32 Remains of the inner defences were uncovered during recent excavations at Trim Castle, Co. Meath. These defences protected the first-floor entrance to the keep.

most early Anglo-Norman fortresses in Ireland the cut-stone surrounds for these opes (or windows) were of sandstone.

Excavation results and the historical background suggest that the early gate-tower dates to the late twelfth century and that its replacement was erected by William Marshal in the thirteenth century.[22] The later gateway, with its twin subrectangular-shaped towers, did not have a drawbridge pit and depended on a portcullis and flanking fire from plunging arrow loops for its defence. There are five loops in each tower and these were accessed via a mural passage which leads into a rectangular-shaped chamber. Besides the portcullis, which was set behind the line of the outermost pair of arrow loops, there was a wooden gate which provided the first line of defence for the gateway.

Although Trim Castle is not in as prominent a siting as Dunamase its defensive features are even more impressive. The castle is built on high ground at the southern side of the River Boyne. This elevated site was scarped back to bedrock all the way round and the curtain wall with its mural towers was built against the exposed rock-face. This gives the added advantage of having the ground high immediately inside the walls and a dramatic fall outside. It also meant that the curtain walls could not be easily undermined since they are founded on and backed by solid rock. A large quantity of the stone required for the building was quarried from immediately outside the curtain walls while creating a large rock-cut moat. At the town side of the castle an early gateway with a barbican (no longer

Fig. 33a   Plan of Trim
Castle, Co. Meath.

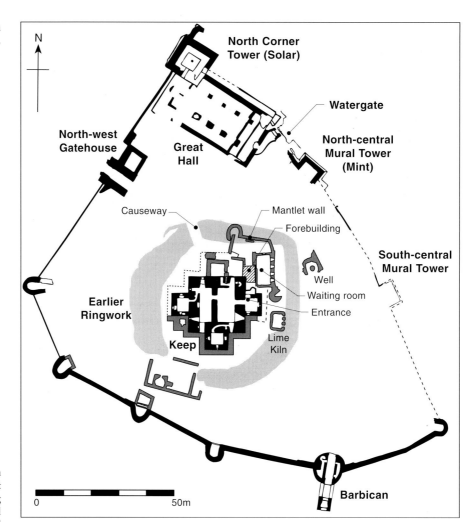

**North Corner
Tower (Solar)**

N

Watergate

**North-west
Gatehouse**

**North-central
Mural Tower
(Mint)**

**Great
Hall**

Causeway

Mantlet wall

Forebuilding

**South-central
Mural Tower**

Well

**Earlier
Ringwork**

Waiting room

Entrance

Lime
Kiln

Keep

0   50m

Barbican

Fig. 33b   Reconstruction
drawing of the north-east
curtain walls showing
the watergate and
the great hall
(Kevin O'Brien).

Mint

Great Hall

Solar

North
Corner
Tower

Friary

Watergate

standing) and portcullis was built. A later gateway, with a large circular gate-tower, centrally pierced, and a rectangular-shaped barbican, was constructed at the Dublin side of the castle. These outer defences are so strong it is highly unlikely that the castle could seriously have been under threat from the indigenous population in the medieval period. Even if the outer defences could have been breached there were substantial inner defences around the keep. Recent excavations have revealed that as well as a fosse running completely around the keep its first floor entrance was protected by a fore-building.[23] By the mid-thirteenth century a mantlet wall inside the line of the fosse was added with a drawbridge entrance across the fosse. There appears also to have been a drawbridge at the entrance to the keep, which was lowered from corbels, and a wooden hoarding at second-floor level in order to bridge a pit-like area formed between the up-standing masonry. The mantlet wall of the defences of the inner ward also contains a number of arrow-loops with narrow, splayed embrasures.

Clonmacnoise, which dates to the beginning of the thirteenth century, is built on the east bank of the Shannon River overlooking the famous monastic site just to its north. It is built on a much smaller scale than Trim but has similar defensive features such as a keep built within earthwork defences. Its gatehouse, which was three storeys high, was pierced in the same way as the townside gateway at Trim. Only its south-west gable remains intact. At each level it had narrow slit opes set in widely splayed embrasures. The most notable feature of this castle is the fore-building which protected the first-floor entrance to the keep. This building, now almost completely collapsed, originally had a drawbridge and pit set laterally to the north wall of the keep. Access to the fore-building appears to have been from the wall-walk area.[24] Its main defences on the landward sides depended on the large earthwork with its wide deep fosse and outer bank. This bank must also have had a substantial palisade set into it since the bank in itself would not have been sufficiently defensive. Another early gateway is to be found at Adare. It is rectangular in plan and is two storeys high, with a chamber to one side of the entranceway and a single chamber overhead. There is a fosse outside the gateway which was fed by the River Maigue and there is a causeway through it opposite the gateway which also must have been defended. If the outer defences were penetrated then there was the wide deep inner fosse which surrounded the keep. A gatehouse and drawbridge structure protected this inner entranceway which led to the inner ward.

At King John's Castle in Carlingford, there are the foundation levels of a rectangular, twin-towered, centrally pierced gateway which dates to the early thirteenth century.[25] This is a rare type of gatehouse in Ireland since the other early examples have the entranceway to one side. Unfortunately, only a few courses of the lower levels of the gatehouse survive and the only feature to be seen is the remains of a stairwell in the northern tower. The

Reconstruction drawing of a wooden hoard on a curtain wall. Wooden hoardings or galleries enabled defenders to shoot arrows and drop stones on attackers below (Katie Sweetman).

Fig. 34 Plan and section of King John's Castle, Carlingford, Co. Louth. The plan shows the site of the original twin-towered gateway, the mural tower and the angle tower.

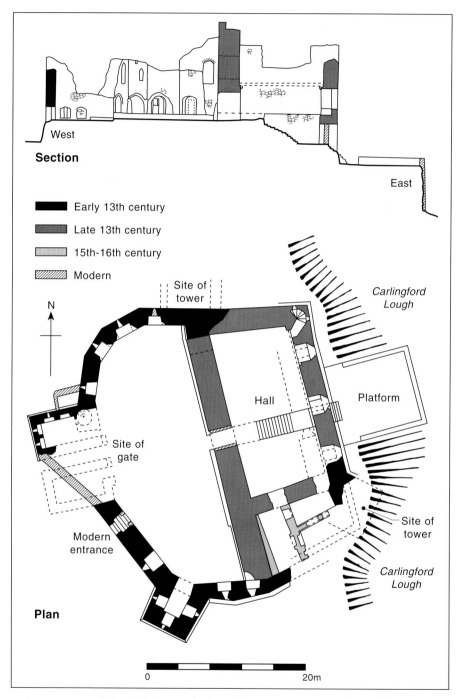

gateway was defended by a series of narrow opes with wide, shallow, squared-off embrasures. The southern tower, which has only a small portion of foundations showing, is also partially covered by a modern enclosing wall. It is therefore not possible to see any defences of the gate-passage such as a portcullis. There is no evidence of a moat outside the

48

curtain walls, which are founded on limestone, and the castle seems to have depended on its position on a steep rock outcrop as a natural defence. However, there is clear evidence for a wooden hoarding having been attached to the curtain walls at parapet level and plunging arrow loops at first-floor level in the west portion of the castle which would have added considerably to its defences. There is a projecting tower at the south-west angle, another one at the north and a possible third one at the south-east angle.[26] Recent cleaning and conservation work below the level of the modern platform, outside the east side of the curtain wall, revealed two garderobe chutes at the base of its north wall. There was, therefore, a fourth projecting tower at the east side overlooking the sea. This projecting tower may be a late thirteenth-century addition at the time that the vaults were constructed inside the east wall of the castle. This tower is in an obvious place to defend the seaward side of the castle and to act as a lookout for any movement on the lough.

At Maynooth there is a simple rectangular gatehouse with no side chambers but with first and second floor accommodation above. A map of 1630 shows that the gateway was protected by a barbican wall and an outer ward. This ward could be quite late as it is illustrated as having a bastion at its south angle. The gatehouse is not part of the original stone defences of the castle and may have been built or rebuilt in the later medieval period, certainly after the great stone tower or keep was erected *c*.1200. However, the layout as depicted in 1630 represents the type of defences the castle would have had when it was first built. If the attacker got through the outer and inner defences he would then be faced with the defences of the great tower or keep. This had a first floor entrance, which is a common feature of castles of this period, defended by a large fore-building as is evidenced by tie-stones projecting from the face of the north-east wall.

Fig. 35   Sir Henry Sydney rides out of the gates of Dublin Castle (no longer extant). Dublin is an early example of a keepless castle in Ireland (John Derricke, 1581).

49

Fig. 36 Plan of Dublin Castle showing wall foundations uncovered during recent excavations.

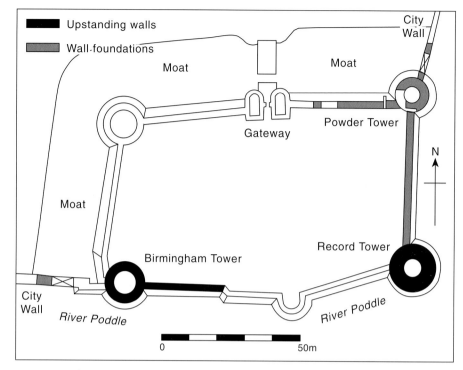

Two of the early thirteenth-century castles, Dublin and Limerick, were built under Royal command. This is not usual for Ireland where most castles were built by the great lords such as Marshal, de Lacy, de Courcy, etc. The gateways of both of these castles, which were built shortly after the first decade of the thirteenth century, had twin D-shaped towers. That at Limerick had a building at the back of the gate-tower which was in effect an extension of the entranceway created by building a wall each side of the passage. This rear portion of the gateway has been destroyed but the tie-stones for it can still be seen and excavations in 1993 uncovered the remains of the walls below the modern ground surface. Presumably there was also a chamber over the back portion of the gateway as indicated by the tie-stones at the rear of the building. No evidence of the Dublin gateway other than the causeway was unearthed during archaeological excavation in the mid 1980s. However, seventeenth-century plans of the castle show it to have been a subrectangular enclosure with the gateway in the centre of the north wall, a round tower at each angle and a small tower in the middle of the south wall. This type of defence with its open plan and no free-standing great tower or keep appears to have developed in France at the beginning of the thirteenth century and is also seen in Wales at sites such as Montgomery and Usk. Kilkenny Castle, recently partially excavated, also seems to have had the same ground plan. In the cases of Dublin and Kilkenny a considerable amount of modern building within the castles has removed much of the medieval fabric. Excavations at both sites uncovered a surprising number of medieval

Fig. 37 A seventeenth-century plan of Limerick Castle from *Pacata Hibernia*.

Fig. 38 Early eighteenth-century drawing of the gateway at Limerick Castle (W.H. Bartlett).

Fig. 39 Plan of Kilkenny
Castle, Co. Kilkenny.

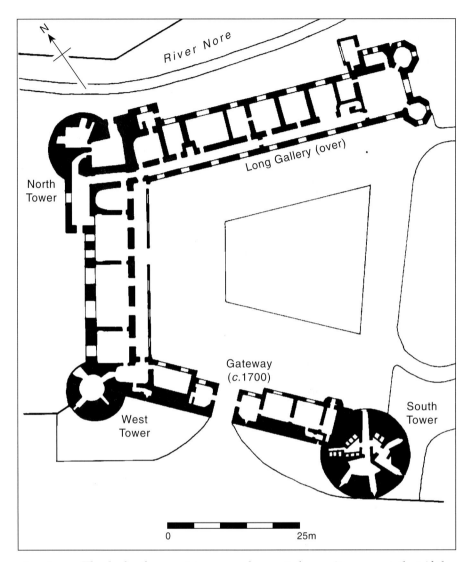

structures. The lack of a great tower or keep at these sites meant that if the
outer walls were breached there was no strong point within the castle to
retreat to. The strength of the castle's defences therefore lay in their enclosing
walls, wide moats and strong gateways. In addition, all of the castle
gateways would have been protected by a portcullis, a drawbridge and a
moat. Some of the gate passages also had murder-holes over them. Many like
Trim, Dunamase, Maynooth, etc. would have stone and/or wooden defences
outside the line of the gateway and/or the fosse. At Trim both gateways were
protected by a barbican, drawbridge, portcullis and murder-hole.

The great gatehouse at Carrickfergus is sited at the northern end of the
rock on which the castle is built and gives access through the outer curtain
which appears to have been constructed in the second quarter of the
thirteenth century.[27] It originally had two completely round towers prior to

Fig. 40   Aerial view of Kilkenny Castle showing the remaining towers which contain medieval fabric.

alterations in the first part of the fourteenth century. This gateway was also defended by a portcullis and a bridge pit which had been cut into the bedrock. However, there is no evidence of a drawbridge in the gatehouse and nothing was found in the pit during the course of its excavation which would indicate any method of pivoting such a bridge. The pit must therefore

Fig. 41   Reconstruction drawing of Kilkenny Castle in the thirteenth century.

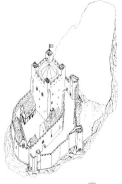

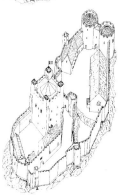

Reconstruction drawings of Carrickfergus Castle, Co. Antrim, *c.*1225 (top) and *c.*1250 (bottom) showing its two main phases of construction (after McNeill).

have been spanned by a structure like a ship's gangway. The earliest castle here, which was probably built by John de Courcy *c.*1178, consisted of a great tower at the north end of its small ward protected by a stone wall at the south end of the rock. This early castle had no projecting towers on its curtain wall and had only a simple gateway. It therefore relied on the strength of its curtain wall and its naturally defended position, with the lough surrounding it on all but the north side, where it was protected by a rock-cut fosse. However, like some of the other early Irish stone castles it had a keep or great tower that could be retreated to if the curtain walls were breached.

Nenagh Castle has a twin-towered gateway but only the eastern tower still stands. The towers were round but with straight sides at the south wall of the gatehouse facing the passageway. The excavation of the gatehouse passageway revealed a drawbridge slot and pit at the front of the entrance.[28] An English short-cross coin (1205-1217) was found in the foundation trench for the gatehouse which puts the building of the castle firmly in the first quarter of the thirteenth century. The drawbridge was a counterbalance one. Although neither of the pivot stones survived, the slots

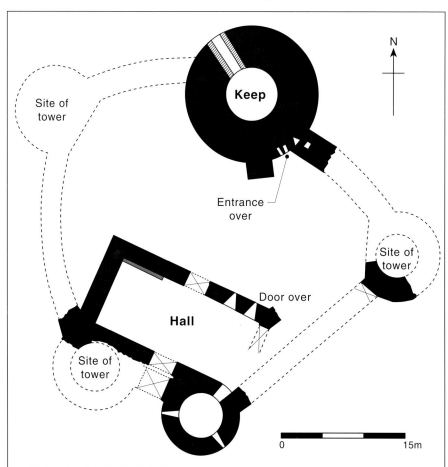

Fig. 42   Plan of the gateway, circular keep and hall, Nenagh Castle, Co. Tipperary.

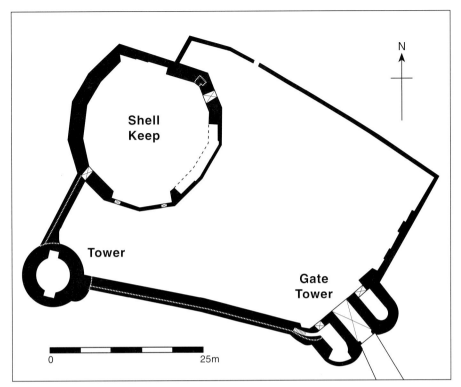

Fig. 43 Plan of
Dungarvan Castle, Co.
Waterford. The castle has
a shell keep and a D-
shaped, twin-towered
gateway.

which had been cut into boulder clay at the back of the pit, to allow for the swing of the counterweight arms of the bridge, were found in the gate passage. The standing remains of the eastern gate-tower contain plunging loops like those in the curtain walls at Dunamase and it had a base-batter from the eastern curtain wall around to the gate passage. There are also the remains of a portcullis slot made with sandstone in the east side of the passageway near the rear arch. The western tower of the gateway only survives at its northern side which also acts as the south wall of the gatehouse. Unlike the eastern tower there is no access to it at ground-floor level from the gatehouse. Access to its lower level was from the first floor which may have been used as the castle prison like that in the south-east angle tower at Ferns, Co. Wexford. Immediately behind the gateway and towers is a rectangular building used as a first-floor hall. This is an unusual plan for an Irish castle although there are examples of substantial accommodation behind gatehouses as at Greencastle, Co. Donegal, and Castleroche, Co. Louth. The great hall is normally in a separate building or contained within the great tower or keep. The hall at Nenagh is a late thirteenth-century addition based on the cut stone of that date retrieved from the drawbridge pit.[29] Like many of these early thirteenth-century Irish castles there must have been a moat around the curtain walls. The castle is five-sided in plan with a twin-towered gateway at the south, circular projecting towers at the west and east angles and the great circular

Fig. 44 Plan of
Castleroche, Co. Louth.

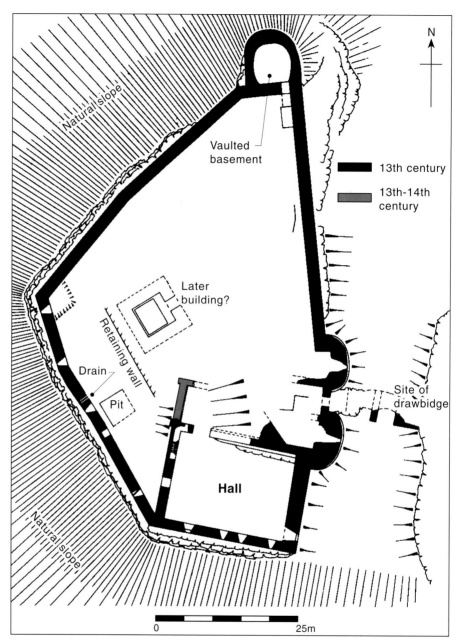

keep/tower in its north angle. Most of the curtain walls are missing and there are only fragmentary remains of the east angle tower. It would appear from the limited remains of the curtain walls that they did not run in a straight line but were slightly rounded making it difficult to have flanking fire along the walls from the towers.

Dungarvan Castle is basically subrectangular in plan and is similar to Nenagh in that it has a tower/shell keep on the opposite side of the enclosure to the gateway. Although the castles are of much the same date,

56

Fig. 45 Twin-towered gateway and great hall (left) at Castleroche, Co. Louth.

the twin towers of the gateway at Dungarvan are D-shaped and not basically circular like Nenagh. The keeps are also different: Nenagh has a great circular tower while Dungarvan has a shell keep. The Dungarvan gatehouse has obvious parallels with that at Dublin, which was also a royal castle, and with slightly later examples such as Castleroche, Co. Louth, Kiltartan Castle, Castletown, Co. Galway, and Ballylahan, Co. Mayo. Dungarvan Castle, of course, was afforded the natural protection of water at the river mouth and must have had a moat on the landward side. There is also a projecting circular tower on the south-west angle to give flanking fire.

Most of the castles of the late twelfth and early thirteenth centuries have a twin-towered gateway, some being more elaborate than others but all following a fairly set pattern. This continues into the middle of the thirteenth century although the ground plan or layout of the entire castle complex may change. One of the most spectacular castles of this mid-thirteenth-century period is Castleroche, Co. Louth, which was thought to have been built in 1236 by Rohesia de Verdun. It is constructed on the edge of a very precipitous rock which protects it on all but the east side where there is a rock-cut fosse. The castle is subrectangular in shape with only one projecting tower which is at the north-east angle. The gatehouse is situated near the south end of the east wall. The twin towers are rounded at the front but squared-off at the rear, behind the line of the curtain wall, where there were two floor levels above the entranceway providing considerable living space. The gateway was also protected by a drawbridge as is evident by the remains of masonry within the rock-cut fosse and its narrowing at this point. The entranceway across the fosse was also protected by a barbican. The gate towers and the curtain walls adjoining them have a number of narrow arrow

Fig. 46 Plan of the
gateway at Dundrum
Castle, Co. Down
(after Jope, 1966).

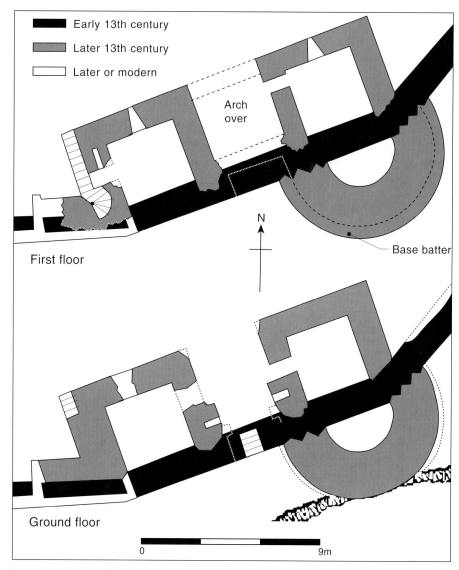

Fig. 46 Plan of the gateway at Dundrum Castle, Co. Down (after Jope, 1966).

loops at various levels and facing in several directions to protect this side of the castle. The well-preserved curtain walls have a line of small rectangular holes below the merlons at wall-walk level. These holes were used to carry a covered wooden hoarding (gallery) around the exterior of the curtain walls to allow the defenders protection while repulsing the attackers by dropping stones and shooting arrows directly down to the base of the wall. However, if the curtain walls were breached, there was no great tower or keep to retire to. Therefore, the defence of the castle totally depended on its natural position and the strength of the curtain walls and gatehouse.

The gatehouse of the upper ward at Dundrum, Co. Down, which dates to the mid thirteenth century, is unique in Ireland in that it has only one half-round tower outside the line of the curtain wall and has two almost square

Fig. 47 Gateway at
Ballylahan Castle, Co.
Mayo (David Sweetman).

ones at the rear.[30] The castle occupies the summit and upper slope of a
prominent hill on the west shore of Dundrum Bay. The upper ward is
enclosed by a rubble-built wall with a rock-cut fosse outside. The curtain
walls of the upper ward follow the natural contour of the hill in the same
manner as Castleroche where the walls followed the edge of the rock
promontory. Originally Dundrum Castle was entered through a late
twelfth/early thirteenth-century simple gateway close to the east angle. This
gateway had a rock-cut drawbridge pit in front of it. The drawbridge was
operated from a platform over the gateway. Dundrum, like Castleroche, had
a wooden hoarding around its curtain walls since it also has small square
holes directly below the parapets. The present gateway was built in the mid
to late thirteenth century and was reached by a narrow path from the
southwest. The gatehouse was two storeys high and was built against and
over the original curtain wall which was reduced in height to accommodate
the new gateway. The reduced curtain wall was retained and thickened in
the gate passage so that a timber ramp would have to have been set in place
to get over it. If the timber ramp could easily be removed when the castle
was under attack then it would have made the gateway more secure.

Rindown, Co. Roscommon, is another example of an early to mid-
thirteenth-century castle (*c.*1227-1235). The castle is on the north-east side of
a peninsula in Lough Ree and is protected on the landward side by a deep
and wide fosse which cuts across the narrowest point. Although the gateway
appears now as a small, centrally pierced gatehouse, it had a substantial
gatehouse with barbican and drawbridge to protect the outer entrance. The
present gateway is quite narrow and has portcullis grooves and a chamber

over it in order to operate the portcullis and a murder-hole. The castle is, like many others, dependent on its naturally defensive position, with water on all but the north-west side and the deep fosse which cuts across the peninsula as well as running right around the curtain walls. To the north-east of the gatehouse are the remains of the original hall-keep, with its north-west wall built into the line of the curtain with loops at ground-floor level. There were no projecting towers on the curtain except at the north-west angle of the later hall so the walls could not be defended by flanking fire.

Two phases of building can be observed in the curtain walls, especially at the south-west and north-east sides. Here one can see that the walls were originally defended by plunging arrow-loops but later the walls were heightened, the loops blocked and a wooden hoarding added. These alterations took place at the same time as the later hall was added (*c.*1270), when large amounts of money were spent on the castle. The later hall was built onto the south-west angle of the curtain and the way it projects out from the line of the original enclosing walls of the castle made it very vulnerable. The defenders of this castle would therefore be very dependent on the wooden hoarding and outer defences, namely the fosses which were presumably filled with water from the lake. Although this was one of the few royal castles in Ireland and was built in a very strategic position, it is not that well defended. It was subjected to many attacks and was captured in 1270 and 1272, being levelled on the second occasion. The castle was frequently repaired and improved upon and Geoffrey de Geneville, who was justiciar and whose domain manor was at Trim Castle, repaired it from 1273 to 1275. These repairs included the construction of wooden towers, repairing and improving the fosse and the drawbridge. It is clear from this, and the present lack of masonry around the fosse in front of the gateway, that the outer defences in front of the drawbridge were constructed of wood. Between 1299 and 1302 over £113 was allowed to the sheriff for the building of a new hall – presumably that which can seen today at the north-west angle of the curtain wall.

A group of Anglo-Norman fortresses in Leinster, which can be dated to the first quarter of the thirteenth century, are so similar in style that they must have been built by the same person. They have in common a large square or rectangular block with round towers at each angle. They are to be found at Ferns, Co. Wexford, Lea, Co. Laois, Carlow town and Terryglass, Co. Tipperary, with a fifth example from Wexford town known only from antiquarian drawings.

Lea is the only castle of this group that has an extant gateway. It has twin-towers which are rounded outside the line of the curtain wall but squared-off behind, like those of the mid to late thirteenth-century castles at Roscommon, Ballylahan and Ballintober. The keep or great tower at Lea is built in two phases and, since this gateway has parallels with others

Fig. 48   The remains of the gateway at Rindown Castle, Co. Roscommon. From broken masonry it is clear that the gateway was originally three storeys high (David Sweetman).

belonging to the second half of the thirteenth century, it is not part of the original fortification. The gatehouse is not bonded to the curtain walls. Ferns Castle is the other castle in this group that has been excavated and here clear evidence of a drawbridge structure and barbican was uncovered at the south side of the castle near the south-west tower. Lea, Ferns and Carlow were built on earlier ringworks. The defences of these early earth and timber

Fig. 49 Ferns Castle, Co. Wexford. This aerial photograph shows the keep after excavation and restoration. Note the rock-cut fosse and the modern bridge where the medieval drawbridge and gatehouse were originally positioned.

castles at the three named sites depended to a large extent on the fosse which at Lea and Carlow made them into islands. It was on these islands and on the ringwork that the great tower was built, and it was these structures which provided the main focus of the defences. Once the defenders raised the drawbridge, closed the doors and shuttered the windows there was little the attacker could do to break into the great tower.

Carlow Castle in 1782 from a drawing by Austin Cooper.

Fig. 50 Little remains of the original four-walled keep at Carlow Castle (David Sweetman).

It was a passive defence and few of these early castles provided the means to actively defend their strongholds; they depended on their invulnerability rather than on their ability to repel the attackers. It is also highly unlikely that the garrisons within the castle were large enough to defend all sides of the castle at the same time. They 'holed-up' in their great towers and waited for the attackers to go away. However, when we move towards the mid-thirteenth century, the defences take a more aggressive role and the emphasis moves away from the keeps or great towers to the gateways and curtain walls. At Castleroche, for instance, there is no great tower but the towers of the well-defended gateway are commodious and the curtain walls have a wooden hoard for repelling attackers.

There are many other examples of early thirteenth-century stone fortresses in Ireland but few of them have gateways or curtain walls remaining which would add to our knowledge of the outer defences. The reader requiring a full inventory of all the castles in Ireland should consult the county archaeological inventories.

DONJONS, KEEPS AND GREAT TOWERS

The previous section examined the outer defences of some of the Anglo-Norman fortresses. These early stone fortresses in Ireland, the Anglo-Norman castles of the late twelfth and early thirteenth centuries, frequently had a massive square or rectangular tower which was often isolated within an inner ward. The term 'keep' is widely used to refer to a strong tower either isolated or incorporated in the curtain wall, which contained the essential rooms of the castle, and could also be used as a place of final retreat should the outer defences be breached. If the tower also acted as the long-term domestic quarters for the lord and his inner household it is properly referred to as a 'donjon'. The word 'keep' was first applied to Guines Castle near Calais which had a cylindrical tower with gabions around the top and marked bands of masonry resembling weaving.[31] The middle English word *kipe* is used to describe weaving on a basket. A reference of 1375-6 states, 'Guines, a tower called *le kype* was heightened'. However, there is no problem with using the sixteenth-century word 'keep' as a catch-all term. For instance the great tower at Trim should properly be called a 'donjon' since it contained, in the late twelfth and early thirteenth centuries, all the domestic accommodation for the lord and his inner household. However, by the mid-fourteenth century, a large double-aisled hall with store rooms was built in the north angle of the ward with a solar for the lord in the square tower.[32] Therefore some of the domestic emphasis was moved away from the great tower and it should be called a keep (and not a donjon) after the mid-thirteenth century.

At Dunamase there was no great tower but rather a large, single-storey hall with a two-storey solar at one end.[33] This building is sited on the highest

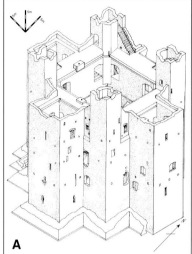
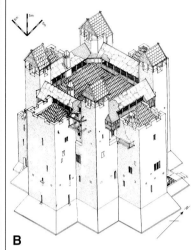
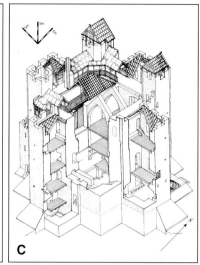

Fig. 51 Isometric drawings of the keep at Trim Castle. A) The remains of medieval fabric. B) The keep as it would have looked in its final phase of building. Note the tiled roofs and sections of hoarding. C) A cutaway view showing floor levels and the divided hall (Kevin O'Brien).

and most easily defended part of the rock. The structure should be called a hall-keep and illustrates how difficult and dangerous it is to pigeon-hole keep-like structures into more rigid classifications. The main structure within the curtain walls of a castle was a tower; this could be a great tower like those at Carrickfergus and Trim or a hall-keep like those at Dunamase and Rindown. In the Anglo-Norman fortresses of Ireland the keep sometimes had a hall within it but, at a later stage, a separate more grandiose one was built elsewhere, isolated from the great tower. This occurred at Trim Castle. At Trim, however, it is difficult to see where a great hall could have been accommodated within the keep, since the first-floor level is divided by a large north-south cross-wall and its only fireplace is in the west wall. The recent excavations uncovered a large well-dressed stone pillar at ground-floor level which may have been intended to support the timbers of the first floor, indicating that there may have been no cross-wall at this first phase of building (*c*.1175-1180). When the final building took place *c*.1204 a large chamber was constructed at third-floor level but this would seem too far removed from the entrance to have acted as a public hall. This problem was resolved *c*.1300 by filling and raising up the ground level behind the north-east curtain wall and building a large, three-aisled hall with large windows piercing the existing curtain and looking out over the Boyne River. This leaves a gap of almost 100 years between the building of the great hall and the large chamber at the top of the keep.[34] The large chamber in the keep with its large fireplace was subdivided around 1300 at the same time that the new hall was constructed.[35] So, regardless of how inconvenient the chamber at the top of the keep was for public access, it must have been used as a hall for about 100 years.

Attached to the south-east of the later hall and at a level below the ground floor a vaulted chamber for storage was constructed. A slipway was built beside this to allow provisions to be taken from the boats coming up-river from the port of Drogheda. At the north-western end of this single-storey hall, in the angle of the curtain walls and within the existing rectangular-shaped tower, chambers were constructed which had direct access to the hall. Presumably these were private and could be used by the lord should he not wish to walk across the ward to his chambers in the keep. A storage area was also provided here with a slipway into the basement at the south-west side and internal stairs up from it to the hall and chambers above. Only the foundation levels of the pillars of the hall and only the below-floor level of the south-western wall remained, so the doorway(s) to the hall were not found. Steps lead up from the storage area outside the south-west end of the building so that there was no direct access here to take provisions to the hall.

As a result of the recent detailed study of the keep at Trim it can be seen how the building functioned as a private residence and how the hall at the top was made accessible to the public without endangering the defences of the castle or invading the privacy of the lord. In the south-west angle of the keep there are stairs which give access to the west and south side towers and the second-floor main chambers. These towers have fireplaces and high-pitched roofs whereas the north and east ones do not. Therefore these more commodious chambers were set aside for the lord and could not be readily accessed from the east side of the building where the entrance and chapel were located. There is a second stone stairs in the north-east angle of the main block, not far from the entrance into the keep through the eastern tower. These stairs lead to the large hall at third-floor level. The hall also had a wooden gallery running right around its inner face which allowed access to all parts of the castle at the uppermost level. There were also steps down into the hall from the stairs which lead from the private chambers in the west and south towers. When the hall was subdivided at the end of the thirteenth century the layout at this high level was changed, presumably because the public no longer had access to the keep and were accommodated in the specially built new hall in the north-east angle of the ward. There was no access to the second-floor level of the now demolished north tower of the keep, except from the wooden hoarding which was attached to the walls around the north-eastern part of the building, and which was part of the defensive mechanism for the protection of the entrance. This tower was only used by those guarding the entrance and controlling access by lowering and raising the drawbridge which was suspended from the walls.

In the area below the first-floor entrance to the tower is a drawbridge feature which consisted of stone walls constructed in such a way as to make what was in effect a drawbridge pit but different from the normal pit in that it rose above the ground to the height of the door jamb of the entranceway.[36]

Fig. 52 Adare Castle, Co. Limerick. Note the two rectangular halls along the riverside and the remains of the great tower or keep in the inner ward.

This entrance feature dates to the second half of the thirteenth century when rebuilding took place and a mantlet wall was constructed inside the line of the fosse and a new entranceway was constructed across the fosse of the ringwork to gain access to the fore-building. Once inside the fosse one could not gain access to the keep unless the drawbridge was lowered onto the stone pit. At Trim one had to cross three drawbridges to gain access to the great tower; first through one of the barbicans and outer gates, then across the bridge over the fosse also protected by gate-towers and then the drawbridge into the keep. This emphasises again the strength of these early fortresses, yet it has to be remembered that they were also the residences of the lord and his retinue.

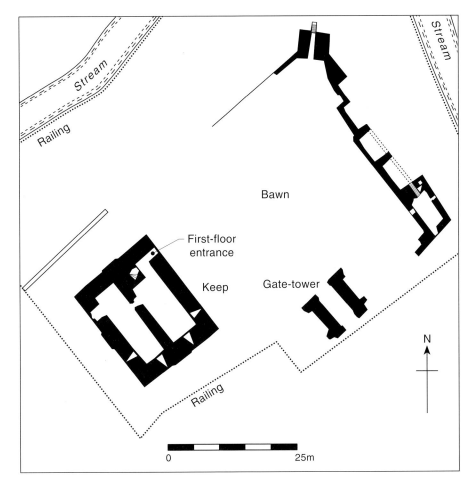

Fig. 53 Plan of Maynooth Castle, Co. Kildare.

At Carrickfergus there was no provision for a hall within the great tower and the early hall was tied into the east curtain wall beside the original entrance.[37] At Rindown the early hall is also set into the curtain wall immediately to the east of the gateway. In this case there is no evidence of a free-standing keep or tower so that this building, with its hall at first-floor level and two large vaulted chambers with slit opes below, must have acted as a hall-keep before the later hall of 1299-1302 was built outside the existing north-west angle of the curtain. Also, at Adare, the early hall is set into the south-west angle of the outer ward close to the gateway. Like Rindown, the hall is at first-floor level. By the end of the thirteenth century another hall was built to the east on the bank of the River Maigue. The kitchens were attached to the east end of the aisled hall as at Trim. The main entrance was through a porch in its north wall. It was very well-lit with two double-light windows in both its north and south walls. Like Trim the halls at Adare are also situated in the outer ward with the keep set inside the inner defences which were originally those of the ringwork castle. The rectangular-shaped keep has only its northern side surviving to full height with the southern

portion only to be seen at ground level. It was built in two phases, the earliest being two storeys high and probably contemporary with the early hall. In the fifteenth century it was raised a further two floors and had vaults inserted over the ground-floor level. Some of the jamb stones of the doorways were also replaced at this time and a north-south cross-wall inserted to carry the vaulting. The angles of the tower all project slightly in one direction either to the east or the west and may be original buttressing since the extra width that they provide is not used to hold stairs, passages or chambers. This tower is quite small when compared to Trim and was never intended to be used as a donjon.

The great towers, keeps or donjons almost always had their entrances at first-floor level which were invariably protected by a fore-building. At Adare, Maynooth and Athenry, for instance, there is clear evidence for such buildings but the recent excavations at Trim give us a much clearer picture

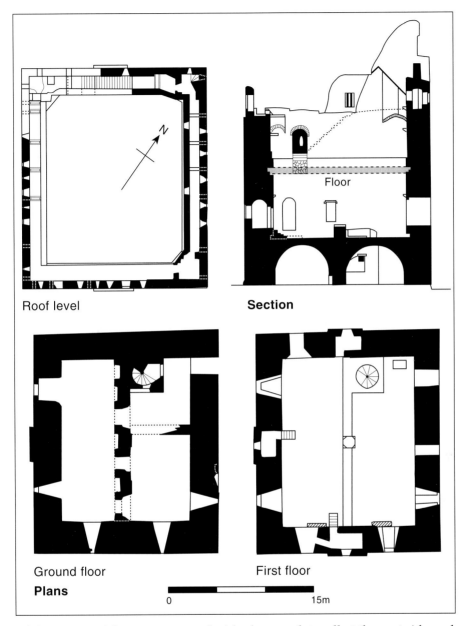

Roof level

Section

Floor

Ground floor

First floor

Plans

0   15m

of the nature of these structures. Inside the mantlet wall at the east side and attached to it are the remains of a rectangular building which has wooden internal walls on stone footings making cubicles along its west wall. These internal structures were used as a waiting area for visitors before entering the keep. The east wall of the building has the remains of four slit opes with embrasures on the inside. This structure, like the other buildings around the entrance to the keep, dates to the second half of the thirteenth century.

At Maynooth, the large hall-keep is not a true rectangle since the sides and diagonals of the building are of differing lengths.[38] Many of the

Fig. 56 The hall-keep and curtain walls of Athenry Castle, Co. Galway.

measurements for the layout of this building, like the keep at Trim, are multiples of 0.7m. At present the ground floor is divided in two and is covered by wicker-centred vaults. The original first floor was of timber and some of the original beam holes can be seen in the side walls. The floor was supported at the centre on three stone piers which are now embedded in the later dividing wall. At first-floor level, where the entrance is in the north wall, there was a small fore-building. This is the level that the original hall was at and other early halls would also have had a high roof. The third-floor hall at Trim clearly has evidence for a gallery around it and at Maynooth there are beam holes in the walls at the height where a second floor could have been carried. However, there are no windows at this level so they may be evidence for a gallery or a later inserted floor. At Athenry, Co. Galway, which is an early thirteenth-century hall-keep (judging by the plunging arrow-loops with crosslits in the merlons), there are also beam holes above the first-floor hall but there are no opes at that level to light it. These beam holes may also have carried a gallery for which there is clear evidence in the form of part of a masonry arch at the south-west gable near the doorway. The vaults over the ground floor of the hall-keep at Athenry have also been inserted at a later stage. The first-floor entrance doorway here and the window embrasures have finely carved stonework indicating that this was undoubtedly a hall and that it was intended to be displayed to the public.

Recent excavations at Limerick and Dunamase have uncovered great halls. That at Limerick, however, dates to *c*.1280, while the hall-keep at Dunamase dates to the later part of the twelfth century.[39] The latter building was sited at the very highest point on the rock and was thought to have been

Decorated capital from the doorway at Athenry Castle.

Fig. 57 The hall-keep at Athenry, Co. Galway, displays evidence that a wooden sturcture was attached; either a small forebuilding or steps.

a keep but recent work there has shown it to be a single-storey hall with a two-storey solar block attached to its north end and a slightly later forebuilding at the north-west angle of the hall. The structure is not purely a hall since it is defended by a fore-building, has very thick walls and is sited in a very defensive position. Therefore, it is more appropriate to call it a hall-keep, linking it to a similar structure at Rindown and the later thirteenth-century hall and solar at Trim.

The early thirteenth-century fortress at Carlingford was almost D-shaped in plan, with a rectangular twin-towered gateway at the west side and probably at least four square towers projecting from various parts of the curtain wall. Only that at the south-west angle is almost complete. The lower portions of one square tower midway along the east curtain is still extant while there is clear evidence for another midway along the north wall and also at the south-east angle. Before the later reconstruction of the eastern half of the castle there may well have been another tower at the north-east angle. There are no internal stone structures within the curtain walls so the accommodation must have been in wooden buildings tied into the enclosing wall. Thus all the private chambers, hall, kitchen, etc. were constructed of

The late thirteenth-century cross-loop in the north face of the south-west angle tower at Castlegrace, Co. Tipperary (Jean Farrelly).

wood when the castle was first built *c.*1200. However, at a later stage towards the end of the thirteenth century, a large north to south cross-wall was built in the middle of the enclosed area, effectively dividing off the west from the east portion and allowing the eastern part to be developed as chambers. At this stage only the first floor of the new structure was large enough to contain a hall. If it was a hall it would have been accessible at first-floor level through a doorway in the north end of the cross-wall. Since there are no windows in the cross-wall, it was possibly used as part of the defences and that the western portion of the castle then ceased to be inhabited and would merely have been used as a ward.[40] Parapets on top of the dividing wall support the contention that it acted as an external wall to the new residential block. However, this would not stop the first floor being used as a hall and there are many examples including Carrickfergus and Rindown where one wall of the hall is also part of the curtain wall.

When Castlegrace, Co. Tipperary, was built *c.*1250 its curtain walls were constructed on a large rectangular plan with a tower at each angle. At the west end of the enclosed area a large north to south cross-wall was built which acted as the east wall of a large residential block. This meant that the entire western curtain and parts of the north and south curtain wall acted also as the walls of the residential area much in the same way as they did at Carlingford, albeit that at Castlegrace was part of the original design of the castle. The walls of the castle are very thick but there are only a few small cross-loops with expanded bases which could provide flanking fire. This made it vulnerable to attack. The hall which was at first-floor level had three large windows in the west wall and one in the south, which still retains part

Fig. 58 Castlegrace, Co. Tipperary, showing its first-floor hall. It has a fine window in the gable end, unfortunately covered in ivy (Jean Farrelly).

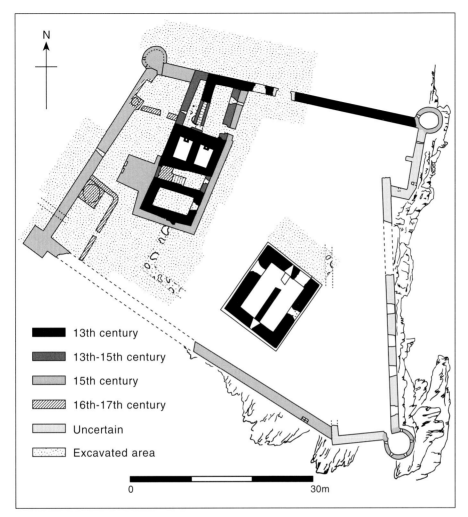

Fig. 59 Plan of
Glanworth Castle, Co.
Cork.

of its tracery and which is very similar to windows in Ferns Castle. They
have trefoil-pointed single or double lights and tympana pierced with plain
or foiled circles. Castlegrace is quite commodious and, because of its being
vulnerable to attack, it has very strong walls. One could almost say that it
looks forward to the late-medieval and early post-medieval fortified houses
rather than back to the large, early thirteenth-century fortresses of the
Anglo-Normans.

At Glanworth Castle, Boherash, Co. Cork, the first building phase
(*c.*1250) consists of a rectangular gateway in the west curtain, a small
rectangular keep close to the south wall and a large rectangular hall
extending along most of the north side which is incorporated in the
curtain.[41] The castle is sited on a cliff in a very strong position overlooking
the River Funshion. This castle has features in common with Castlegrace,
which is only 29km away from it. The main differences are that Castlegrace
encloses a rectangular area whereas Glanworth has an irregular shape,

Fig. 60 Glanworth
Castle, Co. Cork.

which is almost square, except at the south-east and south-west angles, and
there is no evidence of an isolated keep at Castlegrace. The first and second
floors of the keep at Glanworth were originally of wood like many of the
early buildings, especially the halls, but later had a vault inserted to carry
the first floor. The same process took place in the keep at Adare and the hall-
keeps at Maynooth and Athenry. The original great hall at Glanworth was
probably sited along the north side but by the fourteenth century was
relocated to the cliff edge at the east side where there are at least four large
windows piercing the curtain wall. The keep initially also contained a first-
floor hall and its use was changed when the first great hall was built.

Grenan Castle, Co. Kilkenny, is another example of a hall-keep but it has
a ground floor entrance which is unusual. It is three storeys high, has its
entrance in the east end of the south wall and has a mural stairs in the south
which rises straight to the first-floor hall. This castle is situated on low-lying
ground close to the River Nore near Thomastown and is sited on what might
be an earlier earth and timber castle. It is a substantial building 19.5m long
and 13.1m wide, with a base-batter at least 3.4m high and walls 3.5m thick
at the base. It has a chapel in its south angle at first-floor level directly over
the entranceway, a feature of Anglo-Norman fortresses. There is a fireplace
in the north gable and a garderobe chamber in the north-east angle. The
first-floor level was divided into a hall which occupied two-thirds of the

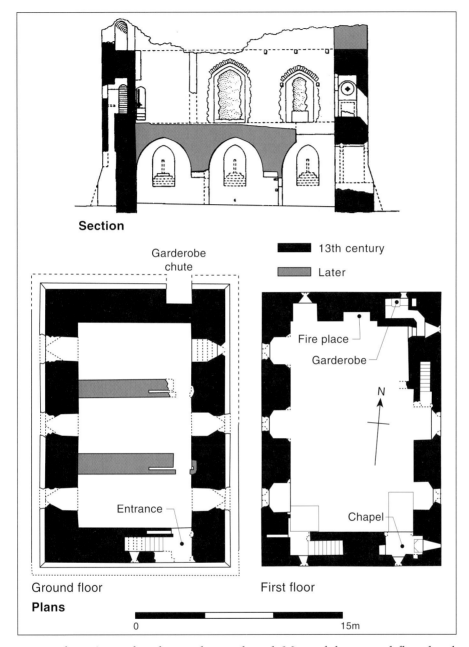

Fig. 61 Plans and section of Grenan Castle, Co. Kilkenny (after Waterman, 1968).

area and a private chamber at the north end. Most of the second-floor level is missing but the stairs which gave access to it is in the northern end of the east wall. The use of Dundry stone (a type of limestone from the Bristol area) and the building of a chapel again indicate that it was designed as a residence but that it was also well fortified despite its ground-floor entrance. The fosse and the wall which once surrounded the hall-keep formed the outer defences and also enclosed other buildings, possibly of wood, which have now disappeared.

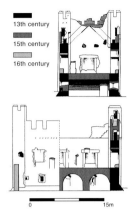

13th century

15th century

16th century

Sections of Greencastle
Co. Down (After
Jope, 1966).

At Greencastle, Co. Down, there is a large hall-keep which was built by Hugh de Lacy II, around 1240 or at least before 1242 when he died and the castle reverted to the Crown. Here, as with most hall-keeps, there is a first-floor entrance leading to a hall, with a garderobe chamber. Diagonally opposite angle vaults were added over the ground floor to replace what was originally a wooden, first-floor level. A broad stairs was inserted from ground to first floor at the west gable end. The building was originally two storeys high but a third floor was added in the late-medieval period. The ground floor, as with the other buildings of this type, has slit opes with embrasures. In the fifteenth century the wide windows of the hall were blocked and narrow lights inserted at a slightly higher level. The castle is sited on low rock about 300m north of Carlingford Lough. Its curtain walls which enclose an irregular quadrilateral area had a tower at each angle but little evidence of these or the curtain remain. The north-east angle tower of the curtain had private chambers and a latrine.[42] Directly to the south of this tower and connected to it, as well as being built into the curtain wall, was a rectangular-shaped great chamber. The plan of the castle and layout of the buildings is quite similar to that of Glanworth and Athenry.

Two-storey rectangular buildings associated with fortresses are not always hall-keeps. Clough, Co. Down, which is a small castle, has a two-storey rectangular structure on top of the motte. It was built of boulders with pinnings and had a first-floor entrance. The ground floor was unlit while the upper storey, which had a wooden floor, was only lit by three small splayed loops and could not have acted as a hall. The hall, as revealed by an excavation in 1951-2, was in fact a large rectangular wooden building occupying most of the northern portion of the motte.[43] It dates to the middle of the thirteenth century and was a single-storey structure with stone-built lower walling and a timber frame.

Castleroche, Co. Louth, like many of the early thirteenth-century castles in Ireland relied on its naturally defensive position and on the strength of its curtain walls. Other than the well-defended twin-towered gate there is only one projecting tower on the curtain, that at the north-east angle to provide flanking fire. However, its position close to the edge of a steep rock outcrop, except at the east side where there is a rock-cut fosse, provided a natural barrier against attack. The tops of the walls carried a wooden hoarding to enable the defenders to attack anyone attempting to undermine the walls. Rohesia de Verdun built her fortress here after she had abandoned her earth and timber castle at Castletown, near Dundalk. It was to be her main residence and the castle reflects this in its internal structures. For instance, unlike most of the early Irish fortresses, it was designed to hold substantial accommodation within its four-storey gatehouse. Accommodation within the gatehouse tends to be associated with the later thirteenth-century castles like Greencastle, Co. Donegal, the later structure added to the back of the gateway at Nenagh, Co. Tipperary, and the late gateway of the outer ward at Lea, Co. Laois.

In the south portion of the ward at Castleroche, to the south-west of the gatehouse, there are the remains of a large rectangular building which uses the curtain as its east and south walls. The ground floor of this building is one storey below the level of the gatehouse since the rock on which it is built drops away sharply to the south and west. The first-floor level of the building contained a hall which was lit by three large windows in the south wall. The entrance to the hall was by a short flight of steps at the north-west angle of the building. The ground-floor level of the building has four opes in the south wall. The two central ones have long narrow slits while the outer ones have windows with round arches of sandstone. The east wall of this building has evidence of a third-floor level which would have risen above the level of the curtain wall. The projecting tower at the north-east angle, which is D-shaped in plan, is very fragmentary but it can be seen that it was four storeys high. Only its south wall is extant and anything which existed outside the line of the curtain wall, other than its basement level, has been completely destroyed. Judging from its size this tower must also have contained considerable accommodation.

Clonmacnoise Castle is built on a low-lying floodplain of the River Shannon. It is set inside a large earthwork which was built sometime shortly before 1215 when Ralph Derevaus and Walter Reboth were requested to hand it over to Geoffrey de Marisco. It comprises a rectangular two-storey keep with a courtyard area adjoining it on the river side. The keep is much ruined but it can be seen that it had a first-floor entrance at the north or river side which is the only side not protected by the earthwork. A fore-building now much destroyed was constructed against the north wall and contained a drawbridge which was set sideways so that one did not approach the doorway head-on but along the wall of the castle from the curtain wall-walk. This fore-building, which was illustrated in 1739, has collapsed and is detached from the keep.[44] However, the drawbridge slots can still be clearly seen. The ground floor of the keep was only lit by narrow slit opes set in wide embrasures. The first floor, which appears to have lancet windows, contained the hall.

The term 'towered keeps' is used to describe a small group of six castles in Leinster: Lea, Co. Laois; Ferns, Enniscorthy and Wexford town, Co. Wexford; Carlow town; Terryglass, Co. Tipperary.[45] There is no physical evidence of a castle in Wexford town and there is general agreement that the castle at Enniscorthy, although somewhat similar, is in fact a smaller sixteenth-century castle possibly modelled on Ferns.

The earliest of these towered keeps is Carlow which was built by William Marshal between 1208 and 1211.[46] Lea Castle was built shortly afterwards in two stages. The mid-thirteenth-century windows of the upper

Two decorated stones from Ferns Castle, Co. Wexford; a thirteenth-century stone head found in the moat (top) and a gargoyle (bottom).

level belong to the later phase.[47] Lea, which has the most extensive remains, was built by Maurice FitzGerald as a direct copy of his Lord's castle in Carlow shortly after 1216 when Marshal returned the property to him.[48] Terryglass was also under the control of William Marshal through his nephew John and is very close in design (but not size) to the others. In 1219 Henry III instructed the Justiciar not to dispossess John Marshal of Terryglass of his lands even though he had not fortified them.[49] This indicates the castle was not then complete.

Ferns Castle, also built in Marshal territory, is so similar to Carlow and Lea that it too must belong to this early thirteenth-century period. Although it has been argued that Ferns should be dated to the mid-thirteenth century because of its traceried windows, few medieval buildings survive without some alteration to their fabric.[50] A good example of this is at Trim where a later thirteenth-century hall was built and new large window opes were inserted into the earlier curtain wall. At Ferns the larger two-light windows are on the first- and second-floor levels while at ground-floor level there are narrow cross-loops. The internal area of Ferns measures almost 20m by 18m and there are no internal walls. Excavation there in the 1970s revealed no evidence for any internal structures so we must assume that there were internal wooden buildings tied into the curtain wall as at Lea and Carlingford Castle. There are several references to Ferns having been burnt down and rebuilt shortly afterwards indicating that there were internal wooden structures rather than stone. The first-floor level must have contained the hall and has a fine fireplace in the east wall. There is also a

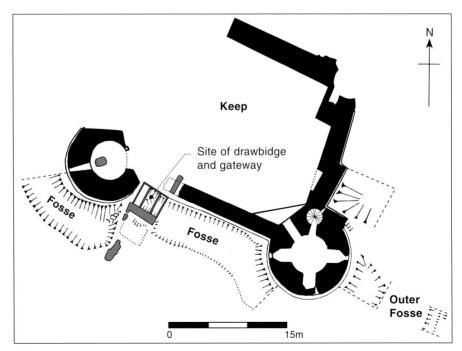

Fig. 62 Plan of Ferns Castle (after Sweetman, 1971).

N

Keep

Site of drawbidge and gateway

Fosse

Fosse

Outer Fosse

0   15m

Plate 8   Clogh Oughter Castle, Co. Cavan, was built on a small island in Lough Oughter. It is one of a small number of circular keeps found in Ireland.

Plate 9   King John's Castle, Carlingford, Co. Louth, from the west overlooking Carlingford Lough.

Plate 10   Kiltartan Castle, Castletown, Co. Galway. The twin-towered gateway has obvious parallels with that at Dublin, Dungarvan, Co. Waterford, Castleroche, Co. Louth and Ballylahan, Co. Mayo.

Plate 11   Castleroche, Co. Louth. This view of the east side of the castle clearly shows holes below the battlements where the wooden hoarding would have been inserted.

Fig. 63 This fine
vaulted chapel is in the
south-east tower at Ferns
Castle, Co. Wexford.

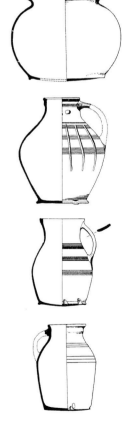

Medieval cooking pot
(top) and wine jugs from
the excavations at Ferns
Castle.

very fine chapel at second-floor level in the south-east angle stair tower. It has a vaulted roof with six moulded ribs springing from corbels which are in the form of capitals with truncated shafts. The chapel is lit by two trefoil-pointed windows. The architectural details of the chapel as well as the traceried windows elsewhere in the castle have led people to believe that this is a mid-thirteenth-century castle. However, there are different building lines using quite different stone in the standing remains. This suggests two building phases at Ferns so there is every reason to assume that the stone castle was first erected *c.*1220. Multiple building phases were noted at Lea and Carlow castles as well.

Ferns, Lea and Carlow all had first-floor entrances with their halls and garderobes at that level and the ground floor was only accessible from above. Another common feature is at Carlow, Terryglass and Ferns where

Fig. 64 The keep at Lea
Castle, Co. Laois.

one of the angle towers had a ground-floor chamber that was only accessible
from above. A similar feature was also noted in the earlier gatehouse at
Trim. Carlow and Ferns are quite alike with wooden internal structures and
probably only two storeys high originally but with at least some of the outer
walls rising above the roof level. At Carlow there were drain holes in the
walls for the roof which was sunk down below what is now the second floor
level. At Lea the windows of the lower levels are round-headed while its
uppermost levels have flattened segmental arches. This method of building
in stages, with the roof sunk well below the line of the outer walls, was also
observed at Trim Castle where there are definite dates for the three building
phases. The chapel at Trim was not part of the original building; the altar,
piscina and window were added during later building phases.

People studying castles or other medieval structures often date the
buildings from architectural details. This is a dangerous thing to do as can
be seen from the detailed study of the keeps at Trim, Lea and Carlow.[51] It
is likely that most castle owners will make alterations to their buildings
and probably the easiest thing to do is to insert new more up-to-date
windows and provide extra accommodation by adding an extra storey to
an existing building.

There are at least a dozen Anglo-Norman stone fortresses in Ireland
which have round or polygonal keeps and most of these belong to the early
part of the thirteenth century. The cylindrical keep appears to have its
origins in France in the early twelfth century but never was very popular in

Plan of the keep at
Lea Castle.

Great Britain, although there are examples in Wales which date to the early thirteenth centuries. It is difficult to understand what the rationale was behind the idea of making these structures circular since the area enclosed was so small compared to that of the masonry of the enclosing element. They are, therefore, unsuitable and uneconomical for residential quarters and must be a defensive feature. However, the keep at Nenagh was four storeys high, had a fine sandstone fireplace and window seats at second-floor level, which was obviously the principal room before it was heightened to take the top storey. At third-floor level there is a room *c.*11m in diameter which is well lit and was obviously the principal living area. The two floor levels below the top storey had slit opes with embrasures which were purely defensive while the ground level had none and was only accessible through a trap-door in the first floor. At third-floor level the only complete window is built of sandstone and has a moulded segmental rear arch supported by sandstone shafts which can be dated to the early thirteenth century. The doorway to the tower was at first-floor level close to where the curtain wall joined it at the south-east side. There is clear evidence here for a fore-building. The intra-mural stairs which rises to the second floor is located immediately to the left of the entrance and rises as a spiral all the way to the top. The keep is set in the north curtain opposite the gateway and is much more massive than the gate-towers or the remains of the tower at the north-east angle. The keep was therefore built mainly as a defensive feature and as a place of refuge should the castle be attacked.

Clough Oughter Castle, Inishconnell, Co. Cavan, is one of two circular or polygonal keeps that have been excavated, the other being Dungarvan,

Fig. 65 The circular keep and the remains of the gatehouse at Nenagh Castle, Co. Tipperary. The crenellations on the keep are a recent addition.

Co. Waterford. The castle of Clough Oughter was built in the 1220s on a very small island in the lake of Lough Oughter close to its south-eastern shore. The lake is part of the River Erne system and the castle was sited here so that it could control traffic through a very narrow point in the lake to points further south. The south wall of the castle was blown up when Colonel Jones of Cromwell's army had it 'slighted'. The tower has walls which are 2.5m thick enclosing an area 15.5m in diameter whereas that at Nenagh had walls 4.6m thick and only enclosed an area of 9.5m in diameter. Clough Oughter had room on the island for only one substantial structure so the tower had to act both as a residence and a fortress whereas that at Nenagh was used mainly for defensive purposes. The original ground floor was made of mortar while the three floors above were all of wood. The ground-floor level had two wide embrasures with plank centring and simple slit opes whereas there were six opes on the floor above, three of which were doorways with the main entrance at the south-west. The other doorways apparently gave access to buildings attached at the north and to the curtain wall at the south-east. No evidence of a fore-building was found so it seems there must have been a wooden structure in front of the doorway, or else all remains of a stone building were destroyed when the castle was 'slighted'.[52] This first-floor level must have been the hall because it is better lit than those above and is readily accessible from the outside. Access to the upper levels was gained from a building which was attached to the north side as evidenced by tie-stones which run the full height of the tower. The castle was built in two phases: the first around 1220 which consisted of the ground and first floors while the second saw the erection of a further two storeys and the external stair-tower by *c*.1226.[53] The completed tower, therefore, dates to the first quarter of the thirteenth century and would not be far removed in time from Nenagh Castle.

During recent excavations at Dungarvan, Co. Waterford, most of the polygonal shell keep was examined and clear evidence for a first-floor entrance was found in the east wall with a drawbridge outside it.[54] The keep was originally only two storeys high, with a hall at first-floor level in the northern half, and an inserted vault over the ground-floor area also at the north side. The ground floor had three arrow loops in its north wall overlooking the estuary but was otherwise unlit. In the west wall of the first-floor level there are the remains of a pair of two-seater garderobes with a third single garderobe at a higher level which was entered from a passage on the outside of the hall. The finished building had a second-floor level lit by two windows which overlooked the bay. Access to the ground-floor level was gained by a narrow stairs from the first floor. At the east end of the north wall of the ground floor there was a doorway allowing access to the water outside and this must have been used to take in supplies for the hall (as at Trim). Access to the second floor was via a mural stairs at the north-

Fig. 66 Shanid Castle, Co. Limerick, prior to conservation work. The circular keep was built on a pre-existing motte.

east corner of the hall. A water cistern was located at the western end of the hall. The southern half of the keep contained a large structure but without a ground-floor level so that the keep had split-level accommodation.

Probably the most spectacular of the polygonal keeps is to be found at Shanid, Co. Limerick. It is built on a very prominent motte which in turn is constructed on a high natural hillock. The stone castle consists of a keep, which is internally circular but polygonal on the outside, and the remains of a curtain wall which once encompassed the top of the motte. The keep, which has only the south and west portions remaining above ground, was two storeys high with a basement. Its walls are *c*.3.4m thick and the internal diameter is 6.7m, smaller than Nenagh. The roof of the keep was set down inside the walls, like many other early Irish stone castles, to protect it from attack. Some of the battlements remain and have slit opes immediately below its merlons. The remains of the curtain walls, which are *c*.1.5m thick and almost 5m high, also have their crenellations and loop-holes remaining. There is very limited space within the keep and not much more in the ward, so it appears that this site was more defensive in nature and that accommodation was not its primary function. Another polygonal keep once stood on the remains of the motte at Castleknock, Co. Dublin, but little of the castle now remains. A 1698 sketch of Castleknock shows it to be a substantial structure, four storeys high with battlements and a base-batter and large windows at first-floor level, presumably for a hall.[55]

Athlone Castle was built in a very strategic position on the west bank of the River Shannon protecting the gateway to Connacht. It was erected by

1212 on the site of an earlier motte. The Justiciar John de Grey decided to build a castle of stone there after the stone tower of the earth and timber castle collapsed, killing Richard Tuit and eight of his men. The mound of the motte was revetted with stone and a polygonal keep built on its base. The castle had large amounts of money spent on it in 1268 and also between 1276 and 1279, at the same time that Rindown was also being upgraded. The curtain wall, with its remaining angle tower along the river, were probably constructed at this time. Athlone, Rindown and Clonmacnoise were royal castles erected to protect the Anglo-Norman conquests in Connacht; they were bridgeheads of the initial settlement. The Athlone keep, which is ten-sided, is almost centrally placed within the area enclosed by the curtain wall. The upper storeys were removed in 1793 and it was used as a barrack in the nineteenth century. While the fabric of the walls are medieval, all recognisable features of that period have been removed by the building of the barrack.

Hook Head lighthouse, at Churchtown, Co. Wexford is a three-storey cylindrical keep which was built, possibly by Marshal, before 1245 but was modernised when it was used as a lighthouse. Each level has a fireplace and is groin-vaulted with plank centring. It has a ground-floor entrance and the

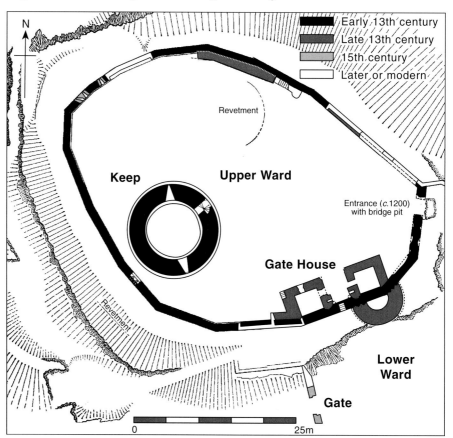

Fig. 67 Plan of the upper ward of Dundrum Castle, Co. Down (after Jope, 1966).

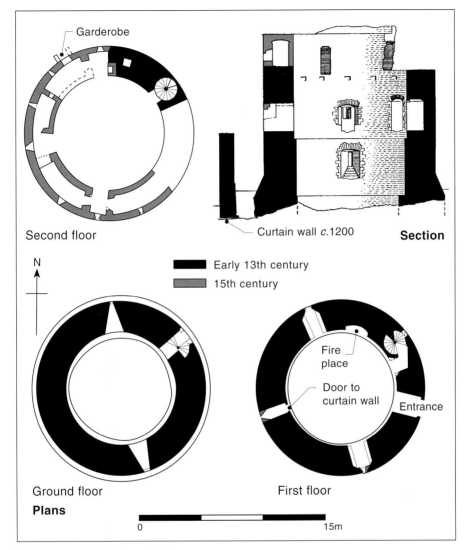

Fig. 68 Plans and section of the circular keep at Dundrum Castle, Co. Down (after Jope, 1966).

stairs is in the body of the wall as are a number of small chambers, mostly at second-floor level. The battlement level is missing but otherwise the tower retains most of its medieval features. The circular keep at Dundrum, Co. Down, is also three storeys high and has a first-floor entrance where there is a fireplace and a circular staircase within the wall up to the second-floor level. The first-floor level also has a doorway opposite the entrance which gave access to the curtain wall. The second-floor level had a garderobe and at least four mural chambers. This upper-floor level, however, was reconstructed in late-medieval times. Above the chambers there are the remains of a wall-walk level at the base of which are holes which served as outlets for rainwater. The first-floor level appears to have acted as a hall when the tower was first built *c*.1200 since it has the only fireplace and windows with seats.

At Inchiquin, Co. Cork, there is a circular keep on the north bank of the River Womanagh. It survives to just over the first-floor level but like some of the towers discussed above it had a mural stairs, window seats, garderobe chamber and fireplace on the first floor. It has a wicker-centred dome-shaped vault over the ground floor which can be attributed to late-medieval restructuring as at Dundrum, Co. Down. The ceiling over the first floor was wooden while that over the garderobe chamber had plank centring. Inchiquin tower, unlike most of the others, had a ground-floor entrance but the hall was apparently on the first floor, as is normal. The walls are 3.8m thick and enclose an area 9.3m in diameter which is similar in size to Nenagh.

The round keep at Kiltinan, Co. Tipperary, although basically early thirteenth century, was also altered in the late-medieval period. The great tower is built in the south-east angle of the curtain walls and also has a ground floor entrance, from which you can either enter the ground floor or else proceed along a mural passage to a spiral stairs, which leads up to the first floor again via a mural passage; a very unusual feature. At Kiltinane the walls are considerably thickened to accommodate the spiral stairs. At Ardfinnan, Co. Tipperary, another circular keep dates to the early part of the thirteenth century. It is perched high up on a rock outcrop overlooking the River Suir to its south. The keep is situated in the north-east angle of what was once a substantial bawn. Its walls, which are over 2m thick, enclose an area of *c*.9m in diameter. Like Kiltinan and Churchtown it had a ground-floor entrance but the spiral stairs is incorporated in a half round projecting tower at the south-west, whereas that at Churchtown is intra-mural. Recent conservation work and historical research indicates that Churchtown was erected by Marshal to act as a lighthouse following a narrow escape from shipwreck.

One further cylindrical keep, that at Aghadoe, Co. Kerry, is sited within an almost square earthwork which is defined by an earthen bank and fosse and is situated on high ground near Lough Leane, 3km west of Killarney. It is right beside the better known early medieval monastic site of the same name. It was originally three storeys high with walls just over 2m thick and enclosing an area *c*.6.4m in diameter. It has a ground-floor entrance like those in south Tipperary, and intra-mural stairs and wooden floors. It also has a number of mural chambers and a fireplace on the first floor indicating that its hall was at this level.

CHAPTER THREE

HALL-HOUSES

In recent years a small type of castle or stronghouse, the hall-house, has come to the notice of some field archaeologists working for the Archaeological Survey. They are two-storey, rectangular-shaped buildings with a first-floor entrance and appear to have originated in the early thirteenth century. They have a defensive ground floor having only slit-opes, while the timbered first floor contained the hall and more open windows. These buildings are in effect constructed in the same way as the hall-keeps discussed already and seen at such sites as Clough, Rindown, Athenry and Glanworth. The main difference between the hall-keep and the hall-house is that the former is only one element of a larger castle complex whereas the latter appears to be an isolated structure. Only at Kindlestown, Co. Wicklow, and Castleconor, Co. Mayo, do there appear to be any substantial outer defences. The distribution of these buildings, on present evidence, is quite haphazard with small clusters in north Tipperary, Galway, Mayo and Limerick. Because of their lack of defensive features it is possible that they should not be classified as castles. However, since most of them date to the early thirteenth century and are virtually indistinguishable from hall-keeps they are included here. They possibly had a wooden stockade, though there are few earthworks remaining to indicate this.[1]

Although many of the hall-houses appear to be isolated they are sometimes found associated with earthworks and/or churches and can therefore be seen as a manor house as well as being a defensive structure. At Tomdeely, Co. Limerick, the hall-house, which is built close to the Shannon estuary, has substantial earthworks close by as well as a later church. There is also a small enclosing fosse around the entire complex, so at Tomdeely we have a manor house with an associated settlement and a medieval church. The hall-house had two large wicker-centred vaults inserted into it to carry the first floor which was originally of timber. Vaults are frequently inserted into earlier medieval buildings including some of the large castles such as Maynooth.

Tomdeely is a large two-storey structure with first-floor entrance and while it is well defended at ground level it has a commodious first floor with large windows. Two of its defensive features are its base-batter and its chamfered angles. A stone stairs now leads down from the first floor to the

Fig. 69   Tomdeely, Co. Limerick. This early thirteenth-century hall-house was modified later in the thirteenth century. It is situated close to a medieval church (David Sweetman).

ground floor through the end of the vault but it originally had a wooden floor and wooden steps. Other alterations have taken place to include an extra stairs for access to the ground floor and a fireplace at first-floor level. The first-floor level was subdivided by wooden screens and there is an intra-mural stairs in the west gable leading to the wall-walk above the roof level. There is a small mural chamber at first-floor level in the west gable which contains the garderobe. The roof of the hall was of cruck construction and

Fig. 70   Moylough, Co. Galway. This hall-house is sited on an inland promontory. It is three storeys high but the top portion is a later addition.

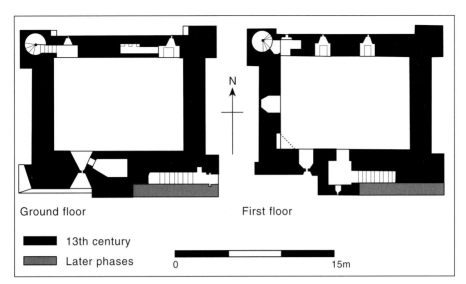

Fig. 71 Plans of
Castlekirk, Lough
Corrib, Co. Galway
(after McNeill, 1997).

Ground floor   First floor

13th century

Later phases

0   15m

was carried on corbels, set into the north and south walls, which appear as
engaged columns. The sides of the roof were set well below the tops of the
side walls as they were in most, if not all, of the earlier stone castles.

A typical example of a hall-house is at Ballyboy East, south Tipperary, a
much ruined small castle, where the later vault is partially carried on the
corbels which were used to carry the original wooden floor. Three hall-
houses have so far been identified in west Co. Limerick; two at Kilfinny and
the other at Castletown Conyers. Twelve hall-houses have been identified in
Co. Galway, most in the northern part of the county. The best known of these
are Ardrahan and Moylough. The latter is sited on high ground on an inland
promontory which is cut off by a fosse. There was a first-floor entrance near
the east angle which has beam holes each side of the doorway to carry a
wooden external stairs. It is now three storeys high with an intra-mural
stairs leading to the upper level which was a later addition. All the floors
were wooden. There are tall narrow windows at the first-floor hall level;
otherwise the building is lit by slit opes or small narrow rectangular-shaped
opes. All of the Galway hall-houses have first-floor entrances with the
possible exception of Carrowmore (Ballynacourty). However, Carrowmore
is so ruined it is difficult to be certain of the entrance. Hall-houses all appear
to have base-batters and clear evidence for external wooden stairs leading to
a first-floor entrance. That at Lough Corrib (Castlekirk), Co. Galway, has
clear evidence for some type of fore-building. At its south-east gable there is
a free-standing masonry pier creating a pit in front of the entrance. This
would have been bridged to gain access to the first floor and there is also the
remains of a small stone structure which was attached to the gable and set
into its thickness. This hall-house also has diminutive square angle towers,
that at the east angle contained a spiral stairs leading down to the ground
floor. On its north-east wall is the remains of a latrine chute and, like most

91

Fig. 72 Inserted late-medieval gun loop and doorway at Castlekirk, Co. Galway.

of the other examples of this type of structure, it has been altered in the late-medieval period by inserting new windows into it.

In other hall-houses vaults have been inserted and extra accommodation provided, as at Castlefarm (Dunmore), Co. Galway, where the later additions almost completely mask the early hall-house which dates to *c.*1225. The original building was almost certainly only two storeys high with the hall at first-floor level and with clear evidence for an external wooden stairs. It had a spiral stairs in the north-east angle to give access to the ground floor and a garderobe in the north-west angle off the hall. It had two further floor levels added to it in the late-medieval period and has a fireplace at each storey above ground level. At Annaghkeen, Co. Galway, the hall-house had a tower added at the west end of the north-west wall which comprises a three-storey garderobe with vaults between each level. It has an intra-mural stairs connecting the first floor hall to the ground level and up to the wall-walk but in different gables. The western part of the hall had a third storey added to it, also in the late-medieval period. There are the remains of a bawn wall to the southwest of the hall-house and if it is contemporary with it, then it is the exception rather than the rule. However it is likely to be an addition in late-medieval times contemporary with the other alterations.

At Cargin, Co. Galway, which is situated on the east shore of Lough Corrib, the hall-house also has a small rectangular tower at its east angle which is a late addition like that at Annaghkeen and probably functioned as a latrine. A doorway was inserted at ground-floor level in the late-medieval

Fig. 73 Dunmore Castle, Castlefarm, Co. Galway. This hall-house was originally only two storeys high but has undergone extensive alterations.

period and a wicker-centred vault inserted to support the first-floor hall. Again the ground floor is connected to the hall by an intra-mural stairs. At Park, Co. Galway, there is a poorly preserved hall-house enclosed by a moated site which raises the question of the relationship of the earthwork to the stone building. If the earthwork is a genuine moated site it would date to the end of the thirteenth century or early fourteenth century but most of the hall-houses seem to date to the first half of the thirteenth century. It could be that the sites are contemporary and the earthworks were built to protect the hall-house.

At Kilmacduagh, Co. Galway, there is a hall-house which is part of an ecclesiastical complex and appears to have been the residence of the abbot or possibly the bishop. Structurally it is no different from any of those mentioned above and, like Annaghkeen, had a third storey added to the western portion of the hall. It has, as is normal, slit opes at ground level and more commodious twin-light windows in the hall. It apparently had an oriel window in the north-east wall of the later medieval second floor. Other examples of hall-houses in Galway are to be found at Castleboy, Kilskeagh and Ardrahan where the castle is set within a rectangular enclosure, possibly of a later date. It has now collapsed but was undoubtedly a hall-house and appears to have had a fore-building attached to its first floor entrance.

Five hall-houses have been identified in north Tipperary while only one has been recorded in south Tipperary (Ballyboy East).[2] Those in north Tipperary are all closely grouped around Theobald Walter's caput at Nenagh and would appear to be manor houses under his control. None of these hall-houses are in particularly good condition but all display the same type of features as those described for the Galway examples. They are all sited on relatively high ground and most have not had major alterations made to them. They are to be found at Ballylusky, Castletown/Kylenamuck, Cloghkeating, Clohaskin and Lisbunny.

They are two storeys high with first-floor entrances and some had later doorways inserted at ground level. The example at Castletown has a garderobe tower at its south-east angle which may be an addition. A third floor may also have been added. Barrel-vaulted chambers were also put in at a later stage in the northern portion of the building and it is similar to that at Annaghkeen, Co. Galway, with its later alterations. At Lisbunny the hall-house had a first-floor entrance at the south end of the east wall and a recess in the south-east angle for a spiral stairs giving access to the ground floor. The hall had large window embrasures in all walls and a later fireplace was inserted into the north wall. At Clohaskin the entrance was at first-floor level at the east end of the south wall and in this angle is a doorway. This leads to an intra-mural stairs which leads up to wall-walk level, while access to the ground floor appears to have been by a wooden stairs. The hall was lit by windows with segmental-arched embrasures which show clear

Fig. 74 Ballylusky, Co. Tipperary, a hall-house which had a late-medieval addition to the rear, now destroyed (David Sweetman).

evidence of plank centring. It has chamfered quoins like those at Tomdeely but not nearly as well preserved. There is evidence of an enclosure in the form of an earthen bank which in places is only a scarp with some evidence of stone facing. These are the remains of earth and timber defences for a bawn. At Cloghkeating there is evidence for the stone footing of a bawn wall. The single-light windows of the hall have window seats. The first floor was carried on corbels and the roof, judging by its crease line, was set well below the level of the tops of the side walls. At Ballylusky the original first floor entrance was converted into a window and a new doorway knocked through at ground level which was protected by a machicolation directly above it at wall-walk level. It has a garderobe in its north angle. A seventeenth-century house was added at the south-west side. Considering the alterations and additions to these hall-houses it is clear that they were used over a long period and must have provided very suitable accommodation as well as having some basic defensive features.

Several hall-houses have been identified in Co. Mayo, the best known of these would be Shrule and Ballisnahyny; others are located at Kinlough, Turin, Ballycurrin Demesne, Ballykine, Cuslough Castle, Castlecarra, Castleconor and Cloghan Lucas.[3] Some of the Mayo examples are not exactly like those referred to already from Galway, Limerick and Tipperary, for instance Ballisnahyny has a vaulted roof over the first-floor hall which is original and is unique. Earlier stone enclosures, as at Ballykine, are used as bawn walls. However, they all have first-floor halls with rectangular-shaped windows, ground floors with simple slit opes and first-floor entrances.[4] At Castleconor, Co. Mayo, there is a much-ruined hall-house located close to the River Moy. It is set almost in the middle of a large earthen enclosure defined mainly by a scarp. There are the remains of a gatehouse in the southern part of this enclosure which appears to be contemporary with the hall-house and is therefore unique in this type of Irish castle.

Other examples of hall-houses have been identified elsewhere in Ireland but as yet no one has completed a study of their morphology and distribution.[5] They appear, however, to be a mainly western phenomenon although there are examples from the eastern half of the country such as Kindlestown, Co. Wicklow, Dunmoe, Co. Meath, and Delvin, Co. Westmeath. At Kindlestown only the north wall of this two-storey hall-house is more-or-less intact. Its ground floor has an original barrel vault over it and has towers at the north-west and north-east angles which project 0.6m out from the line of the wall. The north-east angle tower contained a spiral stairs which gave access to the ground floor. There is an intra-mural passage in the north wall. In the north-west tower there are three garderobes, one of which is below a squinch between the tower and the north wall. There are four windows with round-headed embrasures and external rectangular-shaped opes. This is a late-medieval hall-house,

Fig. 75 Castleconor, Co. Mayo, is a much ruined hall-house beside the River Moy near Ballina. It has only one remaining window on the first floor (Patrick O'Donovan).

probably dating to the late fourteenth century. Like some of the other sites mentioned above there is clear evidence of an enclosing element, in this case it is fossed.

An unusual example of a hall-house is to be found at Rathumney, Co. Wexford, built by the Prendergasts in the early thirteenth century. It is a rectangular building, two storeys high and constructed with fairly rough stone including granite, shale and conglomerates. The ground floor is relatively well lit and has a direct entrance to it from the outside. The south-eastern portion of the structure has been expanded to accommodate two small vaulted chambers, one of which contains a two-hole garderobe. There is a garderobe chute also in the north-east angle at this level and an intra-mural chamber above it on the first floor. It had a ground-floor hall which rose to the full height of the building in the central part of the structure close to the west end as indicated by two large and tall windows, one in the south wall the other in the west. There is also a fireplace close to the south-west angle. On each side of the hall the structure was two storeys high; the north end provided services while the solar was at the south end with its own fireplace. This structure is atypical in that it has a ground-floor entrance and

Plate 12 Shrule, Co. Mayo, a fine example of a hall-house with later additions including a bartizan at each angle. Note also the massive base-batter (Chris Corlett).

Plate 13 Ballycarbery, Co. Kerry, a late-medieval hall-house.

Plate 14 Dunmoe Castle, Co. Meath, stands on the bank of the River Boyne. Originally, it had four angle towers. The house at the right is a much later addition.

Plate 15 Dunmoe Castle, Co. Meath, in 1779 as depicted by Gabriel Beranger.

Fig. 76 Delvin, Co. Westmeath. A hall-house which is very similar to Dunmoe, Co. Meath.

the hall occupies the whole of the central area of the building. A first-floor hall is the norm for this type of building.

Dunmoe Castle is not a typical hall-house nor is it a tower house but has aspects of both. It is probably of the same date as Kindlestown or even later. It has rounded angle towers at each end of the only surviving wall (the south wall) with a spiral stairs in the south-west tower. The hall has one window with a hood moulding and two other large plain opes which are much later in date. The ground floor however was vaulted which is a common feature of the tower house. The vault which runs east to west covers two storeys which are lit by simple arrow-slits. The stairs in the south-west angle tower only gives access to the hall and there are no stairs in the other tower. The roofs of the chambers in the south-east angle tower

Fig. 77 Templehouse,
Co. Sligo has a bellcote;
an unusual feature which
is a later addition
(Patrick O'Donovan).

are corbelled so access to them had to be gained by wooden steps within the hall. Access to the first-floor hall must have been from external steps in the now collapsed portion of the hall-house and the stairs in the tower was only for entry to and from the vaulted areas. The angle towers, therefore, contained the private chamber of the lord.

At Ballycarbery East, on the Iveragh Peninsula, Co. Kerry, there is a building similar to Dunmoe, but of a later date.[6] Ballycarbery Castle is a rectangular three-storey block with vaulting over the first floor which carries the hall above. It has intra-mural stairs and a projecting tower at the north-east angle. A similar building of the same date is found at Carrick, Co. Kildare. Templehouse in Co. Sligo is sited within an enclosure. It was two storeys high with first-floor hall and a divided ground floor which reflects late-medieval alterations to the building. The hall has large plank-centred embrasures and the usual external first-floor entrance from a wooden stairs protected by some type of fore-building at the south-west angle. An intra-mural staircase is in the east angle giving access to the wall-walk. Most of the hall-houses lack garderobes and fireplaces and were heated by a central hearth from which the smoke rose to a high roof where it exited through a wooden louvre.[7]

OTHER 'HALL' CASTLES

A number of castles in Co. Wexford have been classified as 'fortified houses'.[8] Some of these, in particular Coolhull with its service tower, do not fit neatly into any of the categories set out in this book and would appear to be closer in type to the late hall-houses such as Kindlestown and Dunmoe.

100

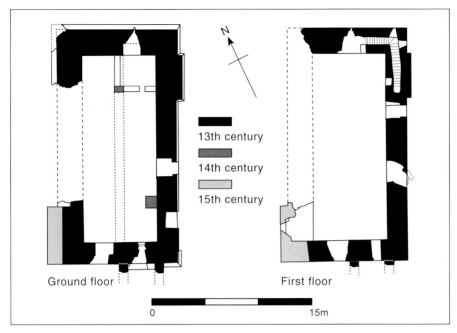

Fig. 78   Plans of
Templehouse Castle,
Co. Sligo (after
Lynn, 1985-6).

Rathshillane and Dungulph are also late-medieval defended houses similar
to hall-houses. Although they lack service towers they are more like hall-
houses than fortified houses.

Coolhull has a three-storey high rectangular block with a four-storey
service tower at the west end. The entrance to the building is through a
doorway at ground level in the service tower which leads to a spiral stairs
and gives access to all the chambers. The first floor of the main block
functioned as a hall and had a fireplace in its north wall. The service tower
had a garderobe at first-floor level for servicing the hall and a larger room
on the third floor, presumably a bedroom. The tower has only slit opes and
a pistol loop and is therefore defensive. Its doorway is also protected by a
machicolation and has evidence for a yett or iron grill. The main block has
simple slit opes at ground level, crenellated battlements and a bartizan with
musket loops at the south-east angle. This building dates to the beginning of
the sixteenth century.

Hilltown, like Coolhull, has a four-storey service tower and three-storey
rectangular block attached which has a hall at first-floor level. It also dates
to the later part of the sixteenth century. At Slade there is a rectangular
house of two storeys with an attached tower. Its ground floor is vaulted and
is divided into three chambers with a large fireplace in the west wall. The
first floor, which contained a hall, is also divided into three chambers and
has a large fireplace in the east wall of the centre room. This chamber is the
only one with double-light windows and must have been the hall. Over the
eastern chamber there is another storey with a room which has a garderobe
in its north-east angle. This is a private room, probably a bedchamber.

101

Fig. 79   Coolhull, Co.
Wexford, hall with
service tower and a
ground-floor entrance.
Note the late-medieval
features such as the arch
of the doorway and the
machicolations.

Fig. 79   Coolhull, Co. Wexford, hall with service tower and a ground-floor entrance. Note the late-medieval features such as the arch of the doorway and the machicolations.

Access to the house was via a ground-floor doorway in the west end of the south wall. This gave access to the intra-mural stairs which went straight up to the first-floor hall in the centre of the block. Bargy, although much modernised, was very like Slade and Coolhull. It has a service tower at the south-west end of the three-storey rectangular block and a hall on its first floor. Hilltown is also very like Coolhull with a small rectangular four-storey service tower and a three-storey rectangular block. Again it had a first-floor hall with double-lit windows and a fireplace in the north wall. A house of relatively modern vintage was built onto the south-west gable and the original house was altered at this time. The tower has no vaulting or stone steps so it must have had wooden floors and stairs. An unusual feature of this house is that it had a first-floor entrance leading directly into the hall like the earlier hall-houses. At Rathshillane there is a rectangular, three-storey building which has stepped crenellations and bartizans at its north-east and south-west angles, while its ground floor entrance is protected by a machicolation. The ground-floor has fifteen gun loops protecting it while the first floor contains a hall with a fireplace in the centre of its west wall. At Dungulph there is also a three-storey, rectangular, much modernised, defended house with first-floor hall, but unusually it has a circular stair tower in its north-east angle. Another example is found at Oldcourt, Co. Wicklow, where only the service tower remains.

The hall-houses discussed above do not include all known sites. Work on them is only at a preliminary stage and more will be identified. Those mentioned provide a flavour of this type of castle, its distribution, location

Fig. 80 Oldcourt, Co. Wicklow, is a service tower for a late-medieval hall which has been completely destroyed. It was probably very similar to Coolhull, Co. Wexford.

and structure. The hall-house is a far more common type of castle than previously thought,[9] and is especially prevalent in the western half of the country. They are associated with manors and tend to be found clustered in fairly limited geographical areas of the west. Only a few examples are located in the east and most of these are late medieval in date. It has been argued by various scholars that tower houses (which are traditionally dated to the fifteenth and sixteenth centuries) can have their origins pushed back to the early fourteenth century. It has also been suggested that the tower house may have originated in the west rather than the east and that this is supported by documentary evidence. However, most if not all of these references are tied to physical remains which turn out to be hall-houses and not early tower houses (see chapter 5).

Fig. 81 Carved stone heads from Bargy Castle, Co. Wexford.

Historical references to hall-houses in the west indicate that they are the manor houses of the Anglo-Normans and date to the first half of the thirteenth century. The few examples in the east are later in date and they have many features in common with the tower house such as vaults over the ground floor, angle towers and machicolations. From our present knowledge it seems that the hall-house in Ireland originated in the west but developed towards the tower house tradition and form in the east. At Templemore, north Co. Tipperary, there are the remains of a tower house. Almost half of it has been destroyed and it has also been altered at one end at a later period. This could be a late hall-house similar to Dunmoe or Kindlestown, thus illustrating the closeness of the two types of structures in the later-medieval period. The tower house clearly owes its origins to the hall-house, especially as some hall-houses, such as Castlemore, Co. Cork, and Coolhull, Co. Wexford, had domestic towers at one end. The Cork example had the tower added to the original structure whereas at Coolhull the tower is designed to service the hall and is contemporary, dating to the sixteenth century and considered a type of hall-house.

104

CHAPTER FOUR

LATER MEDIEVAL STONE FORTRESSES

A feature of the earlier medieval fortresses, as we have seen in chapter two, is the great tower or donjon, though the city castles such as Dublin and Limerick lacked this feature. Towards the end of the thirteenth century and the beginning of the fourteenth a small number of large fortresses were built which lacked a great tower and followed a trend already established in England and clearly seen in the castles of Edward I in Wales. The strength of the early fortress lay in the great tower which was a place of refuge when the castle was under attack. Its defence was passive and depended on the strength of its walls, which were set on rock so they could not be undermined, and on a substantial moat around its curtain wall. The defenders could do little to actively repel the attackers; they merely stayed holed-up in their castles waiting for the enemy to give up. However, the later castles abandoned the great tower in favour of strengthening its outer defences and the development of the gatehouse. Towers were now built on the curtain walls to provide proper flanking fire whereas previously built mural towers were erected in a haphazard manner and often did not give proper cover to the walls.

Four large fortresses, all built much to the same plan, were constructed late in the thirteenth century in the northern half of the country. Of these Ballymote, Co. Sligo, Ballintober, Co. Roscommon, and Greencastle, Co. Donegal, were all built by Richard de Burgh when he was trying to gain control in that area of the north-west. The fourth, Roscommon Castle, was built by Edward I. They all have large twin-towered gateways, angle towers and, in some instances, other mural towers all enclosing what now appear as large open areas. The gatehouse is the most striking and important feature of these later thirteenth-century castles. It is normally a massive rectangular structure with half round towers projecting beyond the line of the curtain and having a large amount of it behind the curtain and containing considerable room for living quarters. The gateway was pierced by a long, narrow entranceway with a chamber over it containing the mechanism for the portcullis and the winding gear for the drawbridge. Some earlier castles such as Lea, Dungarvan, Dundrum, and Carrickfergus had new gateways added or altered to give greater defence and extra accommodation in response to building trends elsewhere in Britain and

Fig. 82   Plan of
Roscommon Castle.

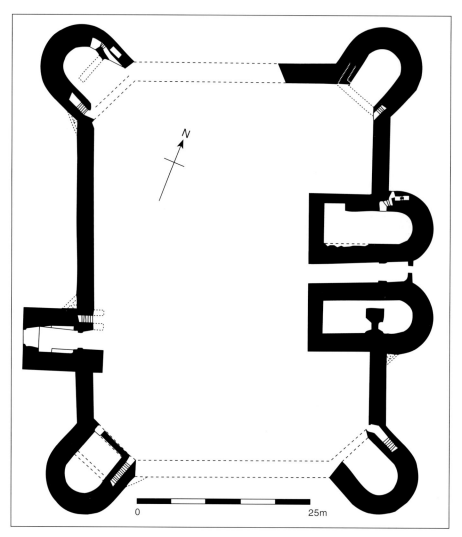

Ireland. The gatehouses at Ballymote, Ballintober, Greencastle and
Roscommon are a logical development from those found at Castleroche and
Dungarvan which could have been built up to 50 years earlier but are also
modelled on the Edward I castles in Wales.

Roscommon Castle is sited on fairly low-lying ground close to a flood
plain or shallow lake. It is an unusual feature of these later fortresses that
most of them, unlike the earlier castles, are not sited close to water. This
means that materials for building the castles and daily supplies for the
residents would have been transported overland; those for Roscommon
probably came overland from the Shannon which lies some distance to the
east. The area enclosed at Roscommon measured *c*.40m by 50m with the
gateway in the middle of the east wall. It was much altered at the end of the
sixteenth century but the gatehouse was three storeys high and contained
the principal room, it being the largest and most commodious part of the

Fig. 83 Roscommon Castle, the large windows show the extent of the late-medieval modification.

castle. The gatehouse here is almost certainly the largest in Ireland but the D-shaped angle towers are also large and were able to contain a considerable number of good-sized chambers. At first-floor level they are equipped with fireplaces and latrines. At the south end of the south wall there is a small rectangular-shaped gateway (postern) with a drawbridge pit

Fig. 84 Ballymote, Co. Sligo, showing the mural towers.

and portcullis slot. The castle also had a moat and outer defences; the latter apparently of earth and timber. Ballymote is very like Roscommon in plan but is almost diamond-shaped rather than rectangular. The angle towers are smaller and half round rather than D-shaped and there are smaller towers, one each mid-way in the east and west walls. The towers of the gatehouse at present only project outside the line of the curtain. No evidence was found for a stone structure at the back of the gate-towers but we must assume that it was intended to build such a structure or else that it was made of timber. Excavation at the back of the castle demonstrated that there was no moat but rather a shallow, water-filled depression and that it was built in a very low-lying area like Roscommon.[1] The angle towers and the gate-towers were partially excavated in 1981 but little of interest was found other than that the walls of the gate-towers had an extra facing within the walls; presumably a defensive mechanism to prevent undermining.

Ballintober Castle, like Ballymote, is also off-square in plan but its angle-towers are also irregular and the gatehouse is smaller. Its towers at the northwest and southwest project off the angle like those at Ballymote and Roscommon but are polygonal. That at the southeast is small and irregular while the one at the northeast projects directly north and has a flat side projecting east making it very vulnerable to attack. There are no additional towers on the walls as at Ballymote and the opes in the existing towers provide for little or no flanking fire. The angle towers at the northwest and southwest contained large, well-appointed chambers but were altered in the

Fig. 85   The much ruined remains of Ballintober Castle, Co. Roscommon. It is similar to Ballymote in plan.

seventeenth century as is evidenced by the late stonework and a fireplace with a date stone of 1627. It would seem that in this case the angle towers rather than the gate tower were lived in by the lord and his retinue.

Greencastle, Co. Donegal, situated on the northern shore of Lough Foyle on a rock outcrop, was built by Richard de Burgh in 1305. Like the three previous castles mentioned its design is based on Edward I examples in Wales and particularly Caernarfon. The twin-towered gatehouse on the other hand is more like that at Roscommon or Harlech. It is a very large three-storey structure and occupies one-third of the site. The gatehouse is much larger than any of the other three castles mentioned above. It has a large square tower added at the north side (probably of fifteenth-century date) which is completely outside the line of the curtain wall and has a great polygonal tower at the west at the opposite end of the ward to the gatehouse. This, of all the castles so far mentioned, was the most commodious. It had considerable accommodation in the gate building, the north tower, the east tower and in the great hall which lay along the north wall between the two towers. The castle was comfortable and fashionable and can be seen as a smaller version of Caernarfon, probably the finest Welsh castle. A strange feature of this castle is that the gateway leads directly into a small courtyard surrounded by bedrock. To gain access to the upper ward and the towers at the north and east one had to go up the stairs at the back of the gatehouse. The upper ward is, therefore, at a higher level than the gatehouse corresponding to its first-floor level. This split level effect is caused by the varying height and uneven nature of the rock on which the castle is founded.

Fig. 86   Greencastle, Co. Donegal, showing the polygonal twin-towered gateway dated to *c*.1305.

Fig. 87   Plan of
Greencastle, Co. Donegal.

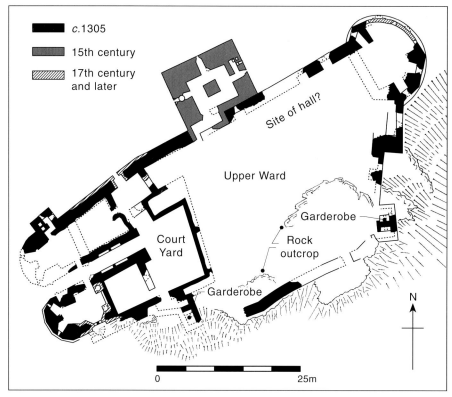

The south gate-tower, which is the most complete, is five-sided to the
front but is otherwise a rectangular block. It has two simple arrow-loops at
the front at ground-floor level and this is also the arrangement on the first
floor. It has an entrance in its north wall leading from the gate-passage
opposite the entrance to the north tower. The towers had wooden floors
which were accessed from a stair tower in the north wall of the now ruinous
north gate-tower. However, there is no access from the ground floor to the
floors above, so entry to the first level must have been from an external stairs
at the back of the north gate-tower from the small courtyard. The chambers
at the back of the gatehouse were barrel-vaulted and had wicker centring, a
feature normally associated in Ireland with tower houses. This centring
appears to be part of the original castle dating to *c*.1305. The gate-passage
was *c*.20m long, 2m wide and was vaulted for its full length. There was no
portcullis but there were two gates in the entrance passage. The first-floor
chamber at the back of the gate-towers appears to have been a hall.

There are two latrine towers other than those in the gatehouse and the
east tower, one is at the south-east angle of the curtain and the other close to
the south-east angle of the gate buildings south of the courtyard. The east
tower has a half-circular lower portion but is polygonal above, and
originally had a straight wall at its back. South-east of the tower and
attached to it are the remains of a rectangular two-storey structure with

garderobes at the southern end. It can be seen from this short description of Greencastle that it had ample accommodation and was well served by numerous latrines. Presumably it also had wooden structures inside the walls and, as if this was not sufficient, the north tower was added for more accommodation.

There are two other castles of this later period that have twin-towered gatehouses and lack a keep: Ballyloughan, Co. Carlow, and Harry Avery's Castle near Newtown Stewart, Co. Tyrone. The Ballyloughan gateway has twin circular towers and an almost square block attached half inside and half outside the line of the curtain. It is quite a small gate-building and although it has two storeys above the level of the gate passage, it contained little accommodation. The courtyard is almost 45m square and has square towers at its north-east and south-west angles which provided further accommodation. The 'enclosure castle' was poorly defended with only thin curtain walls and, as an archaeological excavation showed, only a narrow shallow fosse outside.[2] The finds from the excavation and the stonework in the building indicate a date contemporary with Roscommon and the de Burgh castles mentioned above. Harry Avery's Castle has two half-rounded towers and a rectangular-shaped block attached which leads into an enclosure, now almost completely destroyed. This gateway looks like a smaller version of the ones discussed above but the way it is constructed only allows limited access to the enclosure somewhat like the restricted access at Greencastle, Co. Donegal. Other than the gatehouse there is now little to see at this castle.

Liscarroll Castle, Co. Cork, is situated on a limestone outcrop overlooking flat rolling countryside. It has a large enclosure, quadrangular

Fig. 88 Nineteenth-century sketch of Ballylahan, Co. Mayo, showing the twin-towered gateway and curtain wall. Although similar to Ballyloughan, Co. Carlow and other later medieval fortresses, Ballylahan could be earlier.

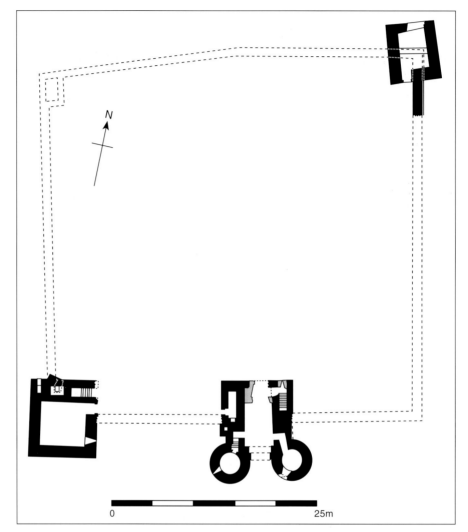

in plan (*c*.62m north-south, *c*.50m east-west) with three-quarter round towers at each angle, a gate-tower midway in the south wall with a smaller tower opposite in the north wall and a small tower in the west. The gate-tower is rectangular and projects 2m beyond the line of the curtain and extends 8.5m back behind it. It has a barrel-vaulted gate passage with plank centring and was protected by a gate at either end and a portcullis in between. There is a spiral stairs leading to the chamber, over the gateway, which is barrel vaulted with wicker centring. There are two further storeys above. The second floor has a two-light ogee-headed window, a blocked ope and a reconstructed doorway indicating a late-medieval rebuild of the gatehouse. The gate-building, which also contained a garderobe, is reasonably large and has enough chambers in it to have been used as the principal accommodation by the owner. The castle would, of course, also have had wooden buildings attached to the inner face of the enclosing walls.

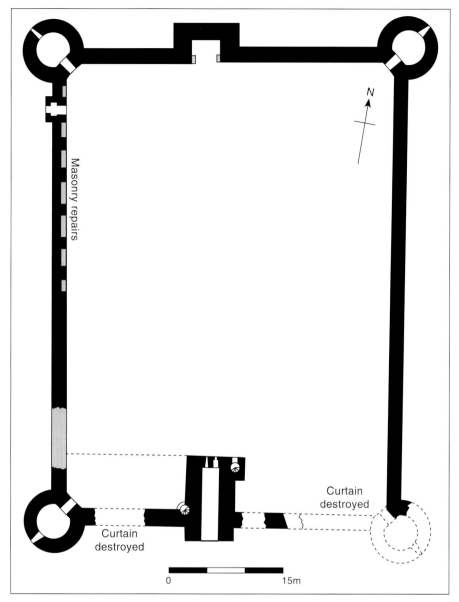

Fig. 90 Plan of
Liscarroll Castle,
Co. Cork.

Masonry repairs

Curtain
destroyed

Curtain
destroyed

0   15m

The tower in the north curtain appears to have been used mainly as a latrine
for it has a large garderobe chute extending from the wall-walk level to the
ground. The second rectangular tower projects almost 1m beyond the line of
the curtain. It is now very ruinous, but originally provided flanking fire. The
angle towers were all originally three storeys high with spiral stairs giving
access to the upper chambers and the wall-walk. The tower at the south-east
contains a well but is now obscured by rubble. There are the remains of a
fosse with a low external bank outside the curtain wall along the north side
and part of the west. Similar outer defences are found at other Irish castles
including Roscommon, Dunamase and Clonmore.

Fig. 91   Liscarroll Castle,
Co. Cork, showing the
large circular corner
towers and rectangular
tower opposite the
gateway.

Fig. 92   Fireplace at
Liscarroll Castle,
Co. Cork.

114

Other than Ballyloughan there are two additional later medieval fortresses in Co. Carlow, at Ballymoon and Clonmore. The latter consists of an almost square enclosure with a range of buildings all along its east side and projecting towers at all its angles other than the north-east where there are only foundations remaining. The building arrangement of the east range is quite complex and a preliminary study of it shows that it was constructed in three phases. There are two large rectangular halls, one in the middle of the range and the other at the north end while the southern end appears to be the main living quarters. The hall in the centre along with the curtain wall is the earliest phase and dates to the end of the thirteenth century as indicated by windows which have trefoil-pointed lights in pairs. In the second phase of building, walls were added to the north-east angle joining the north curtain and north-west angle of the existing hall to form another hall. The final phase saw building and alterations at the south-east angle where two north-south walls with intervening passage were erected between the original hall and the angle tower. Stairs were added to give access to the upper floors, a fireplace inserted in the east wall of the curtain and a garderobe built onto the north-east angle of the tower. The stairs led from the upper storeys of this newly erected solar block into the mural

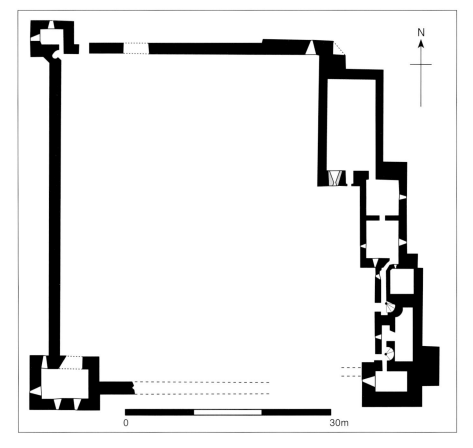

Fig. 93   Plan of Clonmore Castle, Co. Carlow (after McNeill, 1997).

115

passage and down a few steps into the ground level of the original hall which has a plank-centred vault over it. The solar block at Clonmore is four storeys high while the hall blocks have only two storeys. The second-floor level of the solar is the main domestic room and is linked to the first floor of the hall block. It also has a fireplace and access to the latrine which was added to the tower. It is lit by two-light trefoil pointed windows in the east and west walls.

Although there are three distinct phases in the building of the east range of the castle, little time lapsed in their erection as is evidenced by the early windows in the solar which is the latest part of the structure. The south-west angle tower of the curtain is the largest and has domestic quarters at first-floor level while the ground floor is defended by arrow-loops. The southern curtain wall is missing as is the fosse which can be seen immediately outside the north and west walls. The gateway was probably situated on the south side. This castle is one of the few in Ireland that has substantial standing remains of its domestic ranges and loosely compares to the earlier fortress at Adare.

A castle similar to Clonmore and of the same date lies not 32km away to the north-east at Ballymoon. It is almost square in plan, has no angle towers, had building ranges along each curtain, projecting garderobe towers on the north-east and north-west curtain walls, a simple gateway at the south-east and another entrance at the south-west. Unusually, it is built of rough granite boulders and stones. The curtain walls all stop precisely at the second-floor level except for the gate-tower at the south-east which rises to the top of that level. The curtain walls are probably unfinished as it is highly unlikely that they would all have been robbed down to exactly the same level. The gateway at the south-west has tie-stones for a tower over it which was never commenced. Inside the curtain walls along every side there are clear remains of building ranges partly buried in a considerable build-up of rubble. This castle lacks opes at ground level except for two in the south-west wall near the north angle, so that there was no light getting into the ranges through the external walls at ground level.

The walls at first-floor level have numerous opes most of which are loops. However, in the north-east portion of the north-west wall there are the remains of two large windows and almost in the centre of the wall is a double fireplace indicating that this was the area of the hall. Further to the south-west in the same wall is a garderobe tower with two latrines both in the same chamber though partially separated by a wall. Another garderobe tower is in the middle of the north-east wall but in this instance the latrines are separated by a solid wall. There is a fireplace each side of the garderobe tower in the north-east wall. Therefore the main domestic quarters of the castle were in the ranges along the north-east and north-west walls. Although Ballymoon is an impressive castle it was not very

Fig. 94   This aerial photograph of Ballymoon Castle, Co. Carlow, clearly shows the unfinished curtain walls.

Fig. 95   Detail of Ballymoon showing a cross-loop window and a doorway with an arch similar in style to those found at Caernarfon Castle in Wales.

defensive since it lacks flanking towers and strong gateways. It was an adequately fortified and well-appointed residence which could date as late as the middle of the fourteenth century.

There are several large fortresses of this later medieval period in Co. Limerick but best known are Askeaton, Carrigogunnel and Newcastle West. All three, like many of the castles of this later medieval period, have several building phases which can stretch over 300 years of occupation. Carrigogunnel, which is built on a prominent rock outcropping on the south shore of the Shannon estuary, appears as a ruined fifteenth-century fortress but much of its basic fabric dates to the end of the thirteenth or the early fourteenth centuries.[3] The fortress, one of the few to be built by the native Irish, was erected by the O'Briens and consists of a large enclosure with its main building in the north angle and an early hall in the south-east. The domestic quarters were within an upper ward as there is an enclosing wall at the south side and it is situated on a high rock outcrop some distance from the gateway of the outer defences. The curtain walls are of a very irregular shape which is dictated by the rock outcrop. There are no flanking towers and the gateway was a simple breach in the walls, therefore the castle depended to a large extant on its naturally defensive position. The domestic area was built almost as two separate entities, that at the west side is a two-storey block with great chambers which have large windows, fireplaces and garderobes while the chamber tower at the east is four storeys high and has much less commodious rooms. All the accommodation block has been considerably altered and rebuilt in the fifteenth century and new windows and doorways were inserted at that time. At the south angle of the curtain and built into it are the remains of a two-storey hall which is part of the earliest building.

Another Co. Limerick fortress of this period is found at Askeaton sited on a small island encircled by two branches of the River Deel. Most of the standing remains are of fifteenth-century date but the fortification was originally a thirteenth-century earthwork castle. The central portion of the island has a substantial area of high bedrock and has an enclosing wall built around it but the buildings within it, including the Desmond tower and the constables tower, are late medieval. This area of high ground must have had the thirteenth-century fortification sited on it. The siting of the fortification in a low-lying area in the middle of a river is like that of Caher Castle, Co. Tipperary, mentioned below. The most obvious thirteenth-century remains at Askeaton are those of the lower part of a great hall situated at the north end of the west curtain and incorporated in it. The hall is a very fine two-storey structure with a vaulted ground floor and a large aisled hall with great windows. At each end of the hall are chambers for private accommodation and services for the Lord. However, the principal accommodation in the late-medieval period was up on the rock in the inner

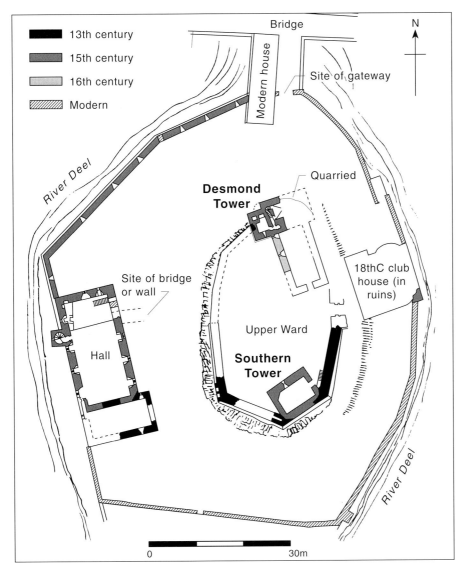

Fig. 96   Plan of
Askeaton Castle, Co.
Limerick.

ward where a large rectangular block now called the Desmond tower was
built. Only the western portion of this domestic block survives. It consists of
a three-storey building with a four-storey tower attached. The tower has
vaulted chambers over the ground and first floor with wicker and plank
centring and a projecting section at the north-west which contains garderobe
chambers. The tower is lit by well-cut windows with ogee-heads, some with
hood-mouldings. The chambers in the main block are more spacious and the
first floor has the remains of a fireplace and a large transomed two-light
window. The second floor level has a finely decorated fireplace and a small
two-light window decorated on the outside. A large chimney-stack remains
perched on the west wall directly over the fireplaces. The inner ward is
accessed through a small gate-tower in the middle of the east curtain. There

are the remains of the three-storey building, called the constable's tower (southern tower), in the south-east angle of the inner ward. It has fireplaces at first and second-floor levels and a latrine. The outer curtain wall has a series of key-hole, square-shaped loops for guns.

A third Co. Limerick fortress of the later medieval period is Newcastle O'Conyll (Castle Demesne, Newcastle West) which is sited on the edge of a steep bank close to the River Arra. When Thomas Westropp was writing about it in 1909, he said it was so modernised and so covered in ivy that it was difficult to give an account of the standing medieval remains. Clearly two halls and two towers could be identified but little or nothing of the curtain wall. Recent work there by Dúchas, the Heritage Service, has removed the ivy and the clutter of modern buildings without revealing anything more in the way of medieval structures. The main interest in the site has always been the remains of two medieval halls. The north hall

Fig. 97 Details of Askeaton Castle, Co. Limerick; the Desmond tower (top left), the constable's tower (top right), the hall (bottom left), and detail of window in the hall (bottom right) (David Sweetman).

(known as Desmond's Hall) is a two-storey building with a vault over the ground floor and a projecting tower at the north-west angle.[4] The hall is unaltered except for the insertion of the vault and insertion of twin-light, cusped, ogee-headed, transomed windows dating to the latter half of the fourteenth century. There are two windows in each of the south and north walls and one in the east wall. They have large embrasures and fine window seats. Access to the hall, the top of the tower and the battlements was via a spiral stairs in the south-west angle of the projecting tower. There is a fireplace in the south wall with a date of 1638.

The south building (known as the Great Hall) is a single-storey building and lacks on present evidence any service rooms. It could be a chapel of the castle.[5] However, it does not work well as a chapel for the following reasons: its east wall is apparently blank; the windows are not convincing as church architecture since they are quite squat; there is only a small single light in the west gable; and finally, the position of the doorway at the east end of the north wall would be very unusual for a church. The windows in the south wall are very fine, two of them being transomed, twin-lighted with cusped ogee-heads and a cusped centre-piece at the head. In the south-west angle of the site there are the remains of a domestic block with a circular tower attached at its south-east angle. Running west-south-west from it is a short stretch of curtain walling which leads to the remains of another tower. This is the only remaining flanking tower of the curtain. It has a vaulted ground floor while the upper floor was converted into a summer house. Loops and a late medieval window have been inserted into the upper-floor level. The tower which is attached to the chamber block was adapted as part of the modern house which was added to it. The modern structure has recently

Fig. 99 A squat traceried window from the great hall, Newcastle O'Conyll Castle, Co. Limerick.

been pulled down. The battlements have been removed and the upper portion modernised. The first-floor level of this tower gives access to the first floor of the chamber block. At the western end of the block is a rectangular tower which has intra-mural stairs in its north wall from first to second floor and a spiral stairs in the north-west angle from that level up to the fourth floor. The chamber block itself is at present only two storeys high with a wicker-centred vault over the ground floor. This block is undoubtedly a domestic range with the round tower at its south-east angle and smaller chambers attached in the rectangular tower at the west end, probably bedrooms.[6] The domestic block and round tower as well as the remaining section of curtain wall are of late-medieval origin but there has been so much rebuilding and alterations that there could be earlier fabric in these structures and we know from historical records that there was a castle here by the end of the thirteenth century.

Caher, Co. Tipperary, is another multi-period castle but with mainly post-1300 standing remains. Like Askeaton it is sited on a rock island in the middle of a river (Suir) in a low-lying situation and dependent on the natural defences provided by the river. Unlike most Irish medieval castles, it is very well preserved partly due to nineteenth-century restoration. The Barony of Caher was granted to Philip of Worcester in 1192 but his first fortification was probably the large motte at Knockgraffon about 6km away to the north. An illustration from 1599 shows the castle much as it is today. There is a large outer ward at the south with circular angle towers at the south-east and south-west but no internal structures. An inner ward with a gatehouse is sited in the middle of its south wall, square towers at the north-east and north-west angles and a small circular tower at the south-east.[7] Recent work has shown that the core of this inner ward dates to the thirteenth century.[8] The 1599 illustration also shows outer defences at the east side fronting onto the river where there is a bridge providing access to the castle. Between the inner and outer wards there is a rectangular walled area of open ground which is termed the middle ward. At the north side of

Fig. 100   Caher, Co. Tipperary. This aerial photograph shows the inner ward and the castle's strategic position in the middle of the River Suir.

123

Fig. 101   Plan of Caher
Castle, Co. Tipperary.

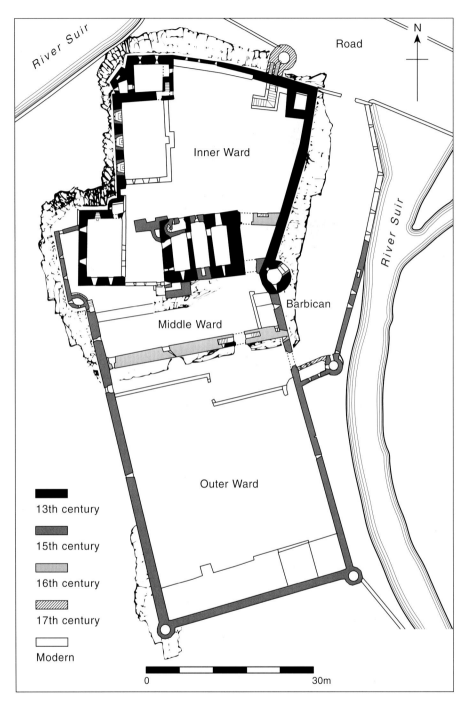

the middle ward are the wall footings of a massive east-west wall which is
thirteenth century in date. The gatehouse and the curtain walls north of this
massive wall are also of the same date.[9]

The inner ward, of mid-thirteenth-century date, consisted of a
gatehouse, angle towers on the curtain, a domestic tower in the south-west

124

Fig. 102 The keep or great tower at Caher was built on a limestone outcrop in the middle of the River Suir.

angle and a great hall along the northern portion of the west curtain wall. The large three-storey rectangular building in the centre of the south wall was originally a centrally pierced rectangular gatehouse. Its passage was blocked in the fifteenth century (its arch can be clearly seen in the south wall) and it was made into a keep. The gate-passage was moved immediately to its east side. The ground floor is divided into three bays on a north-south axis, that in the centre is the blocked thirteenth-century gate-passage, while those on each side were guard chambers and have slit opes in their south walls. The original access to the rooms above the gate-passage was in the north-west angle where there is a stairs. At first-floor level there is a large late-medieval fireplace in the centre of the south wall inserted into where the portcullis mechanism used to be. The original gateway was similar to the one now partially restored at Roscrea Castle which lies about 89km to the north. The present entrance at Caher has a portcullis and archway which are original thirteenth-century structures removed from their primary positions, while the double machicolation over the present gateway is a nineteenth-century restoration.

The north-east tower of the curtain has a first-floor entrance and has no access or light getting into the ground floor. Close to this tower to the west are steps which lead to the base of a well tower outside the curtain walls, something which is not commonly found in Irish castles. At the north-west angle is a large, almost square, three-storey high tower and immediately adjoining it at the south is the great hall which, in its present form, is a mid-nineteenth-century rebuilding. Access to this tower was originally at ground-floor level from the hall. The lower portions of the tower and the adjoining hall were originally built in the mid-thirteenth century. The tower was the solar or private chambers which were equipped with garderobes. The hall was a single-storey building as can be seen from the original roof crease in the south wall of the tower. The west wall has its original embrasures but with fifteenth-century windows inserted. The hall was shortened at some stage and may originally have extended close to the gatehouse. There is a large fireplace, of thirteenth-century date, to the south of the present hall adjoining the north-west angle of the gate-tower which could have been part of the hall.[10] However, it is not parallel with the existing north wall of the hall and it would be unusual for the fireplace to be at one end rather than in the centre of a side wall and therefore it may be a kitchen to service the hall and could be of a later date.

The royal castle at Roscrea, Co. Tipperary was built *c.*1280 after the earthwork fortification fell out of use. It is located on high ground close to the River Bunnow. The castle consists of a polygonal enclosure with angle towers at the south-west and south-east and an almost rectangular-shaped gate-building at the west end of the north curtain. The curtain wall is almost complete despite destruction at the south side to accommodate an entrance for a Georgian house and occupation by the army in the nineteenth century. The gatehouse, which is three storeys high, was centrally pierced. Excavations in the ground floor area of the gatehouse uncovered the slots for a counter-balance drawbridge.[11] Further excavation revealed the remains of the drawbridge pit and part of the moat.[12] Modern alterations to the gatehouse led to the removal of the flanking walls of the gate-passage and the wooden floor of the first level disappeared. The first floor is covered with a fine groin-vaulted roof and has an impressive fireplace midway in the south wall. The first and second floors are accessed from a spiral staircase in the east wall. At the south end of the west wall is a subrectangular projection which at first floor-level contains a garderobe and is accessed via a mural passage. The chamber at first-floor level is the hall. At second-floor level this projection contained steps which led onto the wall-walk of the curtain wall. In the south-west angle is another stairs which leads up to the parapets of the gatehouse and gives access to the machicolation over the gateway. The western end of this building has two further levels with a garderobe in the angle between the west wall and the projection.

The south-east tower at Roscrea Castle is two storeyed with rebuilt spiral stairs in the south-west angle but is otherwise featureless. The three-storey south-west tower (known as the Ormond Tower) is half round and only projects slightly to the west beyond the line of the curtain. It has a fireplace in the north wall at first-floor level with the remains of a coat-of-

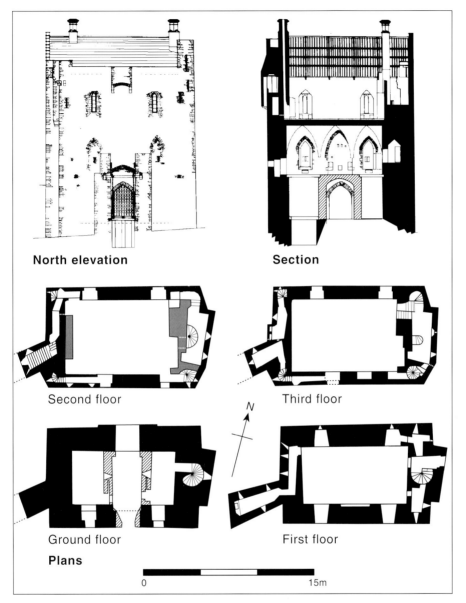

North elevation

Section

Second floor

Third floor

Ground floor

First floor

Plans

0   15m

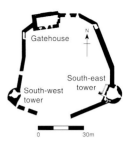

Plan of Roscrea Castle,
Co. Tipperary
(after Stout, 1984).

Fig. 103   Plans, section
and elevation of the
gatehouse at Roscrea
Castle, Co. Tipperary.

arms in stucco which dates to the seventeenth century. Part of the moat was
excavated at the western face of this tower in 1982.[13]

Swords, Co. Dublin, is another castle with several periods of building
within an irregular enclosure. It is built on fairly low-lying ground close to
the River Ward. It was always an Episcopal castle which may account for its
poor defences which consist of a simple gateway, narrow curtain walls and
only one mural tower, that at the north opposite the entrance. It was built at
the start of the thirteenth century but the chapel to the east of the gateway
is a fourteenth-century building. The remains of a hall along the east wall is
late thirteenth century and the north tower is probably even later. The

Fig. 104 The gatehouse at Roscrea Castle, Co. Tipperary, after conservation and reconstruction work.

building is more manorial in character than the other stone castles, although its stepped battlements are typical of the late-medieval period. There is considerable accommodation each side of the gateway and in the great chamber, hall and other buildings along the east curtain wall. In March 1326 an Inquisition taken in Dublin gives a detailed description of the castle:

> There are a hall, a chamber for the Archbishop annexed to it of which the walls are of stone and crenellated like a castle and roofed with shingles and there are a kitchen there with a larder whose walls are stone and roof of shingles. There was a chamber for the friars with a cloister room thrown down; near the gate is a chamber for the constable and four chambers for knights and squires roofed with shingles; under these a stable and bakehouse ...[14]

Fig. 105   Late eighteenth-century illustration of the constable's tower at Swords Castle, Co. Dublin.

Fig. 106   An early photograph of the gateway at Swords Castle.

Fig. 107   Plan of Quin
Castle, Co. Clare. A
Franciscan Friary was
built on the remains of
the castle but its ground
plan is plainly visible.

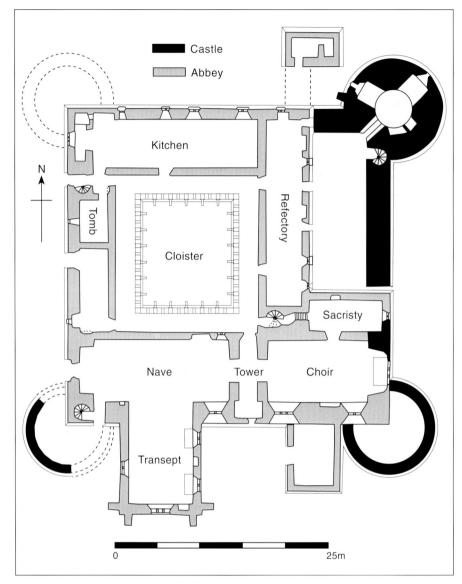

Quin Castle, Co. Clare, was built by de Clare in 1278-80 but captured
and partly destroyed some eight years later. In the middle of the fifteenth
century it was incorporated into a Franciscan friary. The outline of the
original castle, which was almost square in plan with towers at each angle,
can still be seen in the ruins of the friary. The friary church occupies the
southern part of the castle while the cloister and the domestic ranges occupy
most of the remaining portion. The curtain walls were substantial, being
3.3m thick. Little else of the castle can be seen at present but its basic form
fits in well with the Welsh Edward I castles. Kilbolane, Co. Cork, is also
almost square in plan and has circular angle towers remaining at the north-
west and south-west and is therefore similar to the layout of Quin.

130

Plate 16 Ballyloughan, Co. Carlow.

Plate 17 Clonmore Castle, Co. Carlow.

131

Plate 18 Askeaton Castle, Co. Limerick. This photograph clearly shows the inner and outer baileys with their enclosing walls, the hall to the right, and the great tower to the left.

Plate 19 Dunluce Castle, Co. Antrim.

LATE FOURTEENTH/FIFTEENTH-CENTURY FORTRESSES

There is no doubt about the lack of castle building in Ireland in the second half of the fourteenth century.[15] Few totally new fortresses were erected and most of the building activity was concentrated on additions or alterations to existing castles. However, there are some castles, not tower houses, which can be assigned to the late fourteenth or fifteenth centuries.[16] It has also been argued that castles in Carlow, such as Rathnageeragh and Ballyloo, fall within this period.[17] Rathnageeragh Castle is a gatehouse with an entrance through a central vaulted area and a vaulted chamber on each side of the passageway and parallel to it. It has a first-floor hall and a chamber block at the east side. The remains of the associated enclosure is visible in the form of a raised platform. There is, however, no reason to assume that this gatehouse dates any later than the end of the thirteenth century. Ballyloo is clearly a tower house. Three large fortresses from Co. Carlow – Ballymoon, Ballyloughan and Clonmore – have been identified as filling the building hiatus of the later fourteenth century.[18] However, these castles almost certainly belong to the period of great castle building at the time Edward I was actively constructing fortresses in Wales. The problem has been approached from an historical perspective and some tower houses are thought to have been built in this period because of the use of the word 'fortalice'.[19] However, most, if not all, of these examples are hall-houses and the acceptance of the word fortalice as meaning a tower house is extremely dubious. The only type of castle being built in the later fourteenth century appears to be the hall-house. Hall-houses from this period are found in the eastern half of the country. They are clearly the inspiration for the development of the tower house (see chapter 5).

For whatever historical or economic reason, large fortresses were not built in the second half of the fourteenth century. However, we do have examples which can be dated to the fifteenth century such as Granny, Co. Kilkenny. This is a so-called 'enclosure castle', almost square in plan with circular projecting towers at the south-west and south-east angles. It has a five-storey chamber tower inside the north-east angle with the remains of a hall attached at the west which ran the full length of the north wall. It has a simple opening in the centre of the east curtain for the gateway. The castle is sited on the north bank of the River Suir about 5km from Waterford City. The two angle towers are set at the river's edge and there is a third isolated circular tower in a straight line to the west which is joined to the curtain by a length of thin walling as if it was the south curtain of an outer ward. The castle is built very much in the style of the thirteenth- and early fourteenth-century fortresses but its details such as the gun loops and windows are plainly late-medieval.

One possible candidate for a castle of late fourteenth-century origin is Dunluce, Co. Antrim, which cannot have been built before 1360.[20] It is

Fig. 108 The twin-
towered gatehouse with
centrally placed
entranceway at
Rathnageeragh,
Co. Carlow.

constructed on an almost isolated rock peninsula on the north Antrim coast
and is probably the most picturesque castle in Ireland. The original castle
consisted of a rectangular-shaped courtyard with strong walls and angle
towers and a range of buildings along the south curtain but most of the
standing remains can be dated to the sixteenth century. At the south-west
angle is a rectangular gatehouse from the later period. Of the same date are
the extensive remains of the domestic dwellings which now dominate the
castle and can be attributed to the time of its restoration at the end of the
sixteenth century.

There are a number of very large tower houses of this period which
Leask describes as 'larger castles of the fifteenth, sixteenth and
seventeenth centuries'.[21] These include Blarney, Co. Cork, and Fiddaun,
Co. Galway, Bunratty, Co. Clare and Dunsoghly, Co. Dublin. But the only
thing that really distinguishes them from the other tower houses is their
size. They are, therefore, discussed in the following chapter. Leask also
included Caher, Co. Tipperary, Askeaton, Co. Limerick and Newcastle
West, Co. Limerick in this classification but these are certainly earlier in
date. Caher, Askeaton and many other large fortresses have considerable
rebuilding in the later medieval period, as one would expect in high status
castles from an earlier period, and continue to be occupied into the

Fig. 109 Granny Castle, Grannagh, Co. Kilkenny. Remains of curtain walls with late-medieval great tower sited on the River Suir.

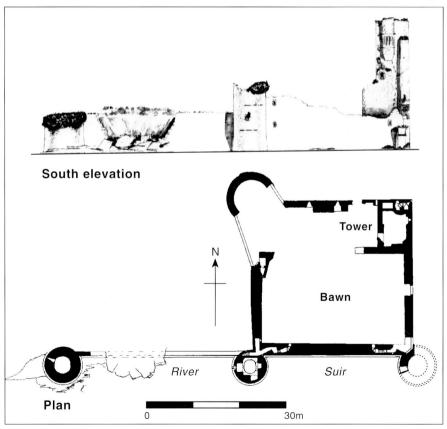

Fig. 110 Plan and elevation of Granny Castle.

Fig. 111   Detail of a
stone carving in Granny
Castle, Co. Kilkenny.

fifteenth and sixteenth centuries, but these examples do not fill the hiatus
in new castle building. We are left with virtually no new castle building
other than tower houses for this period.[22]

CHAPTER FIVE

THE TOWER HOUSE

Tower houses in Ireland are probably the least understood category of castles. Their origins have been questioned and they have often been dismissed as being simple towers, all built more-or-less to the same design, and having poor defensive capabilities.[1] Despite efforts to push their origins back into the fourteenth century, however, there is one inescapable historical fact about the origins of the tower house: a grant of £10 was made available under a statute of Henry VI in 1429 to every man in the Pale who wished to build a castle within ten years and the measurements were to be 20 feet by 16 feet and 40 feet in height or more (6.1m x 4.9m x 12.2m).[2] This grant provided the impetus to build the typical tower house of the eastern half of Ireland.

With most of the survey fieldwork now completed in the Republic of Ireland, a very clear pattern of tower house building has emerged. Those built in the eastern half are generally simple structures, small towers three to four storeys high, usually with one or more projecting towers at the angles to accommodate stairs and garderobes. The further west one travels the more sophisticated and larger these towers become and the later they can be dated. No examples of standing remains have been found which give any credence to alternative theories, whether relating to tower house date or distribution.[3] The later hall-houses have many features in common with tower houses, such as vaults over the ground floor and angle towers with stairs and garderobes, and are patently linked to the development and origin of the tower house in the east. The early small tower house occurs mainly in the east but this type is also found in the west; for instance at Rockfleet, Co. Mayo. Likewise, there are some large tower houses in the east such as Dunsoghly, Co. Dublin, but these are the exceptions rather than the rule. At Leighinbridge, Co. Carlow, there is a tower house on the east bank of the River Barrow. It was constructed mainly in the sixteenth century but according to historical records a castle was built here in 1320 to defend a bridge over the river. Some of this earlier building, which was a Carmelite Friary, can be seen in the tower and curtain walls. This highlights the danger of using historical records on their own to try and prove early dates for tower house building.

Attempts to divide tower houses into regional groups based on their plans has not been convincing. For example 'type 1A', which includes

Fig. 112 Plan of the
Dunsoghly Castle and
Church, Co. Dublin.

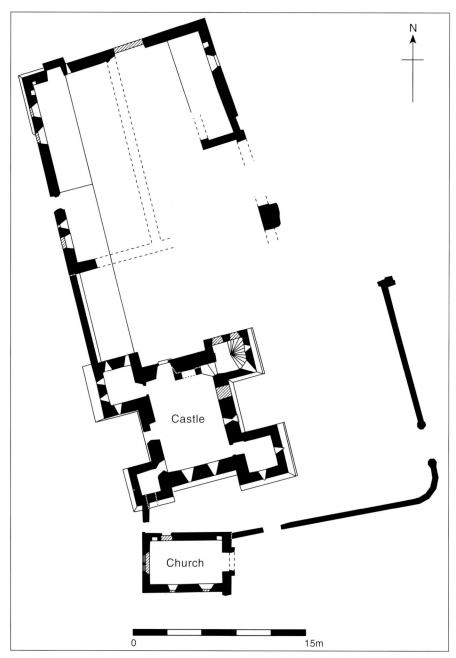

Bourchier's Castle, Lough Gur, Co. Limerick is the commonest type and is
said to be found in a limited area south and west of Limerick City.[4]
However, the description of the type as epitomised by Bourchier's Castle is
typical of the small simple-type tower house found all over Ireland, a type
well illustrated in Louth where the tower house ground plans are basically
the same. The entrance is to be found on the ground floor to one side of a
projecting tower which contains spiral stairs. The entranceway usually leads

Fig. 113 Dunsoghly tower house, Co. Dublin, has four angle towers like Castletown, Co. Louth. The church is on the left.

into a lobby area which has a murder-hole over it and from here one can either enter the stairway or go straight into the barrel-vaulted, ground-floor area. The area immediately underneath the barrel vault often has corbels to carry a wooden floor for storage.

There are the standing remains of 26 tower houses in Co. Louth.[5] Only that at Castletown, Dundalk, which was built *c*.1472, is comparable in any way to the larger examples such as Dunsoghly, Co. Dublin (which is of much the same date). At Milltown there are projecting towers at diagonally opposite angles, one containing the stairs and the other the garderobe. A few kilometres away at Killincoole we have almost exactly the same plan. The

Fig. 114 The late sixteenth- or early seventeenth-century doorway of the church at Dunsoghly Castle, Co. Dublin. A plaque with the tools of the crucifixion is mounted above the doorway.

outer doorway was often protected by a yett (iron grill) which could be pulled up or across by chains from within while the door was also barred from inside. Frequently there was a separate door to the stairs and to the ground-floor chamber so, even if the outer door was broken down, the intruder was faced with further barriers. At Balregan one had to enter the

Fig. 115 Leighlinbridge, Co. Carlow, is an example of a simple early tower house from the east of Ireland.

ground-floor chamber before gaining access to the intra-mural stairs which led straight up to the first floor. The first floor of these tower houses contained the hall and invariably the garderobe, while the private chambers were in the levels above. At Dunmahon there is a large garderobe tower with two chutes exiting into a chamber at ground level. In the Glaspistol tower house, at first-floor level, the west side has a mural passage running most of its length and contains a latrine at its north end.

Other variations such as separate access to the ground-floor chamber and stairs is to be found at Haynestown. Also at this tower house one can clearly see how it was constructed by first building the free-standing barrel

141

Fig. 116 Elevation and section of Bourchier's Castle, Co. Limerick.

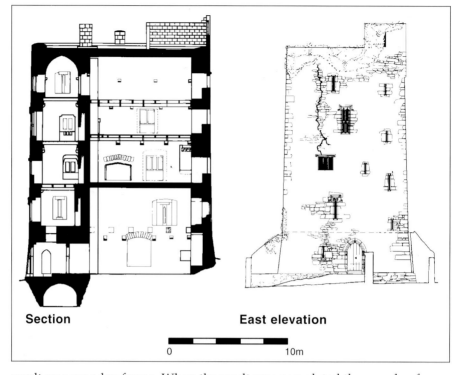

Section   **East elevation**

0   10m

vault on a wooden frame. When the vault was completed the wooden frame was pulled out and the end walls filled in and then the bases of the angle towers were butted on. Everything was then tied together at first-floor level. This method of construction is often seen in tower houses leading some people to mistakenly conclude that there are quite different phases of building. At Haynestown the line of the vault can be seen in the outer face of the east and west walls. At Termonfeckin the doorway is in the centre of the north-west wall but it appears that it was originally intended to place it in the north-east angle where the stairs is now situated. The doorway is protected by a miniature bawn. The ground floor, unusually, has two chambers, a large rectangular one and a smaller almost square one. This plan is repeated at first-floor level except that the south angle which is not utilised at ground-floor level has a substantial garderobe in it above. Another unusual feature of this tower house is that its upper floor is roofed with very fine corbelling, something not seen over a main chamber elsewhere in Louth and rare in this type of building in Ireland. Tower house roofs were gabled and the wall-walk passed between the gable ends and the crenellated battlements. At battlement level there was normally a machicolation over the doorway and frequently chimneys projecting out carried on corbels. The wall-walk was provided with outlets through the bases of the battlements to allow water to run off down the walls. The angle towers usually rose above the level of the battlements and were sometimes

Isometric view of Termonfeckin Castle, Co. Louth.

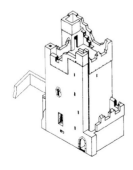

142

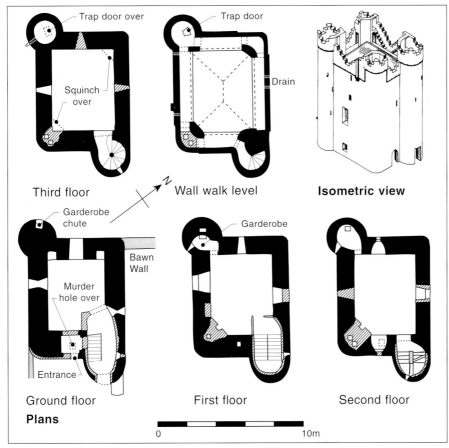

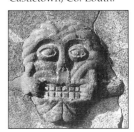

Fig. 117 Plans and isometric view of Milltown, Co. Louth.

Carved stone face from the tower house at Castletown, Co. Louth.

provided with latrines for the sentries on watch. The windows of these tower houses are usually plain, single lights or slit opes at ground-floor level with more elaborate ones on the first floor and above. Double lights or single lights with ogee heads and hood-mouldings are common. Roodstown has some transomed four-lights with cusped ogee heads. A remarkable

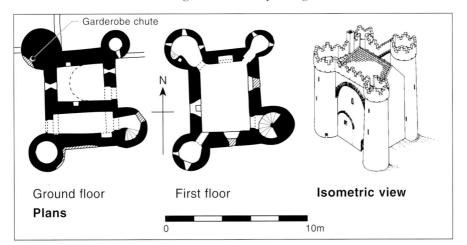

Fig. 118 Plans and isometric view of Haynestown, Co. Louth.

Fig. 119   Plans of
Killincoole, Co. Louth.

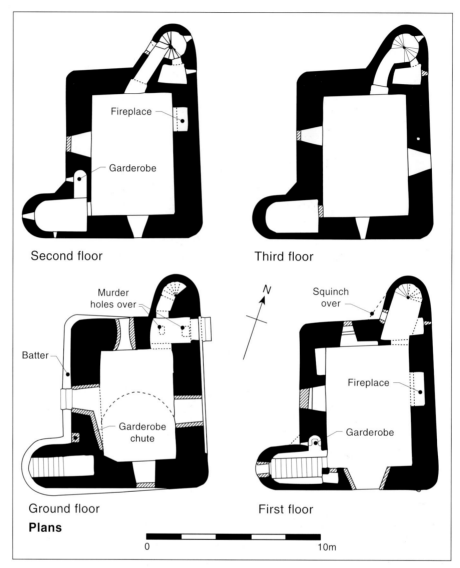

Second floor

Third floor

Ground floor
Plans

First floor

0   10m

feature of the Louth tower houses is the large number of them which were occupied until quite recently or still lived in such as Darver, Richardstown and Smarmore. Others have had houses added to them and in some cases they have been incorporated into later dwellings so that they are almost completely disguised.

In Co. Louth, the most common ground plan for a tower house is two projecting angle towers sited diagonally opposite each other, one carrying the stairs, the other the garderobe and both being almost square. However, within Louth a number of the smaller tower houses have no projecting angle towers, such as the Mint in Carlingford and Athclare near Dunleer, while some have towers at each angle like Balregan and Castletown. Dunmahon has the towers on the north-east and north-west angles but one projects east

Fig. 120 Roodstown, Co. Louth, a typical simple tower house of the Pale. The projecting tower at the angle carries the stairs.

Stone heads on corbels in Carntown tower house, Co. Louth.

and the other north, whereas at Glaspistol there is only one tower and it contains the stairs. The angle towers can sometimes be circular, as at Haynestown, where there is one at each angle, all of different sizes. Milltown not only has diagonally opposing, rounded projecting towers but the angles without towers are also rounded. Finally, the Court House in Ardee has two projecting towers on its west wall while Hatch's Castle, just up the street from it, has two half round towers projecting from its east wall. Co. Louth is the smallest county in Ireland yet there is considerable variation in the ground plans of its 26 tower houses. Most of them date from the early phase of the development of this type of castle.

Fig. 121 Highly decorated windows from the late sixteenth-century urban tower house known as The Mint in Carlingford, Co. Louth.

At Clara Upper, in Kilkenny, there is a very fine example of a small tower house. It is probably one of the best known in Ireland because it was used as a type site by Leask.[6] It is five storeys high with a wall-walk and, unusually, has the remains of a small subrectangular-shaped bawn attached at the north where it protects the doorway. The plan of this tower house is different from the Louth examples (except for Termonfeckin) in that it has a small rectangular chamber close to the stairs at the first, second and third-floor levels. The lower floors of Clara were wooden while it has a stone vault over the third floor which also has a secret chamber accessible from above. The small tower houses in Louth which do not have vaulting over the ground floor, such as The Mint in Carlingford or Carntown, are late in the series as is evidenced by the stonework, especially in the windows of the Mint and its gun loops. This could point towards a late date for the construction of Clara.

The almost 50 examples of tower houses in Co. Meath show little or no differences in their plans and layouts to those in Co. Louth and are typical of the Pale castles of the fifteenth and sixteenth centuries. Some of the tower

Fig. 122 Clara, Co. Kilkenny, a tall rectangular tower house with small bawn. The machicolation at battlement level is directly over the doorway at ground-floor level.

houses have large houses attached to them which in most cases date to the seventeenth century such as Athlumney, Dardistown and Slane Castle Demesne. These houses are also to some extent fortified. At Kilbrew the early eighteenth-century ruined house incorporates part of a tower house as does another eighteenth-century example at Skreen. Bective Abbey and Newtown Trim (the Crutched Friary) both have two tower houses built into the monastic site either after or close to the time that they were suppressed. Building of tower houses in monastic sites is something which is repeated in several of the counties in the eastern half of the country, for example at Mellifont, in Co. Louth, Kells, Co. Kilkenny, and Dysart, Co. Kilkenny.

Ballagh Castle, Ballagharahin, Co. Laois, is a fine example of a late sixteenth-century tower house of medium size. It is five storeys high with a slight base-batter and is impressively defended as well as being well

147

Fig. 123 Liskeveen, Co. Tipperary. Arrow and gun loops indicate the defensive nature of the tower house (David Sweetman).

appointed and having finely dressed stonework. At third-floor level it has a bartizan on the east angle and machicolation on the north-west and south-west walls. The lower floor levels have only slit opes and the impressive doorway was protected by a yett. Immediately inside the doorway is a small lobby which is defended by a cross loop which would have been manned from inside the main chamber and defended by a murder-hole over. The floors were all wooden as is the case with the later tower houses in the eastern half of the country. There are mural passages in the north-west wall at first and second-floor level giving access to garderobes and fireplaces at second and third floor. Ballyadams, Co. Laois, is also a late example but is six storeys high with rounded towers at its south-west and north-west angles and an imposing entrance in the wall between them. Spanning the area between the angle towers and just below the uppermost storey is a segmented arch which carries a machicolation. Below this at first-floor level is a murder-hole over the doorway. A large seventeenth-century, three-storey house is attached to the east side. The distribution of this type of tower house – the main feature being the projecting towers on one side projecting in the same direction – was said to have been confined to an area

Fig. 124 Fireplaces at Rathnaveoge tower house in north Co. Tipperary (Jean Farrelly).

Plate 20   Rockfleet, Co. Mayo. This type of small simple tower house is quite common in the west of Ireland.

Plate 21   Derryhivenny, Co. Galway. This is a late, sophisticated tower house with high chimney stacks on its gables, a style more akin to the later fortified house.

149

Plate 22   Aughnanure Castle in west Galway was the stronghold of the O'Flahertys and is sited on the south bank of the Drimneen river. It is protected by two bawns. The rectangular tower house, which is sited almost centrally in the inner bawn, is six storeys high with a gabled attic. It is defended by bartizans at the south-east and north-east angles.

Fig. 125 Sheela-na-gig (or exhibitionist figure) mounted in the wall of Garrycastle tower house, Co. Offaly.

in south-east Down.[7] However, the occurrence of projecting towers and their positioning is very variable and while a number of tower houses within a region will often have similar plans, these plans do not seem to be exclusive to any particular region.

Laois, which is almost twice the size of Louth, has 29 tower houses.[8] Fifteen of these can be fairly securely dated through historical references to their date of erection, the type of stone dressing, or by date stones. Eleven belong to the sixteenth century and only four appear to be earlier. The early examples all have barrel vaults over the ground floor whereas the later examples seldom have vaults and, if they do, they are over an upper floor as at Gortnaclea. The later examples all have finely dressed windows, usually with ogee-heads, and well-finished doorways with yett-holes. These later examples are also larger and higher and contain fireplaces, sometimes with date stones.

Some of the tower houses appear on architectural and historical grounds to have been built as late as the first quarter of the seventeenth century. For instance Ballinakill, Co. Laois, is said to have been erected by Sir Thomas Ridgeway between 1606 and 1612. Shrule has a stone plaque with a date of 1640 and Tintore has a date stone of 1635 on the fireplace. Two castles can be dated on historical grounds to 1425 (Galesquarter) and 1427 (Castlebrack). These dates tie in well with structural features, in particular a vaulted ground floor. Bawns were found at six tower houses in Laois and at least three of these had gun loops in their walls. One of these is at Galesquarter (built in

Fig. 126   Section and
elevation of Burnchurch,
Co. Kilkenny.

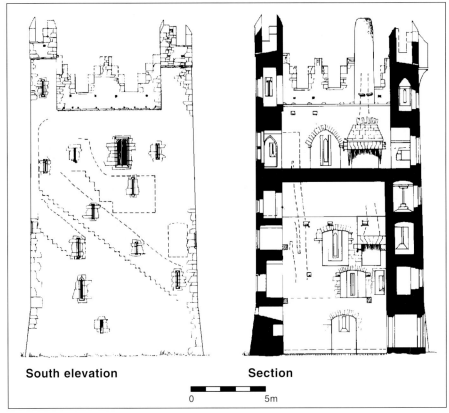

South elevation   **Section**

0   5m

Angle loops, Coole
Castle, Co. Offaly.

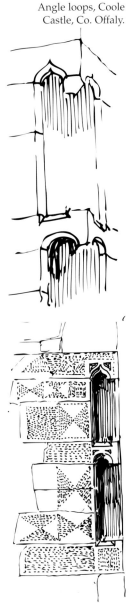

1425), so the bawn must be a later addition. Sheela-na-gigs are known from the tower houses at Galesquarter and Tinnakill. Grantstown is one of the very few circular tower houses in Ireland. It is five storeys high and has an intra-mural staircase and intra-mural passages at second, third and fourth-floor levels with a barrel vault over the third. It has a few gun loops and machicolations at battlement level. Historical references, and features such as gun loops and a vaulted third floor, clearly point to a late date.

Offaly, which lies to the north and west of Co. Laois, and which is of much the same size, has some 43 tower houses.[9] The majority of these, like the Laois examples, can be dated to the later sixteenth and early seventeenth centuries. Many of the tower houses in both counties can be attributed to the Laois/Offaly plantations between 1556 and 1626. Laois/Offaly forms an almost square area in the midlands. The tower houses are fairly evenly distributed except for the central portion in the north-west part of Laois. North-east Offaly, from Tullamore eastwards, has the remains of eight tower houses, most of which can be dated to the fifteenth century and appear to be influenced by the development of those within the Pale, the one exception being Ballydrohid. A striking thing about the Laois/Offaly tower houses is their large size compared to those of the Pale. They also lack projecting angle towers and barrel vaults over the

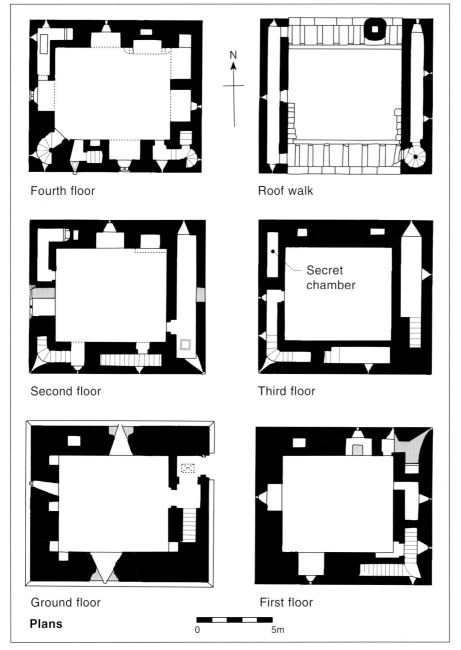

Fourth floor

Roof walk

N

Second floor

Third floor

Secret chamber

Ground floor

First floor

Plans

0   5m

Fig. 127   Plans of the tower house at Burnchurch, Co. Kilkenny.

Two ventilators, Coole Castle, Co. Offaly.

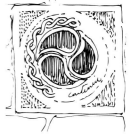

ground floor. The Laois/Offaly examples have large bartizans which are absent from the early Pale examples. The later tower houses are often defended by elaborate machicolations around the wall-walk level of the battlements and many have them directly over the doorway. These later tower houses contain many gun loops of various shapes and sizes.

There are only eight tower houses in Wicklow and most of these are in poor condition. They all appear to have been of the basic simple Pale type

Fig. 128 Plans and
section of the circular
tower house at
Ballynahow, Co.
Tipperary.

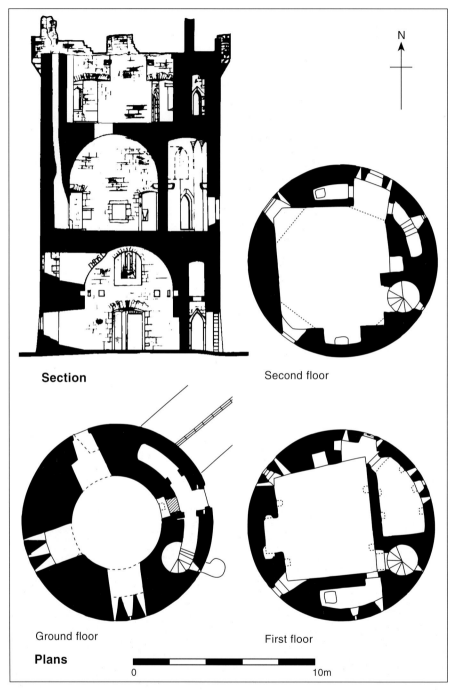

Section

Second floor

Ground floor

First floor

Plans

0   10m

though some of them are quite late in the series. In the neighbouring county of Wexford there are over 60 tower houses and a considerable number of these have substantial standing remains.[10] They vary considerably in ground size but are never more than three or four storeys high and nearly always have a barrel-vaulted ground floor. Few of the Wexford tower houses

154

Fig. 129   Balief, Co. Kilkenny, a circular tower house.

have projecting towers so the stairs and the garderobes are contained within the main block of the building. Those that have projecting towers have only one except at Kilcloggan, where there are two diagonally opposite each other, one with the stairs the other with the garderobes (albeit they only project slightly). Mountgarrett is the only five-storey tower house in Wexford and is one of only two that does not have a barrel vault over the ground floor. A feature of this castle is that it has four garderobes, all in different locations, so that the same chute could not be used for any of them.

Late-medieval pot from Ferns Castle, Co. Wexford.

Fig. 130   Rathmacknee Castle, Co. Wexford.

155

An unusual feature of the Wexford tower houses (also to be found in Cork and Galway) is that several of them, including Butlerstown, Ballyconor Big, Clougheast and Sigginstown, had a portcullis which was operated from a chamber above which also had a murder-hole. Another feature of these

Fig. 132   Bunratty Castle,
Co. Clare, a large tower
house in the west of
Ireland.

castles is an oubliette (secret chamber) as found at Ballyteige, Ballycogly,
Ballyhack, and Clougheast. These tower houses were also protected by gun
loops, whether original or inserted, and yetts to protect the doorways. The
windows are frequently simple rectangular opes or slits but sometimes at
the upper levels ogee-headed examples are found. Virtually all the Wexford
tower houses are well equipped with fireplaces and garderobes, especially
at first-floor level which would have contained the hall.

In Co. Waterford, which is almost as large as Wexford, there are only
about 30 tower houses and most of these are in a very ruinous condition.
Many of these had barrel vaults over one of the upper storeys as well as the
ground floor. The pressure of the upper vault appears to have been the cause
of the collapse. Vaults over the ground floor are evident in most of the
Waterford examples, but they are not an indicator of an early date in this
county, since many of them have musket loops and other late features such
as ogee-headed windows with hood-mouldings. Tower houses in Waterford
that have vaults over upper floor levels such as Ballymaclode are sixteenth-
century in date. Clonea, one of the larger tower houses in the county, is six
storeys high, has no vaults over the ground and first floors, and is enclosed
by a bawn and fosse. Most if not all of the larger tower houses, i.e. those four
storeys high or more, are late in the series and frequently have a vault over
one of the upper floors. Circular tower houses are not common but two
examples, one at Ballyclohy and the other at Mayfield/Rocketscastle, have
barrel vaults over the first-floor level. Fireplaces in these tower houses
appear to be quite late. Many of the Waterford examples have bartizans
while only one, Cappagh, has a projecting tower. The lack of projecting

157

towers and the presence of bartizans appear to be late features. In summary it can be said that the tower houses of Waterford are similar to those of Laois and Offaly but do not compare well to those found within the Pale.

In Co. Cork there are over 125 tower houses, 31 of which have bawns.[11] These towers are, with few exceptions, rectangular in plan, four or five storeys high and have barrel vaults over two floor levels. There are a small number of circular tower houses such as Mahon though they date to near the end of the sixteenth century. The Cork tower houses are nearly all sited close to water with a solid coastal distribution and are often located on promontories some of which are on lakes or inlets. There are no early simple tower houses like those found in the Pale and very few have projecting towers to carry stairs or garderobes, Carrignamuck and Castleinch being some of the exceptions. In some instances however, as at Kilcoe and Dunmanus West, there are subsidiary towers added to the main building to give extra accommodation. These extra towers are often one storey higher than the main block. In the sixteenth-century examples nearly all have gun loops, fireplaces often with date stones and the initials of the original owners, and large windows transomed and mullioned in the main chambers. The tower houses with associated bawns are nearly always late in the series and frequently have bartizans. Most of the towers have two vaults. Where the vault is over the first floor the second vault is over the third but where it is found over the ground floor then the upper vault is over the second level. In some instances, as at Dundeady and Dunlough, the vaulting is corbelled like that found in Termonfeckin, Co. Louth, rather than barrel-vaulted in the normal manner. The principal room and hall are always found directly over the vaulted levels so if, for example, there is a vault over the third floor, the fourth-floor level will have the principal domestic chambers which will contain a large fireplace and possibly smaller fireplaces in the side chambers used for bedrooms. This level is well lit with large windows mullioned and transomed and with seats in the embrasures which are frequently decorated with carved stone. In a few instances carvings such as sheela-na-gigs or human heads are found on the outside of the walls, especially on or near window frames, as at Ballinacarriga and Kilcoe. The windows of the upper floor levels will frequently be ogee-headed with hood-mouldings.

A defensive feature of four of the late sixteenth-century Co. Cork tower houses is a gable-shaped over-sailing found in the side walls of the buildings, as seen at Raheen. The over-sailing is pierced with musket holes so that fire can be directed down to the base of the walls and will also provide flanking fire to cover the angles. Another defensive feature not usually associated with tower houses is the portcullis, or rather the slot for one, which is placed just in front of the door or in the passage behind. It takes the place of the yett which was pulled in front of the door by means of chains that were pulled through the jambs and head of the doorway. Examples of portcullis slots are to be found at Oldcourt, Ballycrenane and Ballinacarriga, as well as examples in Co. Wexford. A small number of tower houses have substantial bawns and these tend to be the later examples. They are defended by projecting mural towers with gun loops for flanking fire. At Ballincollig the bawn walls with mural towers and garderobe chutes assume more importance than the small isolated tower at the centre of the complex. At Mashanaglass the rectangular tower has triangular spurs projecting from its south-west and north-east angles which were used for gun flanking fire. The spurs or projections have a solid ground floor, were only two storeys high and were entered at first-floor level from the main block. Similar-type spurs are to be found on three other Cork tower houses and at Ireton's Castle in Lehinch, Co. Tipperary. Ireton's Castle is, however, a 'Z-plan' fortified house rather than a tower house and was not built until *c*.1650.

Tower houses were built to a great extent by large, wealthy, land-owning families both Gaelic and Old English and they represent places of power and control over most of Munster. Barryscourt Castle near Midleton is typical of the large tower houses found in the southwest of Ireland. It was the chief seat of the Barrys in the cantred of Olethen. Barryscourt, which is built on a slight rise in flat low-lying land, is a rectangular block, four storeys high, with projecting towers at the north-east and south-west angles and a third larger one attached to the south portion of the east wall. It has a barrel vault over the first-floor level which replaced an earlier pointed vault.

Fig. 133 Barryscourt, Co. Cork, a large tower house with bawn walls which are almost completely intact.

Fig. 134 Sections of
Barryscourt tower
house, Co. Cork.

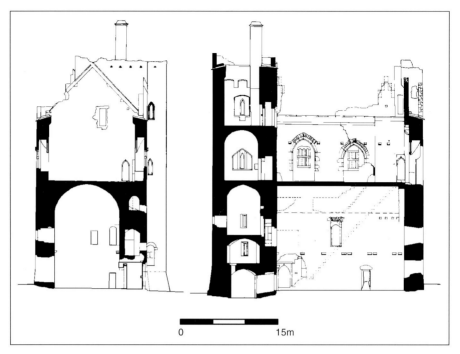

0   15m

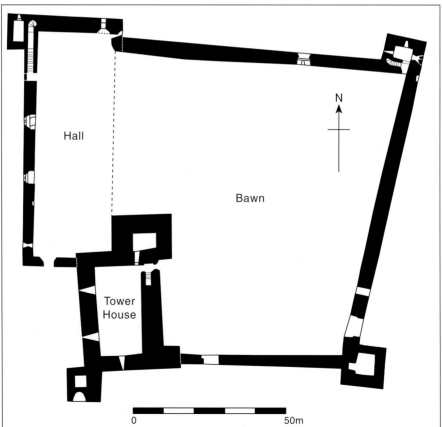

0   50m

Fig. 135 Plan of
Barryscourt Castle.

The second floor, being directly over the barrel vault, is one of the principal rooms; the hall is therefore well lit by two and three-light mullioned and transomed windows which are set in wide embrasures with window seats. In the west wall is a fireplace with carved surround and a date stone of 1588. Unusually for tower houses this one has its own chapel in the north-east tower. A spiral stairs gives access to the upper private chambers which are commodious, being well lit and supplied with fireplaces and garderobes. A substantial amount of the bawn wall remains and the entire structure is being restored. Near the north-east corner of the bawn excavations have revealed part of an early hall possibly dating to the thirteenth century.[12] The site was first occupied by the Barrys in the early thirteenth century but the bawn walls and the tower house are fifteenth-century in origin, with later alterations to the castle.

Blarney, probably Ireland's most famous castle, is only a few kilometres north of Cork City and was the principal residence of the MacCarthys, Lords of Muskerry. It is spectacularly sited on top of a limestone outcrop overlooking the junction of two rivers. The tower house, which also has fragments of its bawn surviving, is built in two distinct phases, a primary tower four storeys high and a slightly later addition of five storeys built against the east wall of the original tower. The addition of another main tower within a short period of time to an existing structure is common in the larger tower houses in the south-western portion of Ireland. It seems that the builders had always planned to add to the original towers and, in the case of Blarney, had left room on the rock to accommodate the addition. The later tower is larger, and when added to the earlier one, gave an unusual L-shaped plan to the structure. The opes for the most part are quite small being either slits or small two and three-light mullioned windows. This, combined with its naturally defensive position and its extensive run of wall-top machicolations, makes it a formidable castle. On the other hand it has some more commodious additions such as the large oriel window in the lower part of the west end of the north wall. Other large windows were inserted elsewhere in the castle in the sixteenth century, as were several opes for guns. The third floor level, which has one of the principal chambers, had two large fireplaces. The two towers work independently of each other and have their own stairways but there is a link by mural passage from the third floor of the earlier tower to the fourth floor of the later one.

The later tower has a spiral stairs giving access to all its main chambers which have mullioned windows, some of which seem to be part of the original structure especially at fourth-floor level. This is in contrast to the earlier tower where they are virtually all single-light windows except for those that were inserted at a later date. Many of the windows on the first, second and third floors have had their embrasures widened and enlarged to take the mullioned windows. At second-floor level almost the entire north

Fig. 136 Blarney Castle, Co. Cork. This magnificent tower house vies with Bunratty for the honour of being Ireland's best known castle.

wall was taken up with a large fireplace. A further fireplace was inserted at third-floor level, while between third and fourth-floor level there are two garderobe chambers. Immediately to the east of the castle there are the remains of a fortified tower built against the rock-face which has been much destroyed by the building of a house. It has double-splayed gun loops and is part of the outer defences of the castle, as are the remains of a smaller tower, now buried in the ruins of the house. Small portions of the curtain wall survive, especially on top of the rock outcrop (total length 64.2m) to the west of the larger tower. The early tower was built *c.*1480 with the second one added early in the sixteenth century with later, possibly early seventeenth-century alterations. The fireplaces and the towers of the bawn are features of these late alterations.

There are well over 200 tower houses in Co. Galway.[13] Because there are so few Anglo-Norman fortresses in evidence it should be assumed that

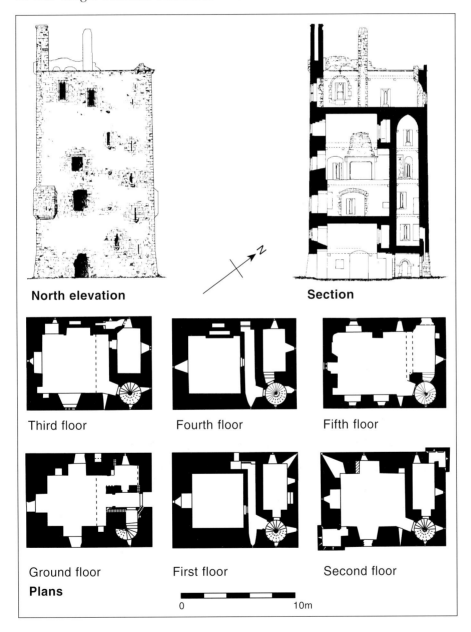

North elevation

Section

Third floor

Fourth floor

Fifth floor

Ground floor
Plans

First floor

Second floor

0   10m

Fig. 137   Plans, section and elevation of the tower house at Fiddaun, Co. Galway.

163

Fig. 138 Overall plan of
the tower house and
bawn of Fiddaun Castle,
Co. Galway.

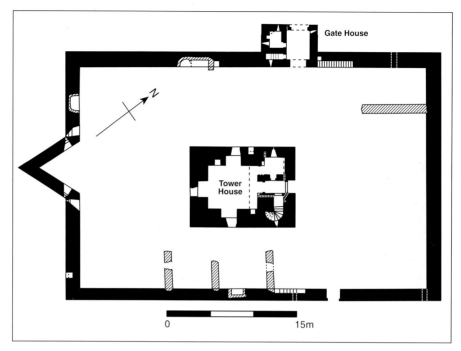

Fig. 138 Overall plan of the tower house and bawn of Fiddaun Castle, Co. Galway.

those sites marked on the Ordnance Survey maps, but which have no standing remains, were for the most part tower houses; a small number may have been earlier hall-houses. The Galway tower houses follow the same pattern as those found in Co. Cork and have much in common with those in the south-western portion of the country such as Limerick and Tipperary. Those found in the western side of the county are frequently situated close to the sea and rivers and are often founded on rock. The larger tower houses are five and six storeys tall, are late in the series and are more commodious, having fireplaces, large windows on the upper floors, mural passages and numerous garderobes. The windows at the upper levels are normally double-lighted, with ogee heads and hood-mouldings, and are sometimes decorated with carvings, especially human heads.

As with the Cork tower houses, if there is a vault over the ground floor the second vault will be over the second floor, and, if over the first floor then the second vault is found over the third or fourth floors. The floor directly over the first vault is used as the hall and at the higher level as the main private chambers. Stairs frequently are intra-mural to the first-floor level and then spiral the rest of the way up. At Derrydonnel More the tower house is six storeys high, is founded on bedrock and was built at the end of the sixteenth century or start of the seventeenth century. The vault here is over the ground floor and it has a series of small chambers from first to fourth floor, but on the fifth, the chamber occupies the whole level. Many of these late tower houses have defensive features such as pistol and gun loops, machicolations, bartizans, portcullises and bawn walls.

164

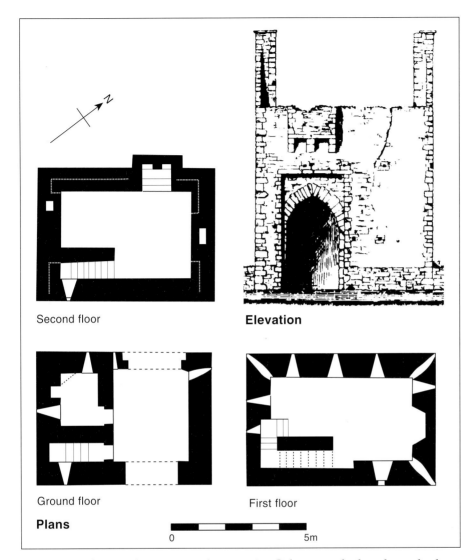

Fig. 139 Plans and elevation of the gatehouse of Fiddaun Castle, Co. Galway.

Second floor

Elevation

Ground floor

First floor

Plans

0   5m

Some of these later tower houses, in Galway and elsewhere, had no garderobes because the use of chamber pots had become fashionable. In a late tower house at Loughlohery in South Tipperary there is a chute in one of the angles at floor level in the wall below an ope and gun loops. This chute goes straight down to ground level to exit outside the building as if it were for a garderobe. However, since there is no seating arrangement for a latrine and since access to the loops would not be possible if it were a garderobe, it was merely designed as a chute to take away waste matter from the hall at second floor level. This system of waste disposal is therefore a link between the garderobe, which was the norm for the tower house, and the sole use of the chamber pot in the seventeenth-century fortified houses.

In Galway a number of tower houses were constructed in two phases, for instance Deerpark which is a four-storey building. The early phase

Fig. 140 Plan and
elevation of Aughnanure,
Co. Galway.

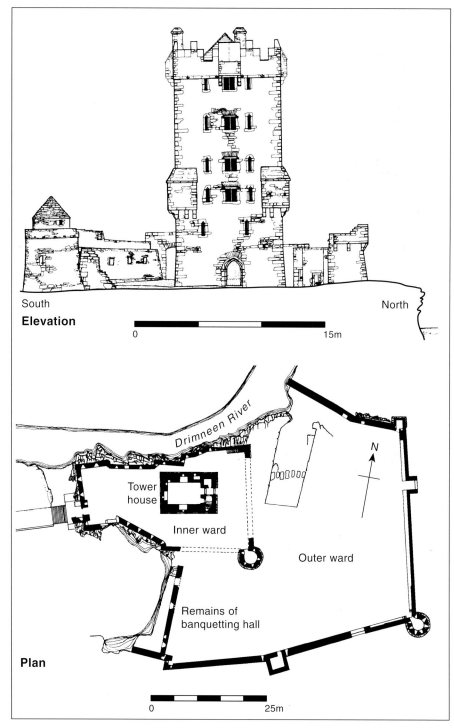

South   North
Elevation

0   15m

Drimneen River

N

Tower
house

Inner ward

Outer ward

Remains of
banquetting hall

Plan

0   25m

contains the stairs and small chambers while the later one has the main
chambers. Some of the earlier tower houses have fireplaces inserted at a
later stage and they sometimes carry the initials of the owners. At Fiddaun

Plate 23   Pallas Castle
and bawn, Co. Galway.
Note the gatehouse at the
opposite end of the bawn
to the tower house.

Plate 24   Rockstown, Co.
Limerick, is located in an
almost impregnable
position on a rock
outcrop.

Plate 25 Nineteenth-century print of Ross Island Castle, Co. Kerry. Situated beside the Lakes of Killarney, Ross Castle was built in the early fifteenth century by one of the O'Donoghue Ross chieftains. It consists of a four-storey tower house surrounded by the remains of a bawn with circular flanking towers.

Plate 26 Carbury Castle, Co. Kildare, is a multi-period fortress sited on high ground. Although it was first mentioned in 1234 the bulk of the remains are an Elizabethan fortified house.

Fig. 141 Derryhivenny,
Co. Galway. Note the
remains of the bawn wall
and angle towers.

there is a well-preserved and partially restored tower house which is remarkable for the fact that it has an inner and outer bawn and the remains of a three-storey gatehouse. The castle is sited on rock outcrop in low-lying ground between Lough Doo and Lough Aslaun. A water-filled channel runs between the two lakes which protects the whole complex. This was spanned by a drawbridge protected by a gatehouse. Both bawn walls have gun loops in them. The tower house is placed almost in the centre of the inner bawn and is seven storeys high. All the floor levels from ground to fifth have a main chamber and a subsidiary one but at the sixth-floor level there is just one large room. There are intra-mural passages with garderobes at one end and fireplaces on the third, fourth and fifth floors, all of which have been inserted. There are bartizans on the south-east and north-west angles at third-floor level.

Aughnanure in west Galway is another substantial tower house with some unusual features. It was the stronghold of the O'Flahertys and is sited near the shores of Lough Corrib on the south bank of the Drimneen river. It is protected by two bawns, the outer one consisting of the remains of a large irregular enclosure of stone with five mural towers. The remains of a great hall can be seen in the south-west angle of this bawn. The earlier inner bawn is wedge-shaped with walls pierced with gun loops, a flanking tower at the south-east and the remains of the gate-building with a drawbridge. The rectangular tower house, which is sited almost centrally in the inner bawn, is six storeys high with a gabled attic. It is defended by bartizans at the south-east and north-east angles.

As in other areas of the country some of the Galway tower houses, such as Ballinderry, have sheela-na-gigs. Similarly, most of the tower houses in

Fig. 142   Plans, elevation and section of Ballymalis tower house, Co. Kerry.

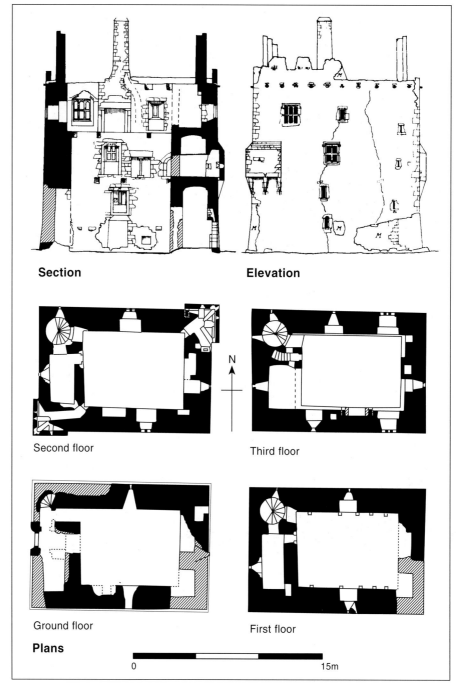

Section   **Elevation**

N

Second floor   Third floor

Ground floor   First floor

Plans

0   15m

Carved window mouldings from Ballymalis tower house, Co. Kerry.

Galway and the western half of the country, are of sixteenth-century date. Some tower houses, especially those with two building phases, could be as late as the early seventeenth century. The late examples invariably have fine transomed and mullioned windows and large fireplaces, often with the owners initials on them.

170

Fig. 143 Ballymalis
tower house, Co. Kerry.
Note the bartizan at first
floor level on the angle at
right and two corbels for
carrying a machicolation
at battlement level over
the doorway.

Carved corbel in the
south-west corner of
Ballymalis
tower house.

The tower house at Ardamullivan, which is a late sixteenth-century structure, is six storeys tall and was built in two phases. There are mural paintings at first- and fourth-floor level, the remains of which are now being conserved. The windows of the first building phase here are all single-light with flat heads, whereas the later building has mainly double-lighted ones with ogee heads. At Castle Ellen, which is also a late sixteenth-century tower house, the outer defences consist of an earthen enclosure with a gateway. At Cahernamuck West the castle is built inside the corner of what appears to be a moated site.

In the northern part of Ireland, most of the tower houses are similar to those found within the Pale and are, therefore, of the less complex type than those in the western half of the country. Many of these tower houses,

Fig. 144 Narrowwater
Castle, Co. Down

especially in Co. Down, have projecting towers breaking forward from the same wall and sometimes, as at Ardglass, have the entrance to the castle set between the two towers. This tower-house plan is not confined to the north of the country and one example can be seen in Ardee town, Co. Louth. The projecting towers, as at those tower houses with projecting towers built on diagonally opposing angles, carry the stairs and the garderobes (see p. 151, note 7). Audley's Castle in Co. Down has a substantial bawn with the remains of a hall-like building in its south-east angle and a tower with gateway in the north-east. A feature of these tower houses is that they have an arch at high level between the two projecting towers which carries a chamber sited over the entrance. Again this is not a feature solely confined to the northern part of the country; examples can be seen at Ballyadams, Co. Laois, and Haynestown, Co. Louth. Many of these northern tower houses have a single vault over the ground floor, some with space for a loft, just like the small early examples within the Pale. Some of the Ulster tower houses, such as Castleward, Co. Down, have no projecting towers, no garderobes, and the stairs is intra-mural. Castleward is a late castle, not unlike The Mint at Carlingford. It has pistol loops indicating that it was built at the end of the sixteenth century. Kirkistown Castle, Co. Down, which was built in 1622, also lacks projecting towers and this appears to be a feature of the later tower houses regardless of their size. At Kirkistown there are remains of a very large bawn with flanking towers at the north-west and south-west angles. Narrow Water, Co. Down and Fiddaun, Co. Galway, also have

Fig. 145 Doe Castle, Co. Donegal, a sixteenth-century tower house with seventeenth-century additions.

simple late towers within a substantial bawn. From recent discoveries at Barryscourt, Co. Cork, we must assume that there were a considerable number of extra buildings within the enclosing walls.[14] At Nendrum, Co. Down, the tower house is rectangular in plan and the ground floor is divided into two separate chambers both with their own entrance but with no communication between the two. One of the chambers contains the stairs

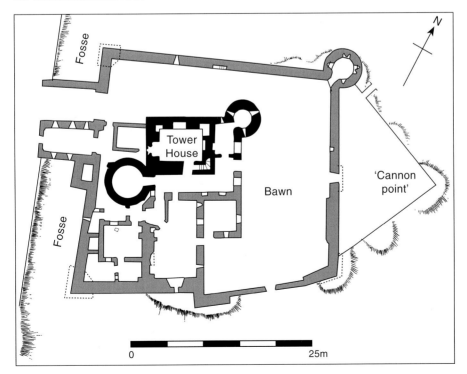

Fig. 146 Plan of Doe Castle.

which gives access to the rest of the building. This same layout can be seen in the tower house at Haynestown, Co. Louth.

Tower houses of the eastern half of the country, whether north or south, whether late or early, tend to be small and simple. Those in the midlands and in the western half of the country tend to be larger and more sophisticated. The earliest examples of this type of castle are found in the eastern half of the country.[15] Tower houses owe many of their features to the later hall-houses (which have their origins in the west) such as Kindlestown, Co. Wicklow, and Dunmoe, Co. Meath. I argue that the origin of the tower house lies in the later hall-houses of the east. On present evidence, there is no reason to assume that tower houses were built before the beginning of the fifteenth century.

CHAPTER SIX

FORTIFIED HOUSES AND STRONGHOUSES

Towards the end of the sixteenth century and in the early seventeenth century two new types of castles evolved, the fortified house and the stronghouse. This period also marked the end of the building of tower houses which had lasted over 200 years. Many of the tower houses built in the early seventeenth century reflect this change as they became less defensive and provided more commodious accommodation while their outer defences became stronger. The fortified houses were usually symmetrical, contained large mullioned and transomed windows, had high gables and massive lozenge or diamond-shaped chimney stacks. Probably the earliest of these was Rathfarnham Castle, Co. Dublin. But perhaps the most perfect and also the latest of the fortified houses is Burncourt, Co. Tipperary. Burncourt has 26 gables, numerous tall chimney stacks, large mullioned and transomed windows with hood-mouldings and clear evidence of stone corbels designed to carry a wooden gallery around the outside of the walls. Inside these houses there was a greater number of private rooms than the earlier castles. The large space within the walls was divided by wooden partitions and there were numerous large fireplaces to warm the accommodation.

Fortified houses were usually no more than three storeys high with an attic and were usually laid out in a rectangular plan but there are alternatives such as the U-plan at Oakley Park, Co. Offaly, and the L-plan as exemplified by Kilcolgan More, also in Co. Offaly. In some instances the stairs are accommodated in an adjoining tower and not in the main block as at Ballycowan, Co. Offaly. Often the fortified houses retained defensive features from the tower house era such as bartizans on the angles and machicolations over the doorway. The builders of these structures were concerned with providing a house of formal and symmetrical plan on Renaissance lines which answered a desire for more luxurious living standards but sacrificed nothing of the defensive nature of the building. They were designed to give flanking fire from the angle towers and the bartizans to protect the doorways and walls. But the main defensive focus moved away from the internal buildings and onto the bawn walls which were provided with a gate house, mural towers and numerous gun loops.

The stronghouses are far less impressive than the fortified houses and are usually only two storeys high with the ground floor defended by slit opes. The first floor is slightly more commodious, having a fireplace and larger plain windows. The chimney stacks are not impressive and are set on either gable. Few of the stronghouses retain their bawn walls but presumably they all had some type of outer defensive works. They also lack other defensive features such as bartizans and machicolations, crenellations and mural stairs and passages. They are in fact, as their name describes them, 'stronghouses'. They mark the end of castle building in Ireland.

THE FORTIFIED HOUSE

There is a continuity of occupation from tower houses to fortified houses which can be plainly seen in the examples found in Co. Meath, where eight of the ten examples are attached to tower houses and have clear evidence of both structures being occupied at the same time, although the fortified houses could have been built up to 100 years later. This pattern of continuous occupation in the sixteenth and seventeenth centuries is seen in most areas of the country but especially from east to west across the midlands. There are a considerable number of two-phase, late sixteenth and early seventeenth-century tower houses, such as Ardamullivan, Co. Galway. There are at least nine other examples in Co. Galway. Some of the fortified houses, especially Killaleigh, Sopwell, Co. Tipperary, show a remarkable resemblance to tower houses except for their gables and high chimney

Fig. 147 Leap, Co. Offaly. A tower house with later houses attached to each side, one of which contains a seventeenth-century fireplace.

Fig. 148 Fortified house at Paal East, Kanturk, Co. Cork. Note the first-floor entrance and the large transomed and mullioned windows of the central block.

stacks. Killaleigh has, for instance, a striking resemblance to the fortified house at Ballycowan, Co. Offaly, which is attached to a tower house. At Tinnahinch, Co. Carlow, there is an early seventeenth-century tower house-like-building that could almost be taken for a fortified house were it not for its lack of high chimney stacks and small opes at ground-floor level. It had wooden floors throughout and a wooden staircase within a projecting tower on its south-west angle. It is, therefore, highly likely that the fortified house developed directly from the later tower houses. Some tower houses such as Leap and Emmel West, both in Co. Offaly, have unfortified seventeenth-century houses attached. Many of the fortified houses stand alone and most of these, especially in Munster, can be associated with the Elizabethan Planters rather than the Old English who would have been responsible for the continuity of occupation from the tower phase of the later medieval period. However, some of the fortified houses were also built by Irish landowners. The large and impressive castle at Coppinger's Court, Ballyvireen, Co. Cork, was built by Sir Walter Coppinger, a businessman from Cork City.[1]

The basic plan of the fortified house is rectangular and is normally three storeys high. The ground plan varied to an extent. At Kanturk (Paal East), Mountlong and Monkstown, Co. Cork, and Burncourt, Co. Tipperary, there are square towers at each angle reminiscent of some of the late tower houses, such as Bunratty, Co. Clare.[2] This type of fortified house appears to be confined to Cork and Tipperary although there is a possible example on Lambay Island, Co. Dublin. The fine fortified house of Coppinger's Court is a three-storey, rectangular block with large towers at its north-east and north-west angles and at the centre of the south wall. The south tower appears to have contained wooden stairs. The windows were transomed and mullioned with hood-mouldings; most of the hood-mouldings have long since disappeared. The house was well provided with fireplaces which fed into seven chimney stacks set onto the various gables. There are five separate runs of machicolations which cover considerable lengths of the wall-tops. There are at least nine loops at ground-floor level and there are traces of a bawn wall at the north side with evidence of outer buildings attached, including one with a bread oven.

There are the standing remains of 22 fortified houses in Co. Cork and these are fairly evenly distributed within the county except for a gap in central Cork. In the south-east part of the county there are ten examples including Monkstown and Mountlong, which have the same ground plan as Kanturk with four angle towers.[3] Ballyannan, which is built close to the inlet of the Owenacurra estuary, is a two-storey house with attic and a rectangular projection at the centre of the west wall and circular towers at its north-east and south-west angles. It has large rectangular chimney stacks on its south gable (also originally on its north gable) and on both round towers. This house was built by a Cromwellian settler, Sir John Broderick, c.1650, on the site of an earlier castle. Ightermurragh, also in Co. Cork, has a cruciform plan with central projecting blocks to the north and the south.[4] It is unusually tall, having four storeys and an attic. It has a large kitchen area with a fireplace and two ovens. It is defended at ground-floor level by thirteen gun loops. As with virtually all of these buildings the internal divisions were of wood but, in this instance, most of the positions of the partitions can be determined by plaster shadows on the wall faces. The north projecting tower contained the wooden stairs which led to all floor levels and the wall-walk. Further defence was provided by gun loops at first-floor level and a machicolation over the first-floor doorway in the south tower. The entranceway was at the opposite side of the house to the private stairs which gave access to the rest of the building. The house contained twelve fireplaces and seven chimney stacks. The surrounds of the fireplaces are finely carved and the one at first-floor level bears an inscription and date of 1642.

Monkstown and Kanturk have the same basic plan, but Monkstown is much more defensive with very large angle towers and a very small central area. Kanturk has a large central block with small angle towers. Monkstown is sited on high ground overlooking the south entrance into West Passage in Cork Harbour. The central block is three storeys high whereas the large angle towers have four plus an attic in the pitch of the roof. There are substantial bartizans on the other angles at wall-walk level. Each tower has a square chimney stack on the inward-facing gables. It has numerous gun-loops, now mostly blocked-up, at various levels. Most of the windows are

Fig. 149 Monkstown,
Co. Cork. Fortified house
with a very small central
block and contrastingly
large angle towers. Note
the bartizans on these
towers.

Fig. 150 Mountlong,
Co. Cork, similar to
Monkstown but with no
bartizans; note the square
two-light windows.

small rectangular double-lighted opes which is in sharp contrast to the large triple-lighted mullioned and transomed ones of Kanturk. The main entrance is via a large door, at ground-floor level in the north wall of the main block. Another unusual feature of this fortified house is that it has a stone stairs in the south-west angle tower. Much of the interior is quite ruined but several fine fireplaces can be seen especially the one at first-floor level which has an elaborate carving and a date of 1636. Mountlong, which is very similar to Monkstown, is sited on the foreshore of Oyster Haven Creek and is also three storeys high with attics under the gables. The main difference between

179

this house and Monkstown is that it lacks bartizans. It has small double-lighted mullioned windows at all but the ground floor where they are single-lighted. Each wall-face is topped by a gable but only some of the inward facing ones as at Monkstown have rectangular chimney stacks on them. The four corner towers have a single chamber at each floor level and are entered from the small central block which appears to act mainly as a service area. The towers are protected by numerous gun loops, especially at ground-floor level, and in some instances are located under the window opes. A feature of the fortified houses of east and south Cork is that they have a very pronounced string course over each floor level. Glinsk, Co. Galway, is also similar in plan but lacks the string courses and has its chimney stacks clustered on the east and west gables.

Mallow Castle (Castlelands), Co. Cork, is sited near the edge of a plateau overlooking the River Blackwater.[5] Its plan, although basically rectangular, is unusual in that it has two, four-storey polygonal angle towers, one at the north-west and one at the south-west.[6] It also has a tower projecting from the centre of the faces of both the east and west walls. The main block is only three storeys high with an attic and a basement under the northern portion. All the floor levels are well provided with windows varying from one to four lights with the larger ones having transoms and mullions. There are numerous gun loops with sandstone surrounds set into the window embrasures at first-floor level. The house has two entrances at ground-floor level leading into the main block, one via a lobby area, the other directly into the ground floor. The house is reputed to have been built by Sir Thomas Norris who died in 1599. If this attribution is correct then it is an early fortified house which may account for its projecting towers.

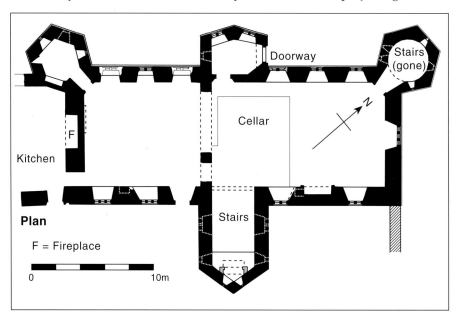

Fig. 151 Plan of Mallow Castle, Co. Cork.

Fig. 152   Elevation and
sketch of Mallow Castle,
Co. Cork.

Kilmaclenine, also in Co. Cork, is two storeys high and is cruciform in plan. The windows have transoms and mullions at both levels and are not defensive but the entrance has holes for a yett and there are gun loops at the north end of the east and west walls providing for flanking fire. It was apparently built by the Barrys *c.*1641.

In Co. Laois there were eleven fortified houses, all but two of which are still standing.[7] One of these, Ballyadams, is attached to a tower house. None of the Co. Limerick fortified houses are attached to tower houses while there

Fig. 153 Ballyadams,
Co. Laois. Plan showing
the T-shaped
seventeenth-century
house atached to the
remains of a
tower house.

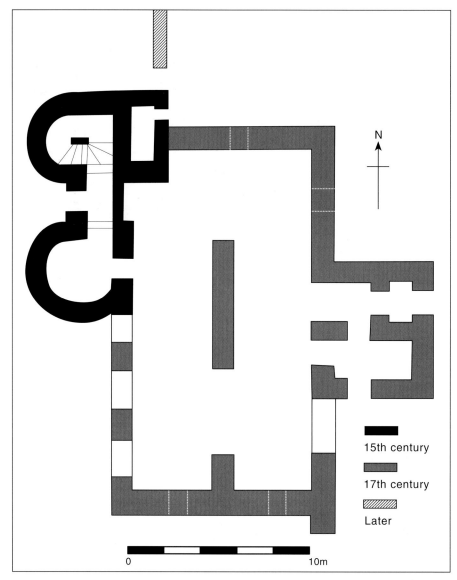

15th century

17th century

Later

N

0   10m

are two examples from Co. Cork and at least one from Co. Clare
(Leamaneh). This trait seems to be an eastern phenomenon, albeit fortified
houses attached to tower houses are absent from Louth, Cavan and Carlow.
At Ballyadams both structures appear to have been used at the same time
because the only access to the various floors of the house is from the north-
west tower of the tower house. At Castlecuffe, also in Co. Laois, the
building, which is a much ruined, three-storey structure, stood isolated
within a large bawn. At Rush Hall, Co. Laois, the fortified house is L-shaped
and is four storeys high and, like Castlecuffe, has large chimney stacks on
the gable ends of a large rectangular block. Rush Hall has a very impressive
bawn, *c*.65m square with walls 3.7m high. It has pentagonal flanking towers

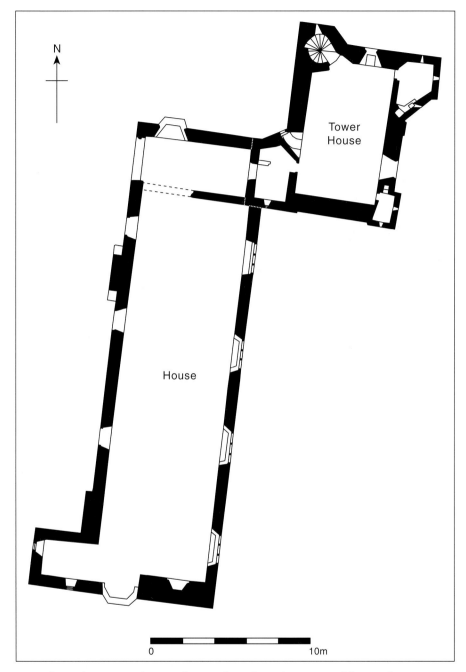

Fig. 154   Plan of Athlumney, Co. Meath, a fortified house attached to a tower house.

at each angle except the northwest, but there is some evidence that a tower once stood in the northwest. The towers are defended by gun loops. These houses are quite different in plan to the fortified houses found at Monkstown, Kanturk and Mountlong. The Co. Laois examples have much more in common with those found in Co. Meath, such as Athlumney and Summerhill Demesne.

Fig. 155 Athlumney fortified house and tower house stand above the Boyne River near Navan, Co. Meath.

Fig. 156 Leamaneh Castle, Co. Clare, a fortified house attached to an earlier tower house which was used as a service tower for the house.

Plate 27   Burncourt, Co. Tipperary.

Plate 28   Fortified house at Ightermurragh, Co. Cork.

Plate 29   Mallow Castle, Co. Cork, showing two of the polygonal angle towers and projecting central tower at the right.

Plate 30   Donegal Castle, an early seventeenth-century gable-fronted fortified house attached to a much-modified tower house.

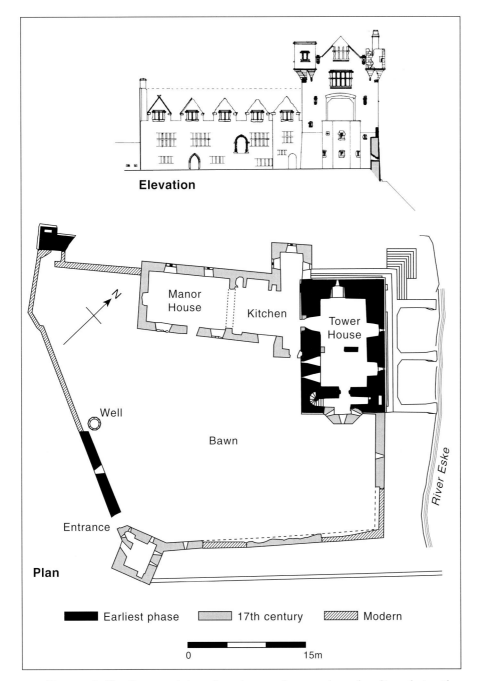

Fig. 157 Plan and
elevation of Donegal
Castle.

Elevation

Manor
House

Kitchen

Tower
House

Well

Bawn

River Eske

Entrance

Plan

| Earliest phase | 17th century | Modern |

0   15m

Donegal Castle consists of a tower house (much altered in the seventeenth century) with an early seventeenth-century gable-fronted fortified house attached at its south-east.[8] The tower house was altered by the insertion of mullioned and transomed windows to match the new house. The fortified house is a slightly skewed T-plan of three storeys. It has two ground-floor entrances and three mullioned windows at the front

Fig. 158 Intricately
carved stonework from
Donegal Castle. The first-
floor doorway in the
fortified house (left), and
fireplace within the
much-altered
tower house.

which makes it vulnerable to attack as does the lack of bartizans and flanking towers. It is heavily dependent on its bawn wall with its defended gateway for its defences.

At Raphoe in the same county, Bishop John Leslie built a palace in 1636-7 which is, in effect, a four-storey fortified house, just off square in plan with flanking towers at each of its angles.[9] The flanking towers are square internally but their outermost angle projects markedly to give an almost lozenge or pear-shaped plan. Each tower has either five or six opes to provide covering fire. Not only is the palace well defended by its angle towers but it is also well sited on high ground and protected by steep slopes on all but the east side. The arms of the Leslie family, surmounted by a bishop's mitre, can be seen on the lintel of what was the original doorway, now rebuilt in the basement. There are also a number of gun loops in the basement at the entrances to the towers where they join the main block. There are three coats-of-arms built into various parts of the eastern portion of the palace.

There are ten fortified houses in Co. Offaly, seven of which have good evidence for bawns. Ballycowan is, probably, the finest fortified house in Co. Offaly.[10] It comprises a long rectangular block, four storeys high dating to *c.*1589 and a five-storey tower added in 1626 by Sir Jasper Herbert and his wife Jane Finglas. Herbert had been granted the land in 1623 and it was subsequently created into a manor subject to the conditions of the plantation. The very tall massive chimney stacks and large transomed and mullioned windows were part of the later building. Sir Jasper's coat of arms with a date of 1626 can be seen over the door to the later tower. The ground floor is divided into four barrel-vaulted chambers some with excellent remains of wicker centring. The upper floors had large fireplaces and were

Fig. 159 Ballycowan Castle, Co. Offaly, a fortified house featuring tall chimney stacks with projecting masonry below to accommodate the fireplace. Note the high gables and the bartizans.

lit by large transomed and mullioned windows. They are reached by intra-mural stairs, an unusual feature in a fortified house. Its defensive features include gun loops, a bartizan on the north-east angle and evidence for a yett at the doorway to the later tower which also has a machicolation over it. The later building acted as a service tower and contained a large winding stairs giving access to the upper floors.

Kilcolgan Castle, Co. Offaly, had an L-shaped plan and was built *c.*1620 but, unfortunately, it was largely destroyed in 1954 to provide filling for the foundations of a power station. It appears to have been two storeys high with a crenellated wall-walk, large chimney stacks and rectangular mullioned and transomed windows. This house had an almost square bawn with a tower at each angle, two of which still stand. The interiors of the towers are circular but have one exterior angle facing directly out from the bawn, not unlike the angle towers of artillery forts of this period. They were three storeys high with a doorway at each level, which was reached from external stairs. There are gun loops in the bawn wall at mid-height, indicating that a wooden gallery was necessary to access them. Ballymooney Castle, Oakley Park, was built *c.*1622 and is a much-ruined U-shaped fortified house with the remains of what was a substantial bawn. The house consisted of a central block with large, tall, gable-fronted towers at the east and west ends which project well forward from the line of the main block. This is an unusual plan but is markedly similar to a sketch plan of Birr Castle in *c.*1668.[11] The entrance was protected by a yett and a

189

machicolation overhead at wall-walk level. The house was enclosed by a bawn but only the east wall and two angle towers survive. The towers are two storeys high with gun loops at each level and a wall-walk at roof height.

Impressive fortified houses are found in Co. Tipperary at Loughmoe, Burncourt, Lehinch (Ireton's Castle), Killaleigh (Sopwell) and Rathnaveoge Lower.[12] Loughmoe Castle, Tinvoher, lies close to the railway line and can be seen by people travelling by train between Dublin and Cork near Templemore. It is an imposing structure consisting of a tower house with a large fortified house added. The tower house is a large rectangular block at the south side while the house is a long rectangular block with a large tower at its north-west angle and a smaller one projecting east from the south end of the east wall. The tower house was re-modelled by widening some of the upper windows and inserting large fireplaces. The house portion looks like Kanturk, Co. Cork, with its string courses marking the different floor levels but the tower house component is like the Meath examples. The main block of the house is three storeys high with attics and a first-floor entrance but the tower house and the large tower have five floor levels. It has the usual large mullioned and transomed windows and numerous fireplaces. On both the angle tower and the main block, at the uppermost level, there is a considerable height of blank unpierced walling which must have contained attics lit by skylights in a series of gabled roofs with valleys in between them. The first-floor level contains the principal reception rooms and has a very large fireplace in the north wall. At ground-floor level there is a basement which is built partially underground.

Burncourt, Co. Tipperary, is like Kanturk in its basic plan, but it is one storey higher and does not have string courses marking the different floor

Fig. 160 Ireton's Castle, Lehinch, Co. Tipperary. Note the pointed bastion of the angle tower (left) to mount a cannon at first-floor level (David Sweetman).

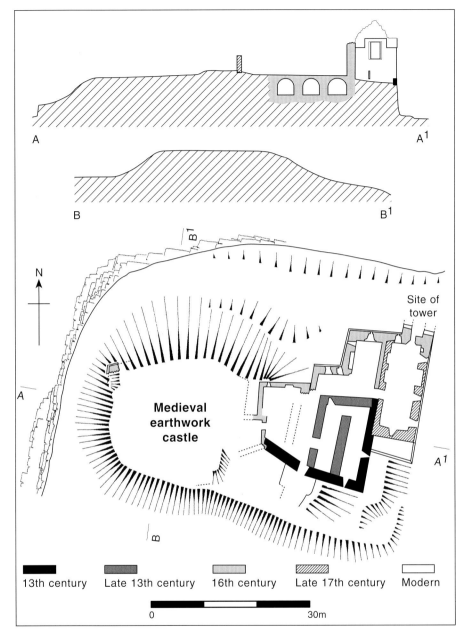

Site of tower

Medieval earthwork castle

13th century | Late 13th century | 16th century | Late 17th century | Modern

0   30m

levels. It was built in 1641 and is one of the most impressive fortified houses in Ireland with its 26 gables and numerous chimney stacks. Both entrances were at first-floor level over half basements and were protected by gun loops. On the main block at a level just below the windows in the gables there are corbels designed to carry a wooden gallery, a possible survival of the medieval idea of wooden hoarding. Another notable feature of this house is that it has plasterwork around the windows marked in such a way as to give the impression that they are bricks. The same method was used to

191

Fig. 162 Fortified house attached to a large rectangular-shaped tower house at Deel, Co. Mayo (David Sweetman).

give the impression of very regular quoins on all the angles of the building. This faking of bricks and quoins is uncommon in Ireland but can be seen in Britain and has also been noted at Roscommon Castle (the late medieval building) and at Portumna in Co. Galway. Burncourt, which was apparently called Clogheen, was burnt to the ground by Richard Everard in 1650 to prevent Cromwell from seizing it.

Ireton's Castle (Lehinch), Co. Tipperary, is situated on a low natural rise on the floodplains of the River Shannon and is described in the *Civil Survey* (1654-6) as 'the castle of Derry McEgan being lately built by Sir Charles Coote'.[13] It is a three-storey Z-plan house of limestone rubble and consists of a central rectangular block with almost pear-shaped angle towers at the north-east and south-west. These towers are similar to ones at Raphoe, Co. Donegal, Carrignacurra, Mashanaglass and Castle Hyde East, in Co. Cork, and Kilcolgan More, Co. Offaly. These bastion-like towers were built towards the end of the sixteenth century and were used for mounting cannon on them at first-floor level. The ground floor is solid and the only access is to the first-floor level which is also the full height of the bastion or projecting tower. The building was erected shortly before 1649 as evidenced by a date stone over the now destroyed entrance.

At Portumna, Co. Galway, conservation and restoration work as well as archaeological excavations have been carried out over a long number of years. Portumna consists of a large rectangular central block with three storeys over a basement and square projecting towers on its angles. It is similar to Kanturk, Co. Cork, but is more in the tradition of a grand house like Burncourt, Co. Tipperary. However, Portumna is not gabled like Burncourt and does not carry impressive rows of large corbels for parapets

192

Fig. 163 Portumna, Co. Galway, more a grand house but still deceptively fortified.

as at Kanturk. It has a grand entrance up a wide flight of stone steps which leads into a large area over the basement and gives access to where there was a large wooden stairs. It gives the impression of not being fortified but there is a machicolation at parapet level over the doorway which itself is defended by gun loops in the towers which provide flanking fire. The doorway itself has holes for a yett. The inner and outer bawns take the form of formal gardens rather than defensive features and provide an impressive approach to the house. It was built by the fourth Earl of Clanricarde *c*.1618, and clearly shows a move away from the emphasis on defence towards the grandisement of a residence.

THE STRONGHOUSE

Few stronghouses have been identified in Ireland but that is not to say that there are not many more to be found. Recent survey work in Laois, Offaly, Tipperary and Wexford has revealed a number of them but they are strangely absent in counties Carlow, Cavan, Cork, Kerry, Limerick and Wicklow.[14] Until an adequate survey is done of this type of castle it is not possible even to give a rough idea of how many of them exist. Their distribution appears to be mainly in the midlands but they are also to be found to a lesser extent in the north of the country and in a different form in the south-east. The basic stronghouse was only two storeys high with a ground-floor entrance. The ground floor is defensive having only slit opes while the second floor was more commodious. The plan of these structures is normally a simple rectangle. They are invariably defended by a good

Fig. 164 Stronghouse and remains of bawn wall at Newtown, Co. Offaly.

strong bawn. Stronghouses are roughly contemporary with fortified houses but are dated mainly to the first quarter of the seventeenth century.

A number of similar structures were identified in Co. Waterford, but they lack the rectangular service tower.[15] However, they frequently have a projecting tower, which is unusually at one of the angles, containing the stairs. At Sleady there is a three-storey garderobe tower attached to the west

Fig. 165 Leitra, Co. Offaly, a much ruined stronghouse.

Fig. 166 Dundonnell, Co. Roscommon, a stronghouse built inside a ringwork castle (David Sweetman).

gable. At Ballynakill, a seventeenth-century, two-storey house of five bays incorporates a tower house while at Ballyduff Lower a house which was built in 1627 has high chimneys on both its gables. At Norrisland, a house of 1641, which is basically a rectangular block, has projecting towers at its north-east, south-east and south-west angles. At Tikincor Lower the stronghouse is three storeys high with an attic and has a stair tower

Fig. 167 Graffan, Co. Offaly, a T-shaped house with the stem of the 'T' (at rear) containing the stairwell.

195

Fig. 168 Plan of a stronghouse within its bawn at Ardtermon, Co. Sligo.

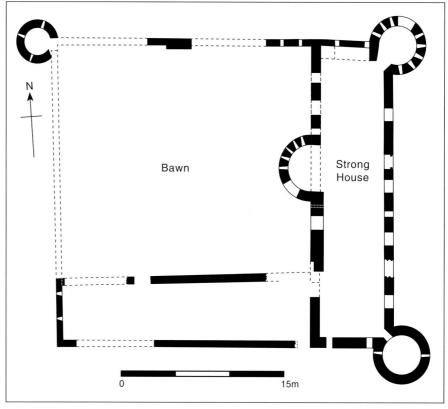

projecting from the centre of the east wall. It has small defensive windows at ground-floor level and a musket loop in the staircase return.

None of the houses in Waterford show the same strength of fortification as the few located in Co. Offaly and, in particular, Leitra and Newtown.[16] Leitra is a small, square, two-storey house built of roughly coursed rubble defended by the remains of a bawn wall. Its ground floor is defended by gun loops and has evidence of a wooden stairs to the first floor which is well lit and has a fireplace. At Newtown, which was built *c*.1622, the strong bawn defends a two-storey house with large chimney stacks on both gables. It has fireplaces at each level in both gables. There is evidence for a wall-walk which was carried on wooden beams supported in the thickness of the walls. The bawn has two surviving flanking towers two storeys high which contain several gun loops.

There is a stronghouse with a substantial bawn at Roosca in south Tipperary, built on the edge of a precipice at the south and west sides.[17] It is a two-storey rectangular building of sixteenth-century date. The ground floor had a stone dividing wall and was lit by simple slit opes. The upper floor was supported on wooden beams carried on sandstone corbels. It has ogee-headed single and double-light windows and had wooden partitions. The rectangular-shaped bawn, which encloses a fairly large area, incorporates the

Fig. 169 Ardtermon, Co. Sligo, a long rectangular stronghouse with flanking towers and bawn.

house in its south-west angle and has a two-storey mural tower at the north-east. The tower has gun loops at both levels.

In Co. Roscommon there are also a small number of stronghouses and these again show a mixture of plans. For instance at Dundonnell there is a plain two-storey house with attic, built within the spectacular earthen defences of a large ringwork castle. It is built of rubble masonry and has a chimney stack on each high gable. It has a very well-defended ground-floor level with numerous gun loops and slit opes. At first-floor level there is evidence for three large windows and a fireplace in each gable. Close to Dundonnell is Cloonbigny, which is also a rectangular-shaped two-storey house with attic. At the south-west angle, but not bonded to it, are the

Fig. 170 The remains of a stronghouse at Roosca, Co. Tipperary. It also has the remains of a bawn with one extant flanking tower (David Sweetman).

197

remains of a tower house. Although the house is on high ground it lacks the defences of Dundonnell, having large window opes on both floors. The tower house was in use when the house was built, and there was communication between the two structures. Tower house and stronghouse were both defended by a bawn wall. Also in the south of Roscommon was Tully, sadly now levelled. It was a rectangular block with angle towers at the south-west and south-east and a chimney stack in the middle of the south wall.[18] It was defended by a bawn wall, now much ruined. Lowberry, also in the south of the county, is similar to Cloonbigny except it has a slight projection in the east wall containing the entranceway. It also has two windows high up in each gable which are more usually seen in later seventeenth-century houses. The chimney breasts and stacks, like the other Roscommon examples, do not project out beyond the line of the gables which is a feature of seventeenth-century houses.

Many of these early seventeenth-century houses have no defensive features but some of them may have had bawn walls to protect them. There are several T-shaped houses such as Derrin, Co. Laois, Graffan, Co. Offaly, and Ballyloughan, Co. Carlow, which are of much the same period but show no obvious means of defence. Ardtermon, near the shore of Drumcliff Bay, Co. Sligo, is a long rectangular two-storey house with circular flanking towers at its north-east and south-east angles. It has a semicircular tower almost in the centre of the west wall which contained the wooden stairs. This tower and the angle towers have gun loops for flanking fire. There is a large bawn adjoining the west side of the house with a gateway in its north wall and a flanking tower at the north-west angle.

It is doubtful if I have mentioned even a fraction of the stronghouses and fortified houses to be found in Ireland. Readers may know of ones that are not included here and many are yet to be recorded by the Archaeological Survey of Ireland. Others have not been recognised or correctly identified. Little work has been done on this final period of castle building in Ireland but I hope that this chapter will contribute to the study of these buildings. Some of these defended houses, such as Kanturk and Burncourt, are easy to classify as are some of the stronghouses, but there are many, such as Mallow that appear to be unique. Intensive fieldwork combined with a re-examination of the sites and monuments records in both the north and south of Ireland will have to be undertaken before a more comprehensive work on this subject can be published.

NOTES

B.G.S.I.H.S.	*Bulletin of the Group for the Study of Irish Historic Settlement*
C.D.I.	*Calendar of Documents Relating to Ireland*
J.C.H.A.S.	*Journal of the Cork Historical and Archaeological Society*
J.G.A.H.S.	*Journal of the Galway Archaeological and Historical Society*
J.I.A.	*Journal of Irish Archaeology*
J.K.A.S.	*Journal of the Kildare Archaeological Society*
J.R.S.A.I.	*Journal of the Royal Society of Antiquaries of Ireland*
J.W.H.S.	*Journal of the Wexford Historical Society*
N.M.A.J.	*North Munster Antiquarian Journal*
R.I.A.Proc.	*Proceedings of the Royal Irish Academy*
U.J.A.	*Ulster Journal of Archaeology*

Preface

1. H. Leask, *Irish castles and castellated houses* (Dundalk, 1941).

Introduction

1. Leask, *Irish castles*, p. 1.
2. J. Ó Meara (trans.), *The history and topography of Ireland* (London, 1982), pp 118-19.

Chapter 1 Earth and timber castles

1. R. Glasscock, 'Mottes in Ireland' in *Château-Gaillard*, vii (1975), pp 95-110.
2. H. Knox, 'The Croghans and some Connacht raths and motes' in *J.R.S.A.I.*, xli (1911), 301-40, see p. 309.
3. B. Graham, 'Medieval settlement in County Roscommon' in *R.I.A.Proc.*, lxxxviii (1988), C, pp 19-38, see p. 26.
4. T. Barry, *The archaeology of medieval Ireland* (London, 1987), pp 37-55; Graham, 'Medieval settlement', pp 19-38; B. Graham, 'Medieval timber and earthwork fortifications in western Ireland' in *Medieval Archaeology*, xxxii (1988), pp 110-20; B. Graham, 'Twelfth- and thirteenth-century earthwork castles in Ireland: an assessment' in *Fortress*, ix (1991), pp 24-34, see pp 24-31; K. O'Conor, 'Irish earthwork castles' in *Fortress*, ix (1992), pp 3-12.
5. R. Higham and P. Barker, *Timber castles* (London, 1992), p. 192.
6. Higham and Barker, *Timber castles*, p. 194.
7. D. King and L. Alcock, 'Ringworks of England and Wales' in *Château-Gaillard*, iii (1969), pp 90-127.
8. By Caimin O'Brien and Jean Farrelly working for the Archaeological Survey of Ireland.
9. P.D. Sweetman, 'Excavations of medieval field boundaries at Clonard, Co. Meath' in *J.R.S.A.I.*, cviii (1978), pp 10-22.
10. By Alan Hayden, excavation report in Dúchas.
11. G. Orpen, *Ireland under the Normans*, (vol. i, Oxford, 1911), p. 338.
12. P.D. Sweetman, 'Archaeological excavations at Ferns Castle, Co. Wexford' in *R.I.A.Proc.*, lxxix (1979), C, pp 217-45.
13. Archaeological excavations by Kieran O'Conor; K. O'Conor, 'The Origins of Carlow castle' in *Archaeology Ireland*, xi (1997), pp 14-15.
14. E. Rynne, 'Was Desmond castle, Adare, erected on a ringfort?' in *N.M.A.J.* viii (1961), pp 193-202.
15. Excavations by Ben Murtagh and Ken Wiggins.
16. Pers. Comm. Kieran O'Conor.
17. Barry, *Medieval Ireland*, pp 46-8.
18. King and Alcock, 'Ringworks', p. 97.
19. Graham, 'Medieval fortifications', p. 117.
20. O'Conor, 'Irish earthwork castles', pp 3-12. O'Conor has studied the medieval earthworks of Leinster, Caimin O'Brien and Jean Farrelly have reassessed the earthwork sites in Offaly and Tipperary, Brian Graham has published widely on medieval earthworks in relation to settlement patterns and historical background.
21. C. O'Brien and J. Farrelly (comp.), *Archaeological inventory of Tipperary North Riding* (Dublin, forthcoming).
22. P. O'Donovan (comp.), *Archaeological inventory of Co. Cavan* (Dublin, 1995), pp 224-5. The present ecclesiastical remains are those of an eighteenth-century church.
23. P.D. Sweetman, O. Alcock and B. Moran (comp.), *Archaeological inventory of Co. Laois* (Dublin, 1995), p. 18.
24. M. Moore (comp.), *Archaeological Inventory of Co. Wexford* (Dublin, 1996), p. 93.
25. I. Bennett, 'Preliminary archaeological excavations at Ferrycarrig ringwork, Newtown townland, Co. Wexford' in *J.W.H.S.*, x (1984-5), pp 25-43, see p. 25.
26. T. Fanning, 'Excavation of a ringfort at Pollardstown, Co. Kildare' in *J.K.A.S.*, xv (1973-4), pp 251-61.
27. M. O'Kelly, 'Beal Boru, Co. Clare' in *J.C.H.A.S.*, lxvii (1962), pp 1-27.

28. C. O'Brien and P.D. Sweetman (comp.), *Archaeological inventory of Co. Offaly* (Dublin, 1997), pp 132-4.
29. Graham, 'Medieval fortifications', pp 19-38.
30. R. Meenan, Deserted medieval villages of Westmeath (unpublished M.Litt. thesis, Trinity College Dublin, 1985).
31. C. Lynn, 'The excavation of Rathmullan: a raised rath and motte in Co. Down' in *U.J.A.*, xliv-xlv (1981-2), pp 65-171.
32. C. Lynn, 'Excavations on a mound at Gransha, Co. Down' in *U.J.A.*, xlviii (1985), pp 81-90.
33. *Ibid.*, p. 81.
34. *Ibid.*, pp 81-90.
35. G. Stout, *Archaeological survey of the barony of Ikerrin* (Roscrea, 1984), p. 26.
36. Graham, 'Medieval fortifications'.
37. G. Orpen, 'Motes and Norman castles in Ireland', *J.R.S.A.I.*, xxxvii (1907), pp 123-52.
38. Knox, 'Connacht raths and motes', p. 113.
39. R. Glasscock and T. McNeill, 'Mottes in Ireland: a draft list' in *B.G.S.I.H.S.*, iii (1972), pp 27-51; Glasscock, 'Mottes in Ireland', pp 95-110.
40. K. O'Conor, 'The later construction and use of motte and bailey castles in Ireland: new evidence from Leinster in *J.K.A.S.*, xvii (1987-91), pp 13-29.
41. A. Otway-Ruthven, 'The partition of the de Verdon lands in Ireland in 1332' in *R.I.A.Proc.*, lxvi (1967), C, 401-5, see p. 415.
42. H.M.S.O., *An inventory of the ancient monuments in Glamorgan vol. III, The early castles* (London, 1991), p. 72.
43. Glasscock and McNeill, 'Mottes', p. 29.
44. *Ibid.*
45. *Ibid.*, pp 29-31.
46. D. Waterman, 'Excavations at Clough Castle, Co. Down' in *U.J.A.*, xvii (1954), pp 103-63; D. Waterman, 'Excavations at Dromore motte, Co. Down' in *U.J.A.*, xvii (1954), pp 164-8; D. Waterman, 'Excavations at Seefin Castle and Ballymoney motte and bailey' in *U.J.A.*, xviii (1955), pp 83-104.
47. Waterman, 'Clough Castle', pp 106-7.
48. *Ibid.*, pp 107-8.
49. Higham and Barker, *Timber castles*, p. 197.
50. D. Waterman, 'Excavations at Lismahon, Co. Down' in *Medieval Archaeology*, iii (1959), pp 139-76.
51. Lynn, 'Gransha'; Lynn, 'Rathmullan', p. 167; A. Hamlin and C. Lynn, *Pieces of the past* (Belfast, 1988); Higham and Barker, *Timber castles*, p. 74.
52. T. McNeill, 'Excavations at Dunsilly, Co. Antrim' in *U.J.A.*, liv (1991-2), pp 78-112.
53. Lynn, 'Rathmullan', pp 65, 148.
54. Waterman, 'Dromore motte'.
55. Waterman, 'Seafin Castle'.
56. McNeill, 'Dunsilly'.
57. C. Dickinson and D. Waterman, 'Excavations at Castleskreen, Co. Down' in *U.J.A.*, xxii (1959), pp 63-77.
58. T. McNeill, *Anglo-Norman Ulster* (Edinburgh, 1980); T. McNeill, *Castles in Ireland: feudal power in a Gaelic world* (London, 1997), pp 66-9.
59. B. Graham, 'The mottes of the Norman Liberty of Meath' in H. Murtagh (ed.), *Irish midland studies* (Athlone, 1980), pp 39-56, see pp 42-3.
60. T. Barry, E. Culleton and C. Empey, 'The Motte at Kells, Co. Kilkenny' in *R.I.A.Proc.*, lxxxiv (1984), C, pp 157-70, see p. 164.
61. Lynn, 'Rathmullan, pp 151-2; McNeill, 'Dunsilly'; O'Conor, 'Irish earthwork castles', p. 5.
62. *Ibid.*; McNeill, 'Dunsilly'.
63. O'Conor, 'Irish earthwork castles', p. 5; McNeill, 'Dunsilly'.
64. A. Otway-Ruthven, 'de Verdon lands'.
65. O'Conor, 'Irish earthwork castles', p. 5; McNeill, 'Dunsilly'.
66. T. Wright, *Louthiana* (London, 1758).

Chapter 2 The Anglo-Norman stone fortress

1. Leask, *Irish castles*.
2. R. Brown, *Castles from the air* (Cambridge, 1989), p. 1.
3. M. Salter, *Castles and stronghouses of Ireland* (Worcester, 1993); P. Somerset Fry, *Castles of Britain and Ireland* (Devon, 1996); McNeill, *Castles in Ireland*.
4. For instance see J. Kenyon, *Medieval fortifications* (London, 1990).
5. Sweetman, 'Ferns Castle'; Carlow Castle was partially excavated by Kieran O'Conor.
6. Excavations by Ben Murtagh in Kilkenny and Ken Wiggins in Limerick.
7. By Alan Hayden.
8. K. O'Conor, 'Anglo-Norman castles in Laois' in G. Lane (ed.) *Laois: history and society* (Dublin, forthcoming).
9. Excavations by Alan Hayden.
10. K. O'Conor, 'Dunamase Castle' in *Journal of Irish Archaeology*, vii (1996), pp 99-105.
11. By Brian Hodkinson in 1996.
12. By Kieran O'Conor.
13. Leask, *Irish castles*, pp 47-51.
14. O'Conor 1997, 'Carlow Castle'.
15. *Ibid.*
16. Excavations undertaken by Dave Pollock in 1995 prior to conservation work.
17. Excavated by Con Manning in 1987 prior to conservation work.
18. Excavated by Brian Hodkinson.
19. *Ibid.*
20. This is Hodkinson's contention.
21. O'Conor, 'Dunamase Castle', pp 99-100.
22. Excavated by Brian Hodkinson.
23. Excavations by Alan Hayden.
24. C. Manning, *Clonmacnoise* (Dublin, 1994), p. 18.
25. V. Buckley and P.D. Sweetman, *Archaeological survey of Co. Louth* (Dublin, 1991), p. 321.
26. *Ibid.*
27. T. McNeill, *Carrickfergus castle* (Belfast, 1981).
28. Excavations by Brian Hodkinson in 1996.
29. The results of Brian Hodkinson's excavation in 1996.

30. E. Jope (ed.), *An archaeological survey of Co. Down* (Belfast, 1966), pp 207-11; D. Waterman, 'Excavations at Dundrum Castle, 1950' in *U.J.A.,* xiv (1951), pp 15-29.
31. J. Kenyon and M. Thompson, 'The origin of the word "keep"' in , *Medieval Archaeology,* xxxviii (1994), pp 175-6.
32. As shown by Alan Hayden's excavation.
33. As revealed by Brian Hodkinson's excavation.
34. As found by Alan Hayden.
35. As recorded by Kevin O'Brien, who has done a detailed study of the keep.
36. As revealed by Alan Hayden's excavation.
37. According to McNeill, who has studied the castle in some detail; McNeill, *Carrickfergus Castle.*
38. As surveyed by Alan Hayden.
39. Excavations by Wiggins and Hodkinson.
40. McNeill, *Castles in Ireland,* p. 193.
41. Where Con Manning excavated parts of the castle in the early 1980s.
42. McNeill, *Castles in Ireland,* pp 88-91.
43. Waterman, 'Clough Castle'.
44. Manning, *Clonmacnoise,* p. 18.
45. McNeill, *Castles in Ireland.* McNeill discusses a group of fortresses in Leinster which Harold Leask referred to as towered keeps. McNeill accuses Leask of the misuse of the term 'keep' and has used the term to mean a place of last resort. McNeill's is a relatively recent interpretation of the term.
46. O'Conor came to this conclusion from his recent excavations and historical research.
47. As pointed out by O'Conor.
48. As argued by O'Conor.
49. Commissioners of Public Records, *Litterarum Clausanrum Vol. I* (London, 1833), p. 408; *C.D.I.* no. 913; my thanks to M. Hennessy for this reference.
50. Leask, *Irish castles,* p. 49; R. Stalley, *Architecture and Sculpture in Ireland, 1150-1350* (Dublin, 1971), p. 27.
51. O'Conor at Lea and Carlow and O'Brien at Trim.
52. C. Manning, 'Clogh Oughter Castle' in *Breifne,* viii (1990), pp 20-61.
53. *Ibid.,* pp 36-8.
54. Archaeological excavations took place at Dungarvan, Co. Waterford from 1995 to 1998 under the direction of Dave Pollock.
55. Sketch by Francis Place; Leask, *Irish castles,* p. 43.

Chapter 3 Hall-houses
1. D. Waterman, 'Rectangular keeps of the thirteenth century, at Grennan (Kilkenny) and Glanworth (Cork)' in *J.R.S.A.I.,* xcviii (1968), pp 67-73. When discussing these keeps, Waterman compared Grenan with Glanworth, yet the former is not found within a castle complex and appears to be isolated except for a possible wall or bank around it.
2. O'Brien and Farrelly (comp.), *Archaeological inventory of Tipperary North.*
3. Identified by archaeologists working for the Archaeological Survey.

4. H.T. Knox, 'Ballisnihiney Castle in *J.G.A.H.S.,* vi (1909-10), p. 179; Knox pointed out that these structures were a distinctive class and were early towers.
5. Identified by the Archaeological Survey archaeologists.
6. A. O'Sullivan and J. Sheehan, *The Iveragh Peninsula: an archaeological survey of south Kerry* (Cork, 1996), pp 365-9.
7. McNeill, *Castles in Ireland,* pp 148-55.
8. Moore (comp.), *Archaeological inventory of Wexford,* pp 180-82.
9. McNeill, *Castles in Ireland,* pp 149-52.

Chapter 4 Later medieval stone fortresses
1. P.D. Sweetman, 'Archaeological excavations at Ballymote Castle, Co. Sligo' in *J.G.A.H.S.,* xl (1985-6), pp 114-24.
2. L. de Paor, 'Excavations at Ballyloughan Castle, Co. Carlow' in *J.R.S.A.I.,* xlii (1962), pp 1-14. The term 'enclosure castle' is generally taken to mean fortifications which do not have a great isolated tower within the enclosed area, and which depend on their curtain walls both for defence and to contain towers and gatehouses which were used for accommodation. It is not a particularly useful classification because the vast majority of castles lack a great tower and those examples that do have a great tower tend to belong to the late twelfth century or very early thirteenth century. Castles that do not have towers have various types of enclosing elements and those from the end of the thirteenth century and the early fourteenth century are modelled on the Edward I examples in Wales.
3. T. Westropp, 'Carrigogunnell Castle and the O'Briens of Pubblebrian, in the County of Limerick, Part II – the ruins and the later families' in *J.R.S.A.I.,* xxxviii (1908), pp 141-59.
4. The hall at the north-eastern part of the site is called Desmond's hall in T. Westropp, 'The Desmond's Castle at Newcastle O'Conyll, Co. Limerick' in *J.R.S.A.I.,* xxxix (1909), pp 361-7 and Leask, *Irish castles,* p. 124. In T. McNeill, *Castles in Ireland,* pp 175-9 it is called the great hall. Westropp named the hall to the south the great hall. To avoid confusion I will follow Westropp's labelling.
5. As suggested by McNeill, *Castles in Ireland,* pp 177.
6. Westropp, 'Desmond's Castle' pp 358-9. Westropp incorrectly considered this to be the keep.
7. P. Holland, 'The thirteenth-century remains of Cahir Castle, Co. Tipperary' in *N.M.A.J.,* xxxv (1993-94), pp 63-71.
8. H. Wheeler, *Cahir Castle* (Dublin, n.d.).
9. Holland, 'Cahir Castle', pp 63-4.
10. Wheeler, *Cahir Castle,* pp 14-15.
11. Con Manning excavated this site between 1989 and 1992.
12. Excavation by Joanna Wren during 1991-2.
13. Stout, *Barony of Ikerrin,* pp 120-1.

14. T. Fanning, 'An Irish medieval tile pavement: recent excavations at Swords Castle, Co. Dublin' in *J.R.S.A.I.,* cv (1975), pp 47-82, see p. 48.
15. What Leask said in his book on Irish castles is still true, despite extensive fieldwork carried out by the Archaeological Survey over the past twenty years. Leask, *Irish castles,* p. 124.
16. T. Barry, 'The last frontier: defence and settlement in late medieval Ireland' in T. Barry, R. Frame and K. Simms (ed.), *Colony and frontier in medieval Ireland* (London, 1995), pp 217-28.
17. T. O'Keefe, 'Rathnageeragh and Ballyloo: a study of stone castles of probable fourteenth to early fifteenth century date in Co. Carlow' in *J.R.S.A.I.,* cxvii (1987), pp 28-49.
18. *Ibid.,* pp 35-6, 42.
19. Barry, 'The last frontier', pp 217-28.
20. McNeill, *Castles in Ireland,* pp 194, 198, 224, 227.
21. Leask, *Irish castles,* pp 113-24.
22. Leask, *Irish castles',* pp 101-11. If we re-allocate the castles that Leask includes in his chapter 'Some other towers' and 'The larger castles of the 15th, 16th, and 17th Centuries' to the section on tower houses and the earlier fortresses, there is virtually no new castle building (other than tower houses) during this period.

Chapter 5   The tower house
1. Barry, 'The last frontier', pp 212-28; T. McNeill, *Castles in Ireland,* pp 201-5.
2. H. Berry (ed.), *Statute Rolls of the Parliament of Ireland, Reign of Henry VI* (London, 1910), pp 33-5.
3. Many students and authors writing on this subject have been at pains to alter this simple basic picture by trying to push the origin of the tower house back into the fourteenth century. This has been attempted by quoting historical references and by trying to attach earlier dates to examples found in the western half of the country. As seen in Chapter 3, the earliest hall-houses lie in the west while the later, larger and more sophisticated hall-houses are to be found in the east, such as Dunmoe and Kindlestown. This obsession of scholars trying to change Leask's initial premise about the dating of the Irish tower house has dogged castle studies. His thesis must stand until we have concrete evidence to prove otherwise. Leask, *Irish castles,* p. 75.
4. McNeill, *Castles in Ireland,* pp 211-13.
5. Buckley and Sweetman, *Co. Louth,* pp 301-49.
6. Leask, *Irish castles,* p. 79-86.
7. McNeill, *Castles in Ireland,* p. 213.
8. Sweetman, Alcock and Moran (comp.), *Inventory of Co. Laois,* pp 110-16.
9. O'Brien and Sweetman (Comp.), *Inventory of Co. Offaly,* pp 139-53.
10. Moore, *Inventory of Co. Wexford,* pp 165-82.
11. D. Power (comp.), *Archaeological inventory of Co. Cork 1: west Cork* (Dublin, 1992), pp 321-30; D. Power (comp.), *Archaeological inventory of Co. Cork 2: east and south Cork* (Dublin, 1994), pp 218-32; D. Power, E. Byrne, U. Egan, S. Lane and M. Sleeman (comp.), *Archaeological inventory of Co. Cork 3: mid Cork* (Dublin, 1997), 356-71; D. Power, E. Byrne, U. Egan, S. Lane and M. Sleeman (comp.), *Archaeological inventory of Co. Cork 4: north Cork* (Dublin, forthcoming).
12. Dave Pollock excavations, 1997-8.
13. Based on the present evidence from the Archaeological Survey and from the number of castle sites marked on the Ordnance Survey maps which have no physical remains.
14. Dave Pollock excavations, 1997-8.
15. As can be readily observed from the large number of tower houses recorded by the Archaeological Survey of Ireland, see T. Barry, 'The archaeology of the tower house in late medieval Ireland' in H. Anderson and T. Wienberg (ed.), *The study of medieval archaeology* (Stockholm, 1993), pp 211-17.

Chapter 6   Fortified houses and stronghouses
1. Power (comp.), *Inventory of Co. Cork 1,* pp 331-2.
2. Leask, *Irish castles,* pp 125-6.
3. Power (comp), *Inventory of Co. Cork 2,* pp 223-7.
4. *Ibid.*
5. Power, Byrne, Egan, Lane and Sleeman (comp.), *Inventory of Co. Cork 4.*
6. Leask, *Irish castles,* p. 131.
7. Sweetman, Alcock and Moran (comp.), *Inventory of Co. Laois,* pp 124-6.
8. B. Lacy, *Archaeological survey of Donegal* (Lifford, 1983), pp 361-5, 376-9.
9. *Ibid.*
10. O'Brien and Sweetman (comp.), *Inventory of Co. Offaly,* pp 154-60.
11. By Dorothy Parsons of Birr castle.
12. O'Brien and Farrelly (comp.), *Inventory of Tipperary North Riding.*
13. *Ibid.*
14. Recent work by Denis Power of the Archaeological Survey strongly indicates that they are totally absent from counties Cork and Limerick, nor do they appear to be in Kerry.
15. Michael Moore following his survey work in Co. Waterford.
16. O'Brien and Sweetman (comp.), *Inventory of Co. Offaly,* pp 158-9.
17. Recently discovered by Jean Farrelly.
18. M. Craig, *The Architecture of Ireland from earliest times to 1800* (London, 1982), p. 131.

BIBLIOGRAPHY

Barry, T. 1987 *The archaeology of medieval Ireland.* London.

Barry, T. 1993 'The archaeology of the tower house in late medieval Ireland' in H. Anderson and T. Wienberg (ed.), *The study of medieval archaeology*, pp 211-17. Stockholm.

Barry, T. 1995 'The last frontier: defence and settlement in late medieval Ireland' in T. Barry, R. Frame and K. Simms (ed.), *Colony and frontier in medieval Ireland,* pp 212-28. London.

Barry, T., Culleton, E. and Empey, C. 1984 'The Motte at Kells, Co. Kilkenny' in *R.I.A.Proc.,* lxxxiv, C, pp 157-70.

Bennett, I. 1984-5 'Preliminary archaeological excavations at Ferrycarrig ringwork, Newtown townland, Co. Wexford' in *J.W.H.S.,* x, pp 25-43.

Berry, H. (ed.) 1910 *Statute Rolls of the Parliament of Ireland, Reign of Henry VI,* London.

Brown, R. 1989 *Castles from the air*. Cambridge.

Buckley, V. and Sweetman, P.D. 1991 *Archaeological survey of Co. Louth.* Dublin.

Commissioners of Public Records 1833 *Litterarum Clausanrum Vol. I.* London.

Craig, M. 1982 *The Architecture of Ireland from earliest times to 1800.* London.

Cunningham, G. 1987 *The Anglo-Norman advance into the south-west midlands of Ireland 1185-1221.* Roscrea.

de Paor, L. 1962 'Excavations at Ballyloughan castle, Co. Carlow' in *J.R.S.A.I.,* xlii, pp 1-14.

Dickinson, C. and Waterman, D. 1959 'Excavations at Castleskreen, Co. Down' in *U.J.A.,* xxii, 63-77.

Fanning, T. 1973-4 Excavation of a ringfort at Pollardstown, Co. Kildare' in *J.K.A.S.,* xv, pp 251-61.

Fanning, T. 1975 'An Irish medieval tile pavement: recent excavations at Swords castle, Co. Dublin' in *J.R.S.A.I.,* cv, pp 47-82.

Farrelly, J. and O'Brien, C. (comp.) forthcoming *Archaeological inventory of Tipperary North Riding.* Dublin.

Glasscock, R. 1975 'Mottes in Ireland' in *Château-Gaillard*, vii, pp 95-110.

Glasscock, R. and McNeill, T. 1972 'Mottes in Ireland: a draft list' in *B.G.S.I.H.S.*, iii, pp 27-51.

Graham, B. 1980 'The mottes of the Norman Liberty of Meath' in H. Murtagh (ed.), *Irish midland studies*, pp 39-56. Athlone.

Graham, B. 1988 'Medieval settlement in County Roscommon' in *R.I.A.Proc.,* lxxxviii, C, pp 19-38.

Graham, B. 1988 'Medieval timber and earthwork fortifications in western Ireland' in *Medieval Archaeology,* xxxii, 110-20.

Graham, B. 1991 'Twelfth- and thirteenth-century earthwork castles in Ireland: an assessment' in *Fortress*, ix, pp 24-31.

Hamlin, A. and Lynn, C. 1988 *Pieces of the past*. Belfast.

Higham, R. and Barker, P. 1992 *Timber castles*. London.

H.M.S.O. 1991 *An inventory of the ancient monuments in Glamorgan vol. III, The early castles*. London.

Holland, P. 1993-4 'The thirteenth-century remains of Cahir castle, Co. Tipperary' in *N.M.A.J.*, xxxv, pp 63-71.

Johnson, D. 1985 *The Irish castle*. Dublin.

Jope, E. (ed.) 1966 *An archaeological survey of Co. Down*. Belfast.

Kenyon, J. 1990 *Medieval fortifications*. London.

Kenyon, J. and Thompson, M. 1994 'The origin of the word "keep"' in *Medieval Archaeology*, xxxviii, pp 175-6.

King, D. and Alcock, L. 1969 'Ringworks of England and Wales' in *Château-Gaillard*, iii, pp 90-127.

Knox, H. 1909-10 'Ballisnahyny castle in *J.G.A.H.S.*, vi, p. 179.

Knox, H. 1911 'The Croghans and some Connacht raths and motes' in *J.R.S.A.I.*, xli, pp 301-40.

Lacy, B. 1983 *Archaeological survey of Donegal*. Lifford.

Leask, H. 1941 *Irish castles and castellated houses*. Dundalk.

Lynn, C. 1981-2 'The excavation of Rathmullan: a raised rath and motte in Co. Down' in *U.J.A.*, xliv-xlv, pp 65-171.

Lynn, C. 1985 'Excavations on a mound at Gransha, Co. Down' in *U.J.A.*, xlviii, pp 81-90.

McNeill, T. 1980 *Anglo-Norman Ulster*. Edinburgh.

McNeill, T. 1981 *Carrickfergus Castle*. Belfast.

McNeill, T. 1991-2 'Excavations at Dunsilly, Co. Antrim' in *U.J.A.*, liv, pp 78-112.

McNeill, T. 1997 *Castles in Ireland: feudal power in a Gaelic world*. London.

Manning, C. 1990 'Clogh Oughter Castle' in *Breifne,* viii, pp 20-61.

Manning, C. 1994 *Clonmacnoise*. Dublin.

Meenan, R. 1985 Deserted medieval villages of Westmeath. Unpublished M.Litt. thesis, Trinity College Dublin.

Moore, M. (comp.) 1996 *Archaeological inventory of Co. Wexford*. Dublin.

O'Brien, C. and Sweetman, P.D. (comp.) 1997 *Archaeological inventory of Co. Offaly*. Dublin.

O'Conor, K. 1987-91 'The later construction and use of motte and bailey castles in Ireland: new evidence from Leinster in *J.K.A.S.*, xvii, pp 13-29.

O'Conor, K. 1992 'Irish earthwork castles' in *Fortress*, ix, pp 3-12.

O'Conor, K. 1996 'Dunamase castle' in *J.I.A.*, vii, pp 99-105.

O'Conor, K. 1997 'The Origins of Carlow Castle' in *Archaeology Ireland*, xi, pp 14-15.

O'Conor, K. forthcoming 'Anglo-Norman castles in Laois' in G. Lane (ed.) *Laois: history and society*. Dublin.

O'Donovan, P. (comp.) 1995 *Archaeological inventory of Co. Cavan*. Dublin.

O'Keefe, T. 1987 'Rathnageeragh and Ballyloo: a study of stone castles of probable fourteenth to early fifteenth century date in Co. Carlow' in *J.R.S.A.I.*, cxvii, pp 28-49.

O'Kelly, M. 1962 'Beal Boru, Co. Clare' in *J.C.H.A.S.*, lxvii, pp 1-27.

Ó Meara, J. (trans.) 1982 *The history and topography of Ireland*. London.

Orpen, G. 1907 'Motes and Norman castles in Ireland' in *J.R.S.A.I.*, xxxvii, pp 123-52.

Orpen, G. 1911-20 *Ireland under the Normans*. 4 vols. Oxford.

O'Sullivan, A. and Sheehan, J. 1996 *The Iveragh Peninsula: an archaeological survey of south Kerry*. Cork.

Otway-Ruthven, A. 1967 'The partition of the de Verdon lands in Ireland in 1332' in *R.I.A.Proc.*, lxvi, C, 401-5.

Power, D. (comp.) 1992 *Archaeological inventory of Co. Cork 1: west Cork*. Dublin.

Power, D. (comp.) 1994 *Archaeological inventory of Co. Cork 2: east and south Cork*. Dublin.

Power, D., Byrne, E., Egan, U., Lane, S. and Sleeman, M. (comp.) 1997 *Archaeological inventory of Co. Cork 3: mid Cork*. Dublin.

Power, D., Byrne, E., Egan, U., Lane, S. and Sleeman, M. (comp.) forthcoming *Archaeological inventory of Co. Cork 4: north Cork*. Dublin.

Rynne, E. 1961 'Was Desmond castle, Adare, erected on a ringfort?' in *N.M.A.J.*, viii, pp 193-202.

Salter, M. 1993 *Castles and stronghouses of Ireland*. Worcester.

Somerset Fry, P. 1996 *Castles of Britain and Ireland*. Devon.

Stalley, R. 1971 *Architecture and Sculpture in Ireland, 1150-1350*. Dublin.

Stout, G. 1984 *Archaeological survey of the barony of Ikerrin*. Roscrea.

Sweetman, P.D. 1978 'Excavations of medieval field boundaries at Clonard, Co. Meath' in *J.R.S.A.I.*, cviii, pp 10-22.

Sweetman, P.D. 1978 'Archaeological excavations at Trim Castle, Co. Meath, 1971-74' in *R.I.A.Proc.*, lxxviii, C, pp 227-98.

Sweetman, P.D. 1979 'Archaeological excavations at Ferns Castle, Co. Wexford' in *R.I.A.Proc.*, lxxix, C, pp 217-45.

Sweetman, P.D. 1980 'Archaeological excavations at King John's Castle, Limerick' in *R.I.A.Proc.*, lxxx, C, pp 207-29.

Sweetman, P.D. 1981 'Some late seventeenth- to late eighteenth-century finds from Kilkenny Castle' in *R.I.A.Proc.*, lxxxi, C, pp 249-66.

Sweetman, P.D. 1985-6 'Archaeological excavations at Ballymote Castle, Co. Sligo' in *J.G.A.H.S.*, xl, pp 114-24.

Sweetman, P.D., Alcock, O. and Moran, B. (comp.) 1995 *Archaeological inventory of Co. Laois*. Dublin.

Waterman, D. 1951 'Excavations at Dundrum Castle, 1950' in *U.J.A.*, xiv, pp 15-29.

Waterman, D. 1954 'Excavations at Clough Castle, Co. Down' in *U.J.A.*, xvii, pp 103-63.

Waterman, D. 1954 'Excavations at Dromore motte', Co. Down' in *U.J.A.*, xvii, pp 164-8.

Waterman, D. 1955 'Excavations at Seefin Castle and Ballymoney motte and bailey' in *U.J.A.*, xviii, pp 83-104.

Waterman, D. 1959 Excavations at Lismahon, Co. Down' in *Medieval Archaeology*, iii, pp 139-76.

Waterman, D. 1968 'Rectangular keeps of the thirteenth century, at Grennan (Kilkenny) and Glanworth (Cork)' in *J.R.S.A.I.*, xcviii, pp 67-73.

Westropp, T. 1908 'Carrigogunnell Castle and the O'Briens of Pubblebrian, in the County of Limerick, Part II – the ruins and the later families' in *J.R.S.A.I.*, xxxviii, pp 141-59.

Westropp, T. 1909 'The Desmond's castle at Newcastle O'Conyll, Co. Limerick' in *J.R.S.A.I.*, xxxix, pp 361-7.

Wheeler, H. n.d. *Cahir castle*. Dublin.

Wright, T. 1758 *Louthiana*. London.

GLOSSARY

BARBICAN	Fore-work situated in advance of gateway or gate tower to protect it, usually sited outside the line of the fosse or moat.
BAILEY	See BAWN.
BARREL VAULT	Vault in the shape of half a barrel split lengthways.
BASTION	Projecting portion of fortification.
BAWN	Bailey or ward, defended courtyard of castle.
BELLCOTE	A small gabled or roofed housing for a bell.
BRETASCH	Wooden tower or wooden defences usually associated with earth and timber castles.
CHAMFER	Made by cutting off the edge of anything right-angled but especially angles on stonework.
CORBEL	Stone block projecting from wall to carry structures, especially floor beams.
CRENELLATION	Notched stone battlements.
CROSSLIT	Arrow loop or slit ope with a horizontal slit for greater range of fire.
CRUCK	Curved timber from ground to roof ridge to support roof.
CURTAIN WALL	Enclosing wall.
CUSP	Projecting point usually in the upper portion of a tracery window and often seen in ogee-headed windows.
DRYSTONE	Method of building without mortar or clay.
FOSSE	Ditch.
GABION	Wicker basket filled with earth and/or stone, used in fortifications.
GARDEROBE	Latrine.
GROIN VAULT	A groin is the line in which two vaults, running at any angle, meet.
HERISSON	Wooden palisade.
INTRA-MURAL	In the body of the wall.
LOOPHOLE	Small narrow light of various forms in wall for shooting arrows etc. out of.
LOUVRE	Wooden slatted opening to allow air in or smoke to exit through a small turret.

MACHICOLATION	Projecting structure supported on corbels outside walls from which stones etc. could be dropped on attackers below.
MANTLET WALL	Wall covering or protecting an entranceway or courtyard.
MERLON	Solid portion of a crenellated parapet.
MULLION	Vertical stone or timber dividing window lights.
MURDER HOLE	Aperture in a floor or vault usually above main entrance to a castle through which intruders could be fired upon.
MURAL STAIRS	Stone stairs in wall.
OGEE	Double curve, partly concave partly convex, usually window or door head.
OPE	Opening.
ORIEL	Large projecting window supported on corbels.
OUBLIETTE	Secret chamber.
PALISADE	Wooden fence used for fortification.
PISCINA	Basin with drain hole for priest to wash hands or vessels, usually set in a niche.
PORTCULLIS	Gate of iron or wood which was made to slide up and down in slots in the jambs of a castle gateway.
QUOINS	Stones, frequently dressed, used in the angles of buildings.
REVETTING	Facing applied to wall or bank.
SOLAR	Private accommodation, usually a withdrawing room, on one of the upper floors of a castle.
SQUINCH	Masonry arch bridging an angle to carry a stone structure in the angle.
TRACERY	Openwork of stone or wood usually for filling the upper part of a window above the transom and mullion.
TRANSOM	Horizontal bar of stone or wood in a window to divide the lights.
TREFOIL	Three-lobed or three-leaved motif.
WICKER CENTRING	Frame of wicker built to hold vault in place while being constructed.
YETT	Iron grille which could be pulled up in front of doorway from inside by chains to protect entrance.

PLACENAME INDEX

Adare Castle, Co. Limerick (14692 14638), 5, *30*, 34, 36, 47, *66*, 67-8, 74, 116

Aghaboe Motte, Co. Laois (23281 18595), *28*, 31

Aghadoe Castle, Co. Kerry (09343 09264), 88

Annaghkeen Castle, Co. Galway (12056 24470), 92-3, 94

Anneville, Co. Meath (see Clonard Old)

Antrim County, 17, 19, 26, 134

Ardamullivan Castle, Co. Galway (14437 19512), 171, 176

Ardee, Co. Louth (see Townparks), 145, 172
    Hatch's Castle (29622 29047), 145
    Court House (29616 29067), 145

Ardfinnan Castle, Co. Tipperary SR (20825 11768), 88

Ardglass (Jordan's) Castle, Co. Down (35601 33713), 172

Ardrahan North Castle, Co. Galway (14609 21228), 91, 93-4

Ardtermon Castle, Co. Sligo (1588234344), *196*, *197*, 198

Arra River, 120

Ash Big Motte, Co. Louth (29769 30504), 31

Askeaton Castle, Co. Limerick (13413 15031), 118-20, *119*, *120*, 123, *131*, 134

Aslaun Lough, 169

Athclare Castle, Co. Louth (30556 28625), 144

Athenry Castle, Co. Galway (15022 22771), 68, 70, *70*, *71*, 74, 76, 89

Athlone Castle, Co. Westmeath (20390 24150), 35, 36, 40, 85-6

Athlumney Castle, Co. Meath (28766 26750), 147, 183, *183*, *184*

Audley's Castle (Castleward), Co. Down (35781 35058), 172

Aughnanure, Castle, Co. Galway (11524 24168), *150*, *166*, 169

Balief Castle, Co. Kilkenny (23223 16352), *129*, *155*

Ballagh (Ballagharahin) Castle, Co. Laois (22244 17661), 147-8

Ballagharahin Castle, Co. Laois (see Ballagh Castle)

Ballina, Co. Mayo, 96

Ballinacarriga Castle, Co. Cork (12875 05080), 158, 159

Ballinakill Castle, Co. Laois (24678 18056), 151

Ballincollig Castle, Co. Cork (15875 06978), 159

Ballinderry Castle, Co. Galway (14457 24623), 169

Ballintober Castle, Co. Roscommon (17260 27478), 60, 105, 106, 108-9, *108*

Ballisnashyny Castle, Co. Mayo (12346 25174), 95

Ballyadams Castle, Co. Laois (26293 19082), 148, 172, 181, 182, *182*

Ballyannan Castle, Co. Cork (18670 07146), 178

Ballyboy East Castle, Co. Tipperary SR (20206 11439), 91, 94

Ballycarbery East Castle, Co. Kerry (04475 07976), *97*, 100

Ballyclohy Castle, Co. Waterford (23219 12111), 157

Ballycogly Castle, Co. Wexford (30379 11122), 157

Ballyconor Big Castle, Co. Wexford (31181 11059), 156

Ballycowan Castle, Co. Offaly (22947 22516), 175, 177, 188-9, *189*

Ballycrenane Castle, Co. Cork (20224 06888), 159

Ballycurrin Demesne Castle, Co. Mayo (11941 24921), 95

Ballydrohid Castle, Co. Offaly (23278 22515), 152

Ballyduff Lower Castle, Co. Waterford (19687 09893), 195

Ballygill North, Co. Antrim (see Doonmore Motte)

Ballyglass Earthwork, Co. Roscommon (17544 28487), 10

Ballyhack Castle, Co. Wexford (27060 11091), 157

Ballykine Lower Castle, Co. Mayo (11136 25699), 95

Ballylahan Castle, Co. Mayo (12747 29892), 57, *59*, 60, 80, *111*

Ballyloo Castle, Co. Carlow (27433 16981), 133

Ballyloughan Castle, Co. Carlow (27459 15851), 111, *112*, 115, *131*, 133

Ballyloughan Stronghouse, Co. Carlow (27456 15861), 198

Ballylusky Castle, Co. Tipperary NR (19122 18847), 94, *94*, 95

Ballymaclode Castle, Co. Waterford (26562 11001), 157

Ballymalis Castle, Co. Kerry (08404 09381), *170*, *171*

Ballymoon Castle, Co. Carlow (27396 16151), 115, 116, *117*, 118, 133

Ballymooney Castle (Oakley Park), Co. Offaly (21282 20185), 175, 189

Ballymote Castle (Carrownanty), Co. Sligo (16605 31548), 105, 106, *107*, 108

Ballynacarrig Earthwork, Co. Offaly (22196 21324), 9

Ballynacourty Castle, Co. Galway (see Carrowmore Castle)

Ballynahow Castle, Co. Tipperary (20829 16020), *154*

Ballynakill Castle, Co. Waterford (26379 11095), 195

Ballyprior Earthwork, Co. Laois (25790 19220), 6

Ballyroney Motte, Co. Down (32162 33948), 24

Ballyteige Castle, Co. Wexford (29670 10444), 157

Ballyvalley, Co. Clare (see Beal Boru Earthwork)

Ballyvireen, Co. Cork (see Coppinger's Court)

Balregan Castle, Co. Louth (30252 31036), 140-1, 144

Bann River, 2, 17

Bannow Bay, Co. Wexford, 1

Bargy Castle, Co. Wexford (30309 10889), 102, *104*

Barrinagh, Co. Roscommon (see Sheeaunbeg Earthwork)

Barrow River, 36, 39, 137

Barryscourt Castle, Co. Cork (18219 07248), 159, *159*, *160*, 173

Beal Boru Earthwork (Ballyvalley), Co. Clare (16960 17429), 5, 7, 8-9, 21

Bective Abbey, Co. Meath (28594 25996), 147

Belfast Lough, 34, 35

Big Glebe Raised Ringfort, Co. Derry (27603 42405), 21

Birr Castle (Townparks), Co. Offaly (20550 20502), 189

Blackwater River, 180

Blarney Castle, Co. Cork (16080 07531), 134, 161-3, *162*

Boherash, Co. Cork (see Glanworth Castle)

Bordeaux Region, France, 26

Bourchier's Castle (Lough Gur), Co. Limerick (16460 14047), 138, *142*

Boyne River, Co. Meath, 29, 34, 45, 64, 98, 184

Bristol, England, 6, 75

Britain, 6, 34, 83, 105, 192

Bunnow River, Co. Tipperary NR, 126
Bunratty Castle, Co. Clare (14498 16092), 134, *157*, 177
Burnchurch Castle (Farmley), Co. Kilkenny (24767 14738), *152, 153*
Burncourt Castle, Co. Tipperary SR (19524 11812), 175, 177, *185*, 190-2, 198
Burren River, 39
Butlerstown Castle, Co. Wexford (30444 10882), 156
Caernarfon Castle, Wales, 109, 117
Cahernamuck West Castle, Co. Galway (16084 21969), 171
Caher Castle, Co. Tipperary SR (20497 12493), 118, 123-26, *123, 124, 125*, 134
Cahir, Co. Tipperary (see Caher Castle)
Callan Motte, Co. Kilkenny (24127 14404), *26*
Calligan River, 40
Cappagh Castle, Co. Waterford (21815 09661), 157
Carbury Barony, Co. Kildare, 38
Carbury Castle, Co. Kildare (26868 23499), 38, *168, 191*
Cargin Castle, Co. Galway (12328 24340), 92
Carlingford (Liberties of), Co. Louth
    King John's Castle (31882 31196), 35, 47-9, *48*, 71-2, 78, *79*
    The Mint (31887 31161), 144, 146, *146*, 172
Carlingford Lough, 35, 48, 76, 79
Carlow Castle, Co. Carlow (27202 17667), 5, 6, 34, 39, 41, 60, 61, 62, *62*, 77, 78, 81-2
Carlow County, 22, 115, 133, 182, 193
Carnbane East, Co. Meath (see Loughcrew Hills)
Carntown Castle, Co. Louth (30916 27954), *145*, 146
Carrick Castle, Co. Kildare (26405 23683), 100
Carrickfergus Castle, Co. Antrim (34143 38725), 34, 35, *35*, 52-4, *54*, 64, 67, 72, 105
Carrignacurra Castle, Co. Cork (12389 06664), 192
Carrignamuck Castle, Co. Galway (14814 07533), 158
Carrigogunnel Castle, Co. Limerick (14980 15523), 118
Carrowmore Castle (Ballynacourty), Co. Galway (13638 21854), 91
Carrownanty, Co. Sligo (see Ballymote Castle)
Castleboy, Co. Galway (15243 21083), 93
Castlebrack, Co. Laois (24047 21644), 151
Castlecarra, Co. Mayo (11717 27535), 95
Castleconor, Co. Mayo (12585 32420), 89, 95, *96*
Castlecuffe, Co. Laois (22814 21123), 182
Castle Demesne, Co. Limerick (see Newcastle O'Conyll)
Castledoe, Co. Donegal (see Doe Castle)
Castle Ellen, Co. Galway (14913 23208), 171
Castlefarm, Co. Galway (see Dunmore Castle)
Castlegrace, Co. Tipperary SR (20298 11432), 72-3, *72*
Castleinch (15345 07208), 158
Castlehyde East, Co. Cork (17841 09853), 192
Castlekevin Ringwork, Co. Wicklow (31835 19854), *14*
Castlekirk (Lough Corrib), Co. Mayo (09961 25022), 91-2, *91, 92*
Castleknock, Co. Dublin (30859 23659), 85
Castleland, Co. Wexford (see Ferns Castle)
Castlelands, Co. Cork (see Mallow Castle)
Castlemore, Co. Cork (14441 066900), 104
Castlerahan Ringwork, Co. Cavan (25355 28636), 6, *8*, 13
Castlering Motte, Co. Louth (29636 30399), 31

Castleroche, Co. Louth (29906 31186), 28, *39*, 55, *56*, 57-8, *57*, 59, 63, 76, 77, *80*, 106
Castleskreen Motte, Co. Down (34658 34000), 21, 26, 27
Castletobin Ringwork, Co. Kilkenny (24249 14511), 6
Castletown, Co. Galway (see Kiltartan Castle)
Castletown, Dundalk, Co. Louth (30318 30866), 139, 144
Castletown Motte, Co. Louth (30295 30831), 28, 76
Castletown Conyers, Co. Limerick (14441 13000), 91
Castletown/Kylenamuck, Co. Tipperary NR (20276 20038), 94
Castleward, Co. Down (35740 34985), 172
Castleward, Co. Down (see Audley's Castle)
Cavan County, 6, 15-16, 22, 182, 193
Churchland, Co. Offaly (see Seirkieran)
Churchtown, Co. Wexford (see Hook Head)
Clara Upper Castle, Co. Kilkenny (25740 15791), 146, *147*
Clare County, 182
Clogh Oughter Castle (Inishconnell), Co. Cavan (23580 30784), 40, 41, *79*, 83-4
Cloghan Lucas Castle, Co. Mayo (12141 28019), 95
Clogheen Castle, Co. Tipperary SR (see Burncourt Castle)
Cloghkeating Castle, Co. Tipperary NR (19353 19077), 94, 95
Clohaskin Castle, Co. Tipperary NR (20037 19972), 94-5
Clonard/Mulphedder Ringwork, Co. Meath (26565 24493), 4, 6, 9, 10, 14
Clonard Old/Anneville Motte, Co. Meath (26575 24506), *19*
Cloncurry Motte, Co. Kildare (28020, 24138), *27*
Clonea Castle, Co. Waterford (23840 11347), 157
Clonmacnoise Castle, Co. Offaly (20076 23055), 5, 7-8, *7, 12*, *29*, 36, 47, 77, 86
Clonmore Castle, Co. Carlow (29608 17616), 113, 115-6, *115*, *131*, 133
Clonmore, Co. Offaly (see Seirkieran)
Cloonbigny Castle, Co. Roscommon (18752 23837), 197-8
Cloonbrackna, Co. Kerry (see Ross Island Castle)
Clough Castle, Co. Down (34092 34029), 19, 20, 24, 26, 76, 89
Clougheast Castle, Co. Wexford (31202 10558), 156, 157
Commons, Co. Meath (see Duleek Motte)
Connacht Province, 2, 17, 40, 85, 86
Coolhull Castle, Co. Wexford (28855 10991) 100, 101, 102, *102*, 104
Coole Castle, Co. Offaly (21342 22274), *152, 153*
Coppinger's Court (Ballyvireen), Co. Cork (12605 03590), 177-8
Cork, Co. Cork, 1, 7, 15, 17, 161, 177, 190
Cork County, 156, 158-9, 164, 177, 178, 180, 182, 193
Cornaslieve Earthwork, Co. Cavan (25967 29036), 16
Corrib Lough, 92, 169
Court House, Co. Louth (see Ardee)
Creeharmore Earthwork, Co. Roscommon (18159 24892), 10
Cuslough Demesne Castle, Co. Mayo (11523 26493), 95
Danestown Ringwork, Co. Meath (29538 26260), 6
Dardistown Castle, Co. Meath (31150 26960), 147
Darver Castle, Co. Louth (30085 29872), 144
Deel Castle, Co. Mayo (11804 31841), *192*
Deel River, 118, 119

Deerpark Castle, Co. Galway (15462 21321), 165-6
Deerpark, Co. Wicklow (see Rathturtle)
Deer Park Farms, Co. Antrim (32866 40878), 21
Delvin Castle, Co. Westmeath (26005 26268), 95, *99*
Derrin Castle, Co. Laois (22602 18839), 198
Derrydonnel More Castle, Co. Galway (14519 22526), 164
Derryhivenny Castle, Co. Galway (18717 20849), *149*, *169*
Doe Castle (Castledoe), Co. Donegal (20871 43198), *173*
Donaghmoyne, Co. Roscommon (see Mannan Castle)
Donegal Castle, Co. Donegal (19291 37854), *186*, 187-8, *187*, *188*
Donohill Motte (Moatquarter), Co. Tipperary SR (19066 14324), *31*
Doo Lough, 169
Doonmore Motte (Ballygill North), Co. Antrim (31187 45256), 21
Douglas River, 16
Down County, 15, 16, 17, 19, 26, 151, 172
Downpatrick Earthwork, Co. Down (34825 34498), 21
Drimneen River, 150, 166, 169
Drogheda, Co. Louth, 34, 65
Dromore Motte, Co. Down (32061 35317), 24
Drumcliff Bay, 198
Drumcor Earthwork, Co. Cavan (23648 29255), 16
Drumharid Earthwork, Co. Cavan (24188 31288), 16
Drumsawry Ringwork, Co. Meath (see Loughcrew Hills)
Dublin, Co. Dublin, 1, 2, 23, 34, 37, 47, 128, 190
Dublin Castle, Co. Dublin (31550 23391), 37, 40, *49*, *50*, 50, 52, 57, 80, 105
Duleek Motte (Commons), Co. Meath (30490 26861), 2
Dunamase Castle, Co. Laois (25300 19818), *30*, 38, 39, 41-3, *42*, *43*, 45, 52, 55, 63-4, 70-1, 113
Dundalk, Co. Louth, 76
Dundeady Castle, Co. Cork (13392 03151), 158
Dundonnell Castle, Co. Roscommon (18939 23799), 4, *195*, 197, 198
Dundrum Castle, Co. Down (34048 33700), 36-7, 40, 58-9, *58*, *86*, 87, *87*, 88, 105
Dundrum Inner Bay, 37, 40, 59
Dungar Ringwork, Co. Offaly (21572 19210), 9-10, *13*
Dungarvan Castle, Co. Waterford (22605 09300), 40, *55*, 56-7, 80, 83, 84-5, 105, 106
Dungulph Castle, Co. Wexford (27795 10757), 101, 102
Dunleer, Co. Louth, 144
Dunlough Castle, Co. Cork (07297 02709), 158
Dunluce Castle, Co. Antrim (29048 44137), *132*, 133-4
Dunmahon Castle, Co. Louth (30362 30204), 141, 144-5
Dunmanus West Castle, Co. Cork (08460 03314), 158
Dunmoe Castle, Co. Meath (29079 27026), 95, *98*, 99-100, 104, 174
Dunmore Castle (Castlefarm), Co. Galway (15006 26402), 92, *93*
Dunsilly Motte, Co. Antrim (31400 38890), 21, 22, 25, 27
Dunsoghly Castle, Co. Dublin (31182 24320), 134, 137, *138*, 139, *139*, *140*
Dysart, Co. Kilkenny, 147
Eleven Ballyboes, Co. Donegal (see Greencastle)
Emmel West Castle, Co. Offaly (19850 18464), 177
England, 4, 6, 13, 14, 19, 20, 24, 105

Enniscorthy Castle, Co. Wexford (29732 13982), 77
Erne River, 84
Eske River, 187
Farmley, Co. Kilkenny (see Burnchurch Castle)
Faughart Upper Motte, Co. Louth (30575 31264), 31, *31*
Ferns Castle (Castleland), Co. Wexford (30175 14985), 4-5, 6, 34, 37-8, 39-40, 41, 55, 60, 61, *62*, 73, 77, 78, *78*, 81-2, *81*, *155*
Ferrycarrig Ringwork (Newtown Ferrycarrig), Co. Wexford (30159 12323), 6-7
Fiddaun Castle, Co. Galway (14101 19586), 134, *163*, *164*, *165*, 166, 172
Foyle Lough, 109
France, 50, 82
Friarsland, Co. Galway (see Meelick Ringwork)
Funshion River, 73
Galesquarter Castle, Co. Laois (23560 17400), 151-2
Galloway, Scotland, 19
Galway County, 89, 91, 93, 94, 95, 150, 156, 163-6, 169-70, 176
Garrycastle, Co. Offaly (20210 21373), *150*, *151*
Glanmorgan, Wales, 6, 18
Glanworth Castle, Co. Cork (17581 10406), 73-4, *73*, *74*, 76, 89
Glaspistol Castle, Co. Louth (31579 28322), 141, 145
Glebe Motte, Co. Westmeath (24893 26123), *20*
Glinsk Castle, Co. Galway (17149 26699), 180
Gortnaclea Castle, Co. Laois (23608 18622), 151
Gortnasillagh Earthwork, Co. Roscommon (17731 28146), 10
Graffan Castle, Co. Offaly (20015 18500), *195*, 198
Grange West Castle, Co. Kildare (26209 23646), *156*
Grannagh, Co. Kilkenny (see Granny Castle)
Granny Castle (Grannagh), Co. Kilkenny (25733 11463), 133, *135*, *136*
Gransha Ringfort, Co. Down (32516 34609), 15, 21
Grantstown, Co. Laois (23322 17977), 152
Greencastle (Eleven Ballyboes), Co. Donegal (26533 44033), 55, 105, 106, 109-11, *109*, *110*
Greencastle, Co. Down (32429 31182), 76, *76*
Greenan Earthwork, Co. Tipperary NR (19525 16561), 10
Grenan Castle, Co. Kilkenny (25929 14139), 74-5, *75*
Guines Castle, Calais, France, 63
Harlech Castle, Wales, 109
Hatch's Castle, Co. Louth (see Ardee)
Haynestown Castle, Co. Louth (30433 30235), 141-2, *143*, 145, 172, 174
Hilltown Castle, Co. Wexford (28847 11493), 101, 102
Hook Head Castle (Churchtown), Co. Wexford (27337 09735), 86-7, 88
Ightermurragh Castle, Co. Cork (19908 07242), 178, *185*
Ikerrin Barony, Co. Tipperary NR, 15
Inchiquin Castle, Co. Cork (20384 07483), 88
Inishconnell, Co. Cavan (see Clogh Oughter Castle)
Ireton's Castle, Lehinch, Co. Tipperary NR (18674 20333), 159, 190, *190*, 192
Iveragh Peninsula, Co. Kerry, 100
Jordan's Castle, Co. Down, (see Ardglass)
Kanturk Castle (Paal East), Co. Cork (13827 10178), 177, *177*, 178, 179, 183, 190, 192-3, 198

Kells Castle, Co. Kilkenny (24977 14322), 147

Kerry County, 17, 193

Key Lough, 40

Kilbolane Castle, Co. Cork (14232 12099), 130

Kilbrew Castle, Co. Meath (30183 25598), 147

Kilcloggan Castle , Co. Wexford (27598 10474), 155

Kilcoe Castle, Co. Cork (10192 03282), 158

Kilcolgan More Castle, Co. Offaly (21460 22461), 175, 189, 192

Kildare County, 6, 7

Kilfinny Castle, Co. Limerick (14627 13984), 91

Kilkenny Castle, Co. Kilkenny (25085 15564), 5, 6, 34, 50, 52, *52, 53*

Killaleigh Castle, Co. Tipperary (see Sopwell Castle)

Killanny Motte, Co. Louth (28927 30101), *31*

Killarney, Co. Kerry, 88, 168

Killincoole Castle, Co. Louth (30008 29978), 139, *144*

Kilmacduagh Castle, Co. Galway (14070 19987), 93

Kilmaclenine Castle, Co. Cork (15044 10624), 181

Kilpipe Ringwork, Co. Wicklow (31111 17718), *9*

Kilskeagh Castle, Co. Galway (14681 23483), 93

Kiltartan Castle (Castletown), Co. Galway (14591 20472), 57, *80*

Kiltinan Castle (Castletown), Co. Tipperary SR (22326 13202), 88

Kindlestown Upper Castle, Co. Wicklow (32793 21175), 89, 95-6, 99, 100, 104, 174

King John's Castle, Co. Louth (see Carlingford)

King's Island, Limerick, Co. Limerick, 36

Kinlough Castle, Co. Mayo (12595 25038), 95

Kirkistown Castle, Co. Down (36450 35800), 172

Knockgraffon Motte, Co. Tipperary SR (20486 12953), 123

Knowth Earthwork, Co. Meath (29956 27291), 15, 38

Kylenamuck, Co. Tipperary NR (see Castletown/Kylena-muck)

Lagavooren Co. Louth (see Millmount Motte)

Lambay Island Castle, Co. Dublin (33101 25089), 177

Laois County, 6, 22, 151, 152-3, 158, 181, 183, 193

Lea Castle, Co. Laois (25709 21205), 6, 36, 60-1, 62, 77-8, 81, 82, *82*, 105

Leamaneh North Castle, Co. Clare (12349 19360), 182, *184*

Leane Lough, 88

Leap Castle, Co. Offaly (21290 19747), *176*, 177

Lehinch, Co. Tipperary (see Ireton's Castle)

Leighlinbridge Castle, Co. Carlow (26916 16545), 137, *141*

Leinster Province, 1, 2, 17, 27, 28, 31, 60, 70

Leitra Castle, Co. Offaly (20062 22676), *194*, 196

Liffey River, 37

Limerick, Co. Limerick, 138, 181

Limerick Castle, Co. Limerick (15734 15769), 5-6, 34, 35-6, *36, 37*, 40, 50, *51*, 70, 105

Limerick County, 89, 91, 95, 118, 164, 193

Lisbunny Castle, Co. Tipperary NR (18916 17936), 94

Liscarroll Castle, Co. Cork (14520 11241), 111-13, *113*, *114*

Liskeveen Castle, Co. Tipperary NR (21711 15240), *148*

Lismahon Motte, Co. Down (34290 33890), 21, 24

Lisnafana Earthwork, Co. Cavan (25737 29108), 16

Lissalway Earthwork, Co. Roscommon (17341 28122), 10

Loughcrew Hills (Drumsawry) Ringwork, Co. Meath (25757 27826), 3, 4, *11*, 15, 38

Lough Gur, Co. Limerick (see Bourchier's Castle)

Loughlohery Castle, Co. Tipperary SR (20862 12384), 165

Loughmoe (Tinvoher) Castle, Co. Tipperary NR (21151 16719), 190

Louth County, 22, 27, 28, 31, 34, 138, 139, 142, 144, 146, 151, 182

Lurgankeel Motte, Co. Louth (30223 31173), 19-20

Lyreen Stream, 37

MacNean Upper Lough, 40

Mahee Castle, Co. Down (see Nendrum Castle)

Mahon Castle, Co. Cork (17235 07143), 158

Maigue River, 30, 36, 47, 67

Mallow Castle (Castlelands), Co. Cork (15698 09775), 180, *180, 181, 186*, 198

Mannan Castle (Donaghmoyne), Co. Monaghan (28535 30742), *22*

Manorland, Co. Meath (see Trim Castle)

Mashanaglass Castle, Co. Cork (13706 07071), 159, 192

Mayfield, Co. Waterford (see Rocketscastle)

Maynooth Castle, Co. Kildare (29356 23762), 37, *38*, 49, 52, *67, 68*, 69-70, *69*, 74, 89

Mayo County, 15, 89, 95

Meath County, 1-2, 6, 22, 26, 27, 33, 146-7, 176, 183

Meath, Liberty of, 26, 35, 190

Meelick Ringwork (Friarsland), Co. Galway (16041 26736), 9, 10, 14

Mellifont Castle, Co. Louth (30129 27816), 147

Middleton, Co. Cork, 159

Millmount Motte (Lagavooren), Drogheda, Co. Louth (30902 27479), 34

Milltown Castle, Co. Louth (30340 29930), 139, *143*, 145

Milltown Motte, Co. Meath (25448 27511), *21*

Mint, The, Co. Louth (see Carlingford)

Moatquarter, Co. Tipperary SR (see Donohill Motte)

Monaghan County, 15, 16

Monkstown Castle, Co. Cork (17658 06621), 178-9, *179*, 180, 183

Montgomery, Wales, 50

Mountbagnall Motte, Co. Louth (31628 30690), 27-8, *31*

Mountgarrett Castle, Co. Wexford (27250 12942), 155

Mountlong Castle, Co. Cork (16757 05110), 177, 178, 179-80, *179*, 183

Moy River, 95, 96

Moydow Glebe Motte, Co. Longford (21457 26885), 17-18

Moylough Castle, Co. Galway (16154 24900), *90*, 91

Mulphedder, Co. Meath (see Clonard)

Munster Province, 2, 15, 16, 159, 177

Muskerry, Co. Cork, 161

Narrow Water Castle, Co. Down (31291 31923), *172*

Navan, Co. Meath, 184

Nenagh, Co. Tipperary NR, 94

Nenagh Castle, Co. Tipperary NR (18667 17908), 38-9, 54-5, *54*, 55-7, 77, 83, *83*, 84, 85, 88

Nenagh River, 39

Nendrum (Mahee) Castle, Co. Down (35239 36394), 173-4

Newcastle O'Conyll (Castle Demesne), Newcastle West, Co. Limerick (12796 13374), 118, 120-3, *121, 122*, 134

Newcastle West, Co. Limerick (see Newcastle O'Conyll)

New Ross, Co. Wexford, 39

Newtown Castle, Co. Offaly (21735 19932), *194*, 196

Newtown Ferrycarrig, Co. Wexford (see Ferrycarrig Ringwork)

Newtown Stewart, Co. Tyrone, 111

Newtown Trim Castle, Co. Meath (28136 25685), 147

Nore River, 74

Norrisland Castle, Co. Waterford (21001 09752), 195

Oakley Park, Co. Offaly (see Ballymooney Castle)

Offaly County, 9-10, 22, 31, 152-3, 158, 188, 193, 196

Old Connell Motte, Co. Kildare (28109 21602), *28*

Oldcourt Castle, Co. Cork (10831 03195), 159

Oldcourt Castle, Co. Wicklow (32599 21751), 102, *103*

Olethen Cantred, Co. Cork, 159

Oriel, 2, 28

Oughter Lough, 40, 79, 84

Owenacurra River, 178

Owenslade Stream, 37

Oyster Haven Creek, 179

Paal East, Co. Cork (see Kanturk Castle)

Pale, The, 137, 146, 152, 153, 171, 172

Pallas Castle, Co. Galway (15565 21992), *167*

Park Castle, Co. Galway (17842 22301), 93

Pollardstown Ringwork, Co. Kildare (27748 21510), 6, 7

Portumna Demesne Castle, Co. Galway (18528 20400), 192-3, *193*

Quin Castle, Co. Clare (14187 17458), 130, *130*

Racraveen Castle, Co. Cavan (24944 28648), 31

Raheen Castle, Co. Cork (11193 03201), 158

Raheen, Co. Roscommon (see Rathmore Earthwork)

Raphoe Castle (Townparks), Co. Donegal (22593 40287), 188, 192

Rathangan Earthwork, Co. Kildare (26708 21944), 13, 14

Rathcroghan, Co. Roscommon (see Rathmore)

Rathfarnham Castle, Co. Dublin (31448 22887), 175

Rathmacknee Great Castle, Co. Wexford (30313 11403), *155*

Rathmore Earthwork (Raheen), Co. Roscommon (18314 28705), 15

Rathmullan Motte, Co. Down (34775 33736), 15, 21, 24, 27

Rathnageeragh Castle, Co. Carlow (27968 15664), 133, *134*

Rathnallog Earthwork, Co. Roscommon (17880 28491), 10

Rathnaveoge Lower, Co. Tipperary NR (20815 18390), *148*, 190

Rathshillane Castle, Co. Wexford (30931 10688), 101, 102

Rathturtle Ringwork (Deerpark), Co. Wicklow (29646 21526), *16*

Rathumney Castle, Co. Wexford (27685 11650), 96

Ree Lough, 40, 59

Relagh Beg Motte, Co. Cavan (26900 29199), *24*

Richardstown Castle, Co. Louth (30151 29057), 144

Rindown Castle (Warren), Co. Roscommon (20060 25427), 40, 59-60, *61*, 64, 67, 71, 72, 86, 89

Rocketscastle (Mayfield), Co. Waterford (24798 11660), 157

Rockfleet Castle, Co. Mayo (09308 29527) 137, *149*

Rockstown Castle, Co. Limerick (16228 14631), *167*

Rodanstown Earthwork, Co. Meath (29016 24170), 6

Roodstown Castle, Co. Louth (29959 29249), 143, *145*

Roosca Castle, Co. Tipperary SR (20509 11956), 196-7, *197*

Roscommon Castle (Cloonbrackna), Co. Roscommon (18726 26507), 60, 105, 106-8, *106*, *107*, 109, 111, 113, 192

Roscrea Castle, Co. Tipperary NR (21368 18940), 125, 126-7 *127*, *128*

Ross Island Castle, Co. Kerry (09495 08874), *168*

Rush Hall Castle, Co. Laois (23102 18993), 182-3

St John's Point, 40

Scotland, 19, 41

Seirkieran Motte (Churchland/Clonmore), Co. Offaly (21394 20222), 9, *11*

Shanid (Upper) Castle, Co. Limerick (12428 14513), *25*, 85, *85*

Shannon River, 7, 8, 12, 15, 16, 17, 29, 35, 36, 47, 85, 89, 106, 118, 192

Sheeaunbeg Earthwork (Barrinagh), Co. Roscommon (15428 27349), 3, 4

Shrule Castle, Co. Laois (27132 18143), 151

Shrule Castle, Co. Mayo (12814 25909), 95, *97*

Sigginstown Castle, Co. Wexford (30628 10702), 156

Skreen Castle, Co. Meath (29537 26016), 147

Slade Castle, Co. Wexford (27464 98490), 101-2

Slane Castle Demesne, Co. Meath (29437 27300), 147

Sleady Castle, Co. Waterford (21888 10182), 194-5

Sligo County, 15

Smarmore Castle, Co. Louth (29454 28592), 144

Sopwell Castle (Killaleigh), Co. Tipperary (19679 19401), 176-7, 190

Stormanstown Motte, Co. Louth (29153 29377), 31

Suck River, 10

Suir River, 88, 123, 124, 125, 133, 135

Summerhill Ringwork, Co. Tipperary NR (16180 31824), *9*

Summerhill Demesne Castle, Co. Meath (28445 24818), 183

Swords Castle, Co. Dublin (31801 24673), 127-8, *129*

Templehouse Demesne Castle, Co. Sligo (16180 31824), 100, *100*, *101*

Templemore Castle, Co. Tipperary NR (21078 17177), 104, 190

Termonfeckin Castle, Co. Louth (31434 28034), 142, *142*, 146, 158

Terryglass Castle, Co. Tipperary NR (18583 20099), 39, 60, 77, 78, 81-2

Thomastown, Co. Kilkenny, 74

Thomond Bridge, Limerick, Co. Limerick, 36

Tikincor Lower Castle, Co. Wicklow (22403 12273), 195-6

Tinnahinch Castle, Co. Carlow (20781 14336), 177

Tinnakill Castle, Co. Laois (25018 20885), 152

Tintore Castle, Co. Laois (23564 18078), 151

Tinvoher, Co. Tipperary NR (see Loughmoe)

Tipperary County, 6, 31, 95, 177, 190, 193
    North Riding, 4, 6, 10, 39, 89, 94
    South Riding, 88, 94, 164

Tomdeely North Castle, Co. Limerick (13236 15199), 89-91, *90*, 95

Tonashammer Motte, Co. Westmeath (25019 27668), *23*

Townparks, Co. Donegal (see Raphoe)

Townparks, Co. Louth (see Ardee)

Townparks, Co. Offaly (see Birr Castle)

Trim Castle (Manorland), Co. Meath (28025 25670), 2, 4, 5, *5*, 6, *29*, 33, 34-5, 36, 41, *44*, 45, *45*, *46*, 47, 52, 60, 63, 64-6, *64*, 67, 68, 70, 71, 78, 82, 84

Tullamore, Co. Offaly, 152

Tully Castle, Co. Roscommon (19408 23086), 198
Turin Castle, Co. Mayo (12570 25757), 95
Ulster Province, 2, 15, 17, 19, 21, 26, 34, 35, 40, 172
Usk, Wales, 50
Wales, 3, 4, 6, 13, 41, 50, 83, 105, 106, 109, 130, 133
Ward River, 127
Warren, Co. Roscommon (see Rindown Castle)
Waterford, Co. Waterford, 1, 133

Waterford County, 157-8, 194, 196
Westmeath County, 13, 26
West Passage, Cork Harbour, 178
Wexford, Co. Wexford, 60
Wexford Castle, Co. Wexford, 60, 77
Wexford County, 6-7, 22, 100, 154-7, 159, 193
Wicklow County, 22, 31, 153-4, 193
Womanagh River, 88